THE SACRAMENTS
IN THE
CHRISTIAN LIFE

J. F. McDonald

THE SACRAMENTS IN THE CHRISTIAN LIFE

St Paul Publications

Unless otherwise stated the law of the Church referred to in this book is that contained in the new Code of Canon Law which was promulgated on January 25, 1983, by the Apostolic Constitution for the Promulgation of the New Code of Canon Law 'Sacrae Disciplinae Leges', and which came into force throughout the Latin Church on the First Sunday of Advent, November 27, 1983. The law it replaces is referred to as the 1917 Code.

St Paul Publications
Middlegreen, Slough SL3 6BT, England

Nihil obstat: Patrick Clancy O.P.
Imprimatur: + Giovanni Canestri
Titular Archbishop of Monterano
Vicariate of Rome, 29 April 1983

St Paul Publications is an activity of the priests and brothers of the Society of St Paul who promote the Christian message through the mass media.

CONTENTS

INTRODUCTION

The documents of the Second Vatican Council and the subsequent teaching given by Pope Paul VI and Pope John Paul II leave us in no doubt about a certain development in the Church's understanding of the significance of the sacraments and the important place they should be given as the principal means of sanctification both in the economy of salvation and in the life of the individual Christian.

The new Code of Canon Law, which is more theologically and pastorally orientated than the Code which it replaces, also reflects present-day thinking in the Church concerning the sacraments.

There is also no doubt that in the past the preparation for the sacraments on the part of the faithful has been inadequate and in many cases lacking altogether. It is, for example, the experience of many priests that many couples show that they have never seriously thought about the real significance of Christian marriage until they come to see the priest shortly before their marriage is due to take place, when there is too little time to make up for what should have been done over a period of years.

And so today greater stress is laid not only on the preparation that the faithful should be given for the reception of the sacraments but also on the length of this preparation first of all for the recipient and then for others who may be involved in the sacrament in question, such as priests, parents, teachers and even the generality of the faithful.

It is also well known that the faithful have at times been led astray either by an incomplete presentation of the teaching of the Church on the sacraments or even by false views about certain matters pertaining to them such as the notion of sin implied by the instruction given concerning the sacrament of Penance or Reconciliation, the sacrament of Matrimony and in some respects the sacrament of Orders.

In his Apostolic Exhortation 'Familiaris Consortio', dated November 22, 1981, Pope John Paul II appeals to priests not to confuse the faithful or lead them astray by teaching them what is at variance with the teaching of the Magisterium — the official teaching of the Church — especially with regard to matters concerning the sacrament of Matrimony. But what Pope John Paul II says applies equally to other areas where the sacraments are concerned.

Some of the views in question have been dealt with in documents issued by the relevant competent authority in the Church.

All this is reflected in this book. The opening chapter gives a general discussion on the sacraments, so that the reader may be enabled to see them in their proper setting as part of God's plan for man's salvation.

Bearing in mind that lay people — as well as priests — are not expected to be theologians, technical terms are kept to a minimum. This chapter also serves the purpose of making it unnecessary to repeat certain matters in the book later.

The discussion of the individual sacraments takes place against the scriptural, theological, liturgical, canonical and pastoral background demanded for an adequate but simplified treatment of the particular sacrament in question. It also takes account of the developments and changes brought about by the revised rites for the celebration of the various sacraments.

Apart from the general purpose of man's sanctification each sacrament is treated according to its own structure and particular purpose in the Christian life.

As sacraments of Christian initiation Baptism, Confirmation and the Eucharist are seen as contributing, each in its turn, to the formation of the complete Christian.

The relation between faith and Baptism which can cause problems especially for those seeking Christian initiation, and in this context, the Baptism of infants, is singled out for special mention. The Eucharist is discussed under its threefold aspect as Sacrifice-Sacrament, Communion-Sacrament and Presence-Sacrament.

In so far as the individual is concerned and apart from other considerations, the rest of the sacraments are seen as meeting a particular need in the Christian life — the sacrament of Penance when there is question of personal sin; the Anointing of the sick when one of the faithful *begins* to be in danger of death; the sacrament of Orders for those who are called to be sacred ministers in the Church and Matrimony for those who choose the vocation of married life.

The particular significance of each sacrament, the special grace attached to its reception, the responsibilities arising therefrom, the difficulties to be met with in living up to the Christian ideals in each case and certain important questions relating to particular sacraments, such as irregular marriage situations, are placed before the reader and explained with appropriate reference to the up-to-date teaching and practice of the Church.

1

THE SACRAMENTS
IN THE CHRISTIAN LIFE

On the occasion of the official presentation of the new Code of
Canon Law by Pope John Paul II on February 3, 1983, Archbishop
Rosalio José Castillo Lara, the Pro-President of the Pontifical
Commission for the Revision of the Code of Canon Law, stated
that in the new Code there "is also to be noted a greater theological
inspiration aimed at underlining the peculiar nature of Canon
Law" and went on to say that "not a few Canons, especially in the
matter of the sacraments and ecclesiology, offer theological syn-
theses of notable precision".

An example of this is to be found in the first Canon in the
section on the sacraments which reminds us that "the Sacraments
of the New Testament, instituted by Christ and entrusted to the
Church as actions of Christ and of the Church, are signs and means
by which faith is expressed and strengthened, worship is given to
God and man's sanctification is achieved. And so they serve
especially to bring about, strengthen and manifest ecclesial communion" (c.840).

The meaning of 'sacrament'

In general the word 'sacrament' means the intervention of God
in history manifesting his will. We speak of the 'sacraments' of
nature, the 'sacraments' of the Old Testament. Christ as the
'sacrament' of God, the Church as the universal 'sacrament' of
salvation.[1] St Paul speaks of marriage as a great 'sacrament',
meaning a mysterious and sacred symbol, a sign of the union of
Christ with his Church (cf. Eph 5 : 32). When applied to one of the
seven sacraments of the New Law the word 'sacrament' has a
special meaning. It means some sign which can be perceived by the
senses, instituted by Christ to signify and actually confer grace on
those who receive it worthily. The signs of the sacraments of the
New Law are material things, gestures and words. Pope Pius XII
tells us that Christ infuses his power into the sacraments as instruments of sanctification.[2]

Divine institution

The divine institution of the sacraments is of the utmost importance. God alone can give to such a sign the power to confer grace. This happens in the sacraments because they have been instituted by Christ who is God.

Actions of Christ and of the Church

The Constitution on the Sacred Liturgy tells us that Christ is present in the sacraments by his active power.[3] The sacraments are acts of Christ who personally sanctifies each individual through contact with him in them.

The sacraments are also acts of the Church which is their common ground or basis. The Church continues the priestly office of Christ because she realises in the world the purpose of the Incarnation. This is summed up in the words of the Nicene Creed: "Who for us men and for our salvation came down from heaven". In so far as the sacraments are concerned the Church is the guardian and interpreter of the will of Christ as made known to the Apostles. She has no power to invent new sacraments. Nor can she change the essential elements determined by Christ her Founder. But her reflections on the sacraments can bring new insights on the riches they contain.

Grace

The saving acts of Christ took place once in history. Through them grace and glory were won for men. In the sacraments *that* grace is actually brought to the individual Christian; *that* glory is given as a pledge or promise. The teaching contained in the antiphon at the Magnificat of Evening Prayer II for the Solemnity of the Body and Blood of Christ applies to the other sacraments as well as to the Eucharist: "O sacred feast in which we partake of Christ: his sufferings are remembered, our minds are filled with grace and we receive a pledge of the glory that is to be ours".

Pope Paul VI speaks of grace as the marvel and mystery of the Christian life; the interior effusion of the Holy Spirit.[4] The grace of God gives us the capacity to will and to work for God's good pleasure (cf. Phil 2:13). Grace is also said to be a mysterious reality capable of illuminating the Christian conscience and of guiding the Christian in his conduct.[5]

St Thomas Aquinas speaks of grace having two effects:

1) It takes away the consequences of sin, i.e. long habits of sin which have left their mark on our nature and our make-up. These consequences are weakened, healed and put right by divine grace.

2) It perfects man according to the requirements of the Christian faith.[6]

Grace is also said to be the principle governing the moral conduct of the baptised together with free-will.[7]

Grace is said to be a spiritual energy, a vital dynamism, a creator of freedom. To possess grace means to live always with a greater awareness of and faithfulness to the Holy Spirit. To lose grace means to be unfaithful to the Holy Spirit.

This grace is chiefly communicated to us through the sacraments. We say 'chiefly' because God's grace is not tied to the sacraments. We must also allow for those moments of actual grace which we all experience.

Signs

The external and perceptible sign is one of the four elements essential to a sacrament. The others being its divine institution, the conferring of sanctifying grace and a duly appointed minister.

The signs referred to in canon 840 have come to be spoken of in sacramental language as the *matter and form of the sacrament*. This terminology reflects the influence of Scholasticism which dates back to the 13th century. The theory of matter and form has been accepted by the Church as the most convenient way of detecting whether there is anything wrong with the sacrament.

The *matter* is spoken of as the indeterminate element; the *form* as the determining element. The matter usually refers to material things or to certain gestures. The form refers to the words used in the conferring of a sacrament.

Christ instituted the sacraments in the way in which he did because man's nature is composite — he consists of body and soul. Spiritual things must reach man through his senses. The knowledge we acquire comes to us through our senses. A sign is the medium through which we arrive at the knowledge of something. Signs which we can perceive are necessary, if we are to know that grace has been given to us. Words are the most appropriate way of indicating what the mind wants to express by the use of material things and gestures. St Paul speaks of Christ delivering himself for the Church that he might sanctify her after having cleansed her by the washing of water with the word (cf. Eph 5 : 25–26). St James speaks of the spiritual effect that anointing with oil accompanied by prayer can have on a person who is sick (cf. Jas 5 : 14).

Guidelines relating to the matter and form

Because the sacraments are personal encounters with Christ it is very important that they be validly administered and received. A valid sacrament is one in which all the essentials for a true sacrament are present.

A sacrament, for example, can be rendered invalid by a substantial change in the matter and/or form:

1) If a substantial change has taken place in the matter for the sacrament, even though inadvertently or in error, the sacrament is rendered null and void. There will be a substantial change if, in the common estimation of men, the substance used is different from that specified, e.g. using eau de Cologne for Baptism or vinegar for the consecration at Mass.

2) A substantial change in the form makes the sacrament invalid. A substantial change in the form takes place when in the common estimation of men the meaning of the words used is not that which Christ intended. We look at the meaning of the words used and also at the intention of the one using them. The sacrament of Baptism would not be validly conferred if the ministers were to say: "I admit you as a member of the Church" because these words do not signify the first effect of Baptism which is to cleanse the individual from sin.

Provided that the substantial meaning of the words has not been changed, a slip of the tongue in uttering the form would not invalidate the sacrament.

Normally one must be certain that valid matter is being used. In certain circumstances, if one is doubtful about having the proper matter, the sacrament is conferred conditionally with the condition 'If this is valid matter'. In acting thus you are doing what you can for the recipient and at the same time you are saving the sacrament from the danger of irreverence and invalidity.

3) In general one can say that in doubt it is lawful to administer a sacrament conditionally as often as it would be exposed to nullity if given absolutely or if the refusal of the sacrament would expose the person to spiritual harm. This teaching has a particular application in the sacrament of Penance as we shall see. The one exception concerns the Eucharist. It is not lawful to use doubtful matter in the Eucharist because there would be a danger of the faithful

adoring something which would not be the body and blood of Christ.

4) If it is certain that a sacrament has been invalidly administered, it must be repeated absolutely, i.e. without any conditions.

Since the sacraments of Baptism, Confirmation and Holy Orders imprint a character, they cannot be repeated. If after careful investigation there still remains a prudent doubt as to whether these sacraments have been validly conferred, they should be conferred conditionally (c.845 nn. 1 and 2).

Faith and the sacraments

The sacraments are "signs and means by which faith is expressed and strengthened" (c.840).

St Thomas Aquinas tells us that Our Lord Jesus Christ, by his life, passion and death and resurrection accomplished the redemption of mankind in general and reconciled it with God. However, by the mere fact of being born we contract original sin and its consequences, by the mere fact of birth we do not automatically receive the benefits of the redemptive act of Christ. The redemption which Christ achieved is not applied to us automatically. Thus there is the problem of how we are to share in that redemptive act of Christ, how we are linked up with it, how it is to reach us and have effect in us. St Thomas gives a very clear answer: "The power of Christ's passion is conjoined to us through faith and the sacraments, yet in different ways. For that continuity with the passion which is achieved by faith takes place through an act of the soul, whereas the continuity which is achieved through the sacraments takes place through the use of external things".[8]

The first link is by faith. Faith puts us into contact with God and by it we come to know his plan and achievements for our salvation. But faith is not merely accepting truths intellectually. It involves a total commitment of the believer to Christ. It also implies a decision to live by these truths. True faith must inspire and colour the whole outlook and actions of the Christian. Without faith God's whole economy for man would pass us by. In this respect faith is the first and essential step towards salvation, it is the "beginning, foundation and root of human salvation", as the Council of Trent put it.

But because faith carries with it an acceptance of God's revelation and the decision to live accordingly, it must lead to the sacraments, for the sacraments are part of the content of God's revelation and plan for our salvation. St Thomas speaks of the sacraments as "the sort of signs in which the faith by which man is justified is explicitly attested".[9] The transition from faith to the sacraments is thus clearly shown. The power of the sacraments can never be divorced from that of faith; the two go hand in hand. Without faith the sacraments would be meaningless, while on the other hand, having regard to man's present state, the sacraments are indispensable to a full life of faith. Faith alone is not enough and where we read in the epistles of St Paul (cf. Romans and Galatians) of the faith which justifies, St Paul is speaking of living faith, a faith which leads to the acceptance of the whole dispensation of Christ, including the use of the sacraments.

The Constitution on the Sacred Liturgy reminds us that the sacraments "not only presuppose faith, but by words and objects they also nourish, strengthen and express it; that is why they are called 'sacraments of faith' ".[10]

Abbot Vonier concludes that "the sacramental system is, then, grafted on to faith; it is essentially the executive of our faith and also its reward. Because of her faith the Church is given these further powers of reaching Christ; powers which make Christ not only the object of contemplation but also of physical possession".[11]

God is worshipped and man is sanctified

The Constitution on the Sacred Liturgy reminds us that "Christ always associates the Church with himself in the truly great work of giving perfect praise to God and making men holy. The Church is his dearly beloved bride who calls to her Lord, and through him offers worship to the Eternal Father.

Rightly, then, the liturgy is considered as an exercise of the priestly office of Jesus Christ. In the liturgy the sanctification of men is manifested by signs perceptible to the senses, and is effected in a way which is proper to each of these signs; in the liturgy full public worship is performed by the Mystical Body of Jesus Christ, that is, by the Head and his members.

From this it follows that every liturgical ceelebration, because it is an action of Christ the priest and of his Body the Church, is a sacred action surpassing all others".[12]

Since the mission of the Church is one of sanctification and this is achieved chiefly through the sacraments, they are numbered among the spiritual goods of the Church, the help of which all the faithful have the right to receive from the sacred pastors (cf. c.213) provided, of course, that they are properly disposed and are not forbidden to receive them by law (cf. c.912).

Pope John Paul II speaks of the sanctification of human beings as a process of transformation when he says that "it is in the sacraments, especially in the Eucharist, that Christ Jesus works in fullness for the transformation of human beings".[13]

Because the sacraments are what they are, they must be celebrated with "the greatest reverence and the utmost care by both the sacred ministers and the faithful" (cf. c.840).

In this context the use of the sacraments for practical reasons is regulated by the Church. She is anxious to safeguard their validity, to save them from the danger of irreverence and to bring about favourable conditions for union with Christ so that the sacraments may bring about the blessings they are intended to produce.

In this respect Pope John Paul II referred to the Code of Canon Law as being extremely necessary for the Church. "Since it is organised as a social and visible structure it must also have norms . . . in order that the exercise of the functions divinely entrusted to her especially that of sacred power and the administration of the sacraments may be adequately organized".[14]

The minister of the sacraments

The minister of the sacraments is the one who in the name of Christ confers it, using the proper matter with the requisite form of words.

Canon 841 of the Code of Canon Law points out that since the sacraments are for the whole Church and belong to the divine deposit, it is for the supreme authority alone of the Church both to define what is necessary for their validity and of the same or another competent authority, in accordance with canon 838 nn. 3 and 4, to determine matters touching their celebration, administration and lawful reception as well as the order to be observed in their celebration.

For a valid sacrament the minister must have the proper power of Holy Orders for those sacraments which require it. In the case of Baptism, when the proper minister is not available, a catechist or anyone else deputed by the local bishop may baptise. In danger of death anyone can baptise, provided he or she has the proper intention (cf. c.861 n.2). With regard to the sacrament of Matrimony, the bride and bridegroom are the ministers.

Secondly the minister must have the proper intention. Because the minister acts in the name of Christ he must have the intention of doing what Christ did or what the Church does.

The ideal is to have what is called an actual intention. This is present when during the rite the minister is all the time aware of what he is doing and why he is doing it. This is not always possible because of the distractions which may arise which cause the minister to be unaware of what he is doing. In such a case the minister is said to have a virtual intention. This means that he is acting in virtue of an explicit intention he had previously made and which he did not retract even though he was not always conscious of it when he was carrying out the rite in question. This type of intention is sufficient to safeguard the validity of the sacrament.

The intention is very important because by it the minister unites himself with Christ who is the principal minister of the sacraments. It also enables him to relate his action to the Church. Without the requisite intention there would only be the simulation of sacrament. If by a positive act of the will, the minister excluded the intention of "doing what Christ or the Church does", he would not be uniting himself to Christ and there would be no true sacrament.

But in accordance with what we have said above, the minister should have something more than validity in mind when he is administering a sacrament. He must make his internal and external actions as conformable as possible to the sentiments and acts of Christ and his Church.[15] What the Ecumenical Directory says about Baptism applies equally to all the sacraments, namely, "its dignity and the manner of administering it are matters of great importance to all Christ's disciples".[16] The faithful are helped by the way a sacrament is administered. That is why the Church requires us to observe the rubrics which are not only aimed at safeguarding the validity of the sacrament.

The obligation of the minister

Sacred ministers cannot refuse the sacraments to those who reasonably request them, provided they are rightly disposed and are not forbidden by law from receiving them. This is a duty on the part of the minister corresponding to the right of the faithful to receive the spiritual goods of the Church about which we have already spoken. Once the sacred minister decides that the request is a reasonable one, he has an obligation to comply with it (cf. c.843 n.1). The request is considered reasonable, for example, when the faithful seek the sacraments in order to make their Easter duties; to obtain peace of soul; to receive them out of devotion, etc. People are presumed to be worthy, unless the contrary is clear. The urgency is even greater when it is a question of someone who is in danger of death.

If the request were made when the priest is rushing out to answer a sick call, it would be unreasonable for the person making the request to expect him to drop everything to hear his confession or give him Holy Communion.

In principle one must refuse the sacraments to those who are known to be unworthy. Reverence for the sacraments demands this. But before refusing the sacraments the sacred minister should try to remove the cause of the unworthiness, so that the individual in question will be disposed to receive them. A person would be considered unworthy, if he were unwilling to give up an unnecessary occasion of grave sin. The minister would try first of all to persuade him to give up this occasion of grave sin.

Canon 915 of the Code of Canon Law states that those who have been excommunicated or placed under interdict may not be admitted to Holy Communion after the penalty has been imposed or declared. The same applies to those who obstinately continue unrepentant in a state of grave public sin.

In spite of this teaching, it is the teaching of moral theologians that it will sometimes be permitted to give the sacraments to those who are known to be unworthy. The reason is that greater harm would come from the refusal of the sacraments than from administering them.

The following reasons are given for justifying this course:

1) The necessity of safeguarding the seal of confession, e.g. a penitent who had been refused absolution might present himself with the rest of the congregation, or even on his own, to the priest who felt unable to absolve him. In these circumstances the confessor would be bound to give him Holy Communion. To do otherwise would be to violate the seal of confession.

2) The necessity of safeguarding a person's good name which would be taken away by a refusal of the sacraments, e.g. someone seeking Holy Communion with others who has committed a secret crime which is known only to the priest.

3) The necessity of preventing scandal being given to the faithful, who would not understand why the person had been refused the sacraments.

It will be seen that a distinction is made between two classes of sinner — a secret or occult sinner, namely one who is known to the priest to be unworthy but not to the generality of the faithful, and a public sinner whose sin is known publicly or his unworthiness is public.

If a secret sinner seeks the sacraments in public, he must be given them. If he seeks them privately, he must be refused unless the priest's knowledge of his unworthiness came through the confessional. The reason is that everyone has a natural right to his good name unless he has done something publicly to lose it. We must also bear in mind what was said above about scandal being given to the faithful by refusing someone the sacraments.

Public sinners are to be refused the sacraments whether they seek them in private or in public. There is no question of their losing their good name. They have already lost it. Before being given the sacraments, such people must do what the Church requires and also be ready to repair the scandal they have given by their crime. Normally going to confession publicly is enough to restore such a person's good name. Complicated marriage situations will be dealt with in the chapter on marriage.

Finally, it is not lawful to administer a sacrament to someone who is not fit to receive it, e.g. to absolve someone who is certainly not sorry for his sins, or to give a sacrament other than Baptism to someone who is not yet baptised (cf. c.842 n.1). In these cases there would be no sacrament. It would be an abuse of a sacred rite.

Preparation for the sacraments

According to the law of the Church, pastors of souls and the rest of the faithful, each according to his position in the Church, have a duty to see that those who request the sacraments are prepared to receive them with due evangelization and catechetical instruction, taking account of the norms laid down by the competent authority (cf. c.843 n.2).

In his Apostolic Exhortation 'Catechesi Tradendae', Pope John Paul II speaks of evangelization and catechesis. Quoting the Apostolic Exhortation of Pope Paul VI, 'Evangelii Nuntiandi', dated 8 December, 1975, Pope John Paul II reminds us that evangelization has the aim of bringing the Good News to the whole of humanity so that all may live by it. It is a rich, complex and dynamic reality, made up of elements, or one could say moments, that are essential and different from each other, and that must all be kept in view simultaneously. Catechesis is one of these moments

— a very remarkable one — in the whole process of evangelization.

Without attempting to give a complete definition of catechesis, Pope John Paul II describes it in the following terms: "All in all, it can be taken here that catechesis is an education of children, young people and adults in the faith, which includes especially the teaching of Christian doctrine imparted, generally speaking, in an organic and systematic way, with a view to initiating the hearers into the fullness of Christian life. Accordingly, while not being formally identified with them, catechesis is built on a certain number of elements of the Church's pastoral mission that have a catechetical aspect, that prepare for catechesis, or that spring from it. These elements are: the initial proclamation of the Gospel or missionary preaching through the kerygma to arouse faith, apologetics or examination of the reasons for belief, experience of Christian living, the celebration of the sacraments, integration into the ecclesial community, and apostolic and missionary witness".[17]

Pope John Paul II goes on to say that "sacramental life is impoverished and very soon turns into hollow ritualism if it is not based on a serious knowledge of the meaning of the sacraments".[18]

May Catholics receive sacraments from non-Catholic ministers?

Treating of this question the new Code of Canon Law states that "as often as necessity demands it or true spiritual advantage urges it and as long as the danger of error or indifference is avoided, the faithful, for whom access to a Catholic minister is physically or morally impossible, are permitted to receive the sacraments of penance, Eucharist and the anointing of the sick from non-Catholic ministers in whose Churches these three sacraments are valid" (c.844 n.2).

May Catholic ministers give sacraments to non-Catholics?

This is the next question dealt with by the same canon where it is stated that "Catholic ministers licitly administer the sacraments of Penance, Eucharist, and Anointing of the sick to members of the Eastern Churches who do not have full communion with the Catholic Church, when such members ask it of their accord and are properly disposed. This regulation is also valid concerning members of other Churches, which in the judgment of the Apostolic See, are in a situation concerning these sacraments equal to that of the above-mentioned Oriental Churches" (c.844 n.3).

"If danger of death is present, or if in the judgment of the diocesan bishop or of the Episcopal Conference, some other grave need urges it, Catholic ministers licitly administer the same three sacraments also to other Christians who do not have full communion with the Catholic Church, cannot approach a minister of their own community, and who ask it of their own accord, provided they manifest the Catholic faith concerning these sacraments and provided they are properly disposed" (c.844 n.4).

"For the cases mentioned in canon 844 nn. 2, 3 and 4, the diocesan bishop or the Episcopal Conference should not issue general norms except after consultation with at least the local competent authority of the non-Catholic Church or community concerned" (c.844 n.5).

Responsibilities arising from the sacraments

Although by reason of their Baptism Christians have a number of responsibilities in common, many of the responsibilities of the members of the Church will vary according to their position in the Church. It is beyond the scope of this book to list all the obligations of the faithful. We will be mentioning a number of responsibilities arising from the individual sacraments when we discuss them. We will limit ourselves to enumerating the main responsibilities or obligations which are directly or indirectly connected with the subject matter in question.

All the faithful should strive to lead a holy life in keeping with their proper condition and to promote the increase of the Church and her continued sanctification (cf. c.210).

So that they may be able to live their lives according to the Christian ideal, to make it known and, if necessary, defend it, and so that they may play their part in exercising the apostolate, the laity have the obligation and the right to acquire a knowledge of that teaching suited to the capacity and the condition of each (cf. c.229 n.1).

The faithful have the duty, each in the way proper to him, of always keeping in communion with the Church (cf. c.209 n.1).

The faithful are called to play their part in carrying out the mission which God has entrusted to the Church in the world (cf. c.204).

All the faithful, each according to his proper condition, should work together to build up the Body of Christ (cf. c.208).

All the faithful have the duty and the right of working so that the divine message of salvation may more and more reach all men of all time in the whole world (cf. c.211).

All the faithful are bound to accept and carry out in a spirit of Christian obedience what the sacred pastors declare as teachers of the faith and lay down as leaders of the Church (c.212).

The faithful are bound to support the Church so that she may have what is necessary for divine worship, for apostolic works of charity and for the decent support of her ministers (cf. c.222 n.1).

Mindful of the commandment of the Lord, they are also bound to promote social justice and to help the poor from their own resources (cf. c.222 n.2).

In so far as temporal affairs are concerned, Archbishop Rosalio José Castillo Lara, Pro-President of the Pontifical Commission for the Revision of the Code of Canon Law, points out that the true and properly specific function of the laity always remains that of "animating and perfecting the temporal order with the spirit of the Gospel" (*AA* 2) so that in the management of temporal affairs and in secular offices the laity may bear witness to Christ (cf. c.225 n.2)".[19]

The appropriateness of the sacraments

St Thomas Aquinas gives three reasons to show how the sacraments are appropriate means for man's salvation.

1) "The first reason is taken from the way in which human nature functions in achieving knowledge of spiritual or intelligible realities. It has the special property of arriving at this knowledge deductively through its experience of physical and sensible realities. Now it is characteristic of divine providence that it provides for each being in a manner corresponding to its own particular way of functioning. Hence it is appropriate that in bestowing certain aids to salvation upon man the divine wisdom should make use of certain physical and sensible signs called the sacraments.

2) The second reason is taken from man's own state. For by sinning he incurred an affection for physical things and so made himself subject to them. Now the remedy designed to heal man has to be applied to that part of his nature affected by the sickness. Hence it was appropriate for God to apply spiritual medicine to man by certain physical signs. For if he were to be confronted with spiritual realities pure and unalloyed, his mind, absorbed as it is in physical things, would be incapable of accepting them.

3) The third reason is taken from the fact that in his activities, man is particularly prone to involve himself with physical things.

Lest, therefore, it should be too hard for him totally to dispense with physical actions he was given certain physical practices to observe in the sacraments. The purpose of these was to enable him to exercise his powers in salutary ways, and so to avoid the superstitious practices of demon worship or of any of the harmful activities consisting of sinful deeds.

Through the sacraments, therefore, sensible signs are used to instruct man in a manner appropriate to his own nature".[20]

Why seven sacraments?

It is the teaching of the Church that there are seven sacraments of the New Law.

Discussing this question, the first reason that St Thomas Aquinas gives for the existence of the sacraments is that they perfect man in all that concerns the worship of God according to the Christian religion, and in other ways as we shall see. This is the background against which St Thomas argues that there should be seven sacraments.

St Thomas makes a comparison between the physical and the spiritual life. First of all man is perfected in himself in so far as his own person is concerned. This happen in two ways:

1) by acquiring a certain perfection of his life and
2) by overcoming the drawbacks in life such as sickness and things of that kind.

There are three stages in this process of perfection:

1) *Generation* — through which a man begins to exist and to live;
2) *Growth* — through which a man reaches his full stature and strength;
3) *Nourishment* — by which a man keeps himself alive and builds up his strength.

The same is true of the spiritual life.

1) Baptism, which is a spiritual regeneration (cf. Tit 3:5), corresponds to the first stage of perfection on the physical level;

2) **Confirmation corresponds to the second stage. In Confir**mation the Holy Spirit is given to strengthen the one being confirmed to help him to become a mature Christian.

3) The Eucharist corresponds to the third stage. Hence we read in John 6:53, "Except you eat the flesh of the Son of Man and drink his blood; you cannot have life in you".

If man's life were free from bodily and spiritual suffering, this would be sufficient. But because man in his physical and spiritual life sometimes experiences sickness of body and that of the spirit, namely, sin, he stands in need of a cure. This can be of two kinds.

The first kind of cure restores health. In the spiritual life the sacrament of Penance corresponds to this according to the words of the Psalmist: "Heal my soul, for I have sinned against you" (Ps 41:4).

The second kind of cure consists in having a suitable diet and taking physical exercise. Corresponding to this in the spiritual life is the Anointing of the sick (Extreme unction). This removes the relics of sin and prepares a man for final glory. Hence it is stated in James 5:15, "And if he has committed sins, they shall be forgiven him".

The second way in which man is perfected as a person relates to the whole of the society in which he lives because man is social by nature.

In this respect the first type of perfection man acquires comes about when he is given the power to govern people and to perform public acts. In the spiritual life the sacrament of Holy Orders corresponds to this because priests offer sacrifices not only for themselves but for the people (cf. Heb 7:27).

Man's perfection is also related to society by the propagation of the species. This happens in the physical and spiritual life through Matrimony by reason of the fact that it is not only a natural function but also a sacrament.

In St Thomas's view seven sacraments are also called for to remedy the human weaknesses caused by sin:

1) Baptism is a safeguard against the absence of the life of the spirit.
2) Confirmation is a safeguard against the spiritual weakness which is found in the newly-baptised.
3) The Eucharist is a safeguard against the liability to sin.
4) Penance is a safeguard against actual sin committed after Baptism.
5) The Anointing of the sick is a safeguard against the relics of sin which have not been completely taken away by Penance, either through negligence or ignorance.
6) Holy Orders is a safeguard against the break-up of society (the Church).
7) Matrimony is a safeguard against personal concupiscence and the diminishing numbers of people caused by death.[21]

St Thomas also divides the seven sacraments into three groups:

1) He calls **Baptism, Confirmation and the Eucharist** sacraments of Christian initiation because they give rise to the Christian life and bring it to perfection. Through them a man becomes a perfect Christian in himself. The law of the Church uses this terminology when it states that the sacraments of Baptism, Confirmation and Holy Eucharist are so related to each other that they are required for full Christian initiation (cf. c.842 n.2).

2) **Penance and the Anointing of the sick** are spoken of as sacraments of reconciliation because they enable man who has lost grace to be reconciled with God and with the Church.

3) **St Thomas calls Holy Orders and Matrimony** sacraments for the renewal of the community or society, because they are related to the perfection of the whole of the Christian society and allow for its continuity and renewal.

References

1. Dogmatic Constitution on the Church, nn. 1, 9, 48; Apostolic Constitution, 'Sacrae Disciplinae Legis' of Pope John Paul II, 25.1.83, L'Osservatore Romano (English Edition), 31.1.83, p.6.
2. Pope Pius XII, Encyclical 'Mediator Dei', C.T.S., n.19, p.14.
3. Constitution on the Sacred Liturgy, *Documents of Vatican II*, Walter M. Abbott, S.J., n. 7, p.141.
4. Pope Paul VI, General Audience, 2.8.72, L'Osservatore Romano (English Edition), 31.8.72.
5. F. Lambruschini, *I Sacramenti nella Teologia Morale e nella Vita Cristiana* (Editrice Ancora, Roma, 1964). p.50.
6. St Thomas Aquinas, *Summa Theologiae*, Part III, Q.62, art.5.
7. ibid., I–II, Q.109.
8. ibid., Vol. 56, pp.71 and 73 (3a 62.6).
9. ibid., p.47 (3a 61.4).
10. Constitution on the Sacred Liturgy n.59, Walter M. Abbott, p.158.
11. A Vonier, O.S.B., *A Key to the Doctrine of the Eucharist*, Collected Works, Vol. II (Burns & Oates, 1952), Ch. II, p.234.
12. Constitution on the Sacred Liturgy, n.7, Walter M. Abbott, p.141; cf. also c.834 C.I.C.
13. Apostolic Exhortation 'Catechesi Tradendae' of Pope John Paul II, 16.10.79, n.23, L'Osservatore Romano (English Edition), 12.11.79, p.4.
14. Apostolic Constitution 'Sacrae Disciplinae Legis' of Pope John Paul II, 25.1.83, ibid., pp. 7 and 8.
15. E. Schillebeeckx, O.P., *Christ the Sacrament* (Sheed & Ward, 1963), pp.126–7.
16. Ecumenical Directory, Part I, n.11, C.T.S. trans., p.10.
17. Apostolic Exhortation 'Catechesi Tradendae' of Pope John Paul II, 16.10.79, n.18, ibid., p.3.
18. ibid., n.23.
19. Address at the official presentation of the new Code of Canon Law, 3.2.83, L'Osservatore Romano (English Edition), 14.2.83, p.9.
20. St Thomas Aquinas, *Summa Theologiae* (Eyre & Spottiswoode, London), Vol. 56, pp. 37 and 39, (3a 61.1).
21. St Thomas Aquinas, *Summa Theologiae*, Part III, Q.65, art.1.

2

BAPTISM

The meaning of Baptism

According to its Greek etymology the word 'baptism' means 'cleansing'. St Paul speaks of Christ loving the Church and giving himself for it "that he might sanctify and cleanse it with the washing of water by the word" (cf. Eph 5 : 25,26). St Thomas Aquinas states that "washing the body with water is of the essence of Baptism".[1] Hence Baptism is called a washing. The new Code of Canon Law makes it clear that Baptism is validly conferred only through a washing with true water accompanied by the correct form of words (cf. c.849).

The transition from Judaism to Christianity was made easier for the Jews because Christ made use of things with which they were familiar. The Jews made great use of washings, even total washings. These signified the legal cleanliness which was required before appearing in the Temple, or as a preparation for various ceremonies.

When John the Baptist baptised on the banks of the Jordan he put the emphasis not on external cleanliness but on the meaning of interior repentance which is required for the forgiveness of sins. John kept repeating that *his* Baptism was but a preparation for the Baptism of Jesus. He also foretold the outpouring of the Holy Spirit at Christian Baptism: "I baptise you with water unto repentance . . . but he that comes after me is mightier than I . . . he shall baptise you with the Holy Spirit and with fire" (cf. Mt 3 : 11).

Faith and Baptism

In several places the documents of the Second Vatican Council speak of the relationship between faith and Baptism.

We read that "by the proclamation of the Gospel, she (the Church) prepares her hearers to receive and profess the faith, she disposes them for Baptism, etc."[2] and, "When the Holy Spirit, who calls all men to Christ and arouses in their hearts the submission of faith by the seed of the word and the preaching of the Gospel, brings those who believe in Christ to a new life through the womb of the baptismal font, he gathers them into one people of God which is a 'chosen race, a royal priesthood, a holy nation, a purchased people' (1 Pet 2: 19)".[3]

The Council also reminds us that "by Baptism men are grafted into the paschal mystery of Christ; they die with him, are buried with him and rise with him".[4]

"**The paschal mystery is the mystery in which the Son of God** became man, accepted an obedience which brought him even to death on the cross, and now, when he is risen from the dead and ascended into heaven, makes it possible for the world to share in his divine life. So it is that men now die to a life of sin, fashion themselves anew according to the model which is Christ, and now no longer live with their own life but with the life of him who died for them and rose again (2 Cor 5: 15). *This comes about through faith and through the sacraments of faith, principally Baptism*".[5]

Thus Baptism presupposes faith in Christ. The Apostles were first of all sent to preach the Gospel and then to baptise. "Go into all the world and preach the gospel to every creature. He that believes shall be saved" (Mk 16: 15–16). Faith is necessary in Baptism, if grace is to be obtained.[6] It is by faith that we are able to contact God initially and it is only against the background of faith that we can see Christ taking the baptised person to himself in the flowing of the water and the invocation of the Blessed Trinity.

According to St Thomas "the faith of the Church and of the person baptised contributes to the efficacy of Baptism; for this reason those who are baptised make a profession of faith and Baptism is called the sacrament of faith".[7]

Can infants have faith?

A difficulty arises in connection with the Baptism of infants who cannot be said to have faith. In treating of this question St Thomas says: "Spiritual re-birth which takes place through Baptism is in some ways similar to physical birth, in this respect that, as the infant in the mother's womb does not receive independent nourishment but is sustained by the nourishment of the mother, so also children not having the use of reason, as if in the womb of Mother Church, receive salvation not independently but through the activity of the Church. Thus St Augustine says: 'Mother Church offers her maternal mouth to her offspring that they may imbibe the sacred mysteries, because they are not yet able to believe unto righteousness with their own heart nor confess unto salvation with their own mouths. But if they are rightly called believers because they confess their faith in a way through the words of their sponsors, why should they not also be considered as repentant since through the same words of the sponsors they show themselves renouncing the devil and this world? For the same reason they can be considered to have the intention of receiving Baptism, not by their own act of intention, since they sometimes struggle and cry, but by the act of those who bring them for Baptism'. . . . But the faith of one person, indeed of the whole Church, profits the child through the working of the Holy Spirit who unites the Church and communicates the good of one to another".[8]

Both faith and Baptism are necessary for salvation. In the Dogmatic Constitution on the Church we read that "He (Christ) himself explicitly asserted the necessity of faith and Baptism (cf. Mk 16:16; Jn 3:5) and thereby affirmed at the same time the necessity of the Church which men enter through Baptism as through a door".[9]

This necessity of actual Baptism or Baptism of desire for salvation is mentioned in the new Code of Canon Law (cf. c.849).

Speaking of Baptism as the gateway to the sacraments (c.849) and pointing out that a person who has not been baptised cannot validly be admitted to the other sacraments (c.842 n.1) the introductory canon to the section on Baptism mentions some of the effects of this sacrament. We will take them in conjunction with the teaching of the Second Vatican Council.

1. *Men are freed from sins:* The Dogmatic Constitution on the Church speaks of the baptised person being "snatched from the slavery of error".[10]

2. *Reborn as children of God:* The various references of the Second Vatican Council to the effects of Baptism each in its turn enriches this notion of rebirth.

We read, for example, that "All Christians — that is, all those who have been reborn in water and the Holy Spirit — are called and in fact are children of God".[11] Then, "They (the baptised) receive the spirit of adoption as sons 'in which we cry, Abba, Father' (Rom 8:15)".[12] And again, "They also *belong* to Christ because by faith and Baptism they have been reborn in the Church, so that by newness of life and work they might belong to Christ (cf. 1 Cor 15 : 23)".[13]

3. *Made like to Christ by an indelible character:* The Dogmatic Constitution on the Church tells us that "through Baptism we are formed in the likeness of Christ".[14]

The character is an important aspect of Baptism as well as of Confirmation and Holy Orders.

In common with the Fathers of the Church St Thomas Aquinas describes the character as a mark or seal. He says that "properly speaking, character is a kind of seal by which something is marked off as ordained to some end, just as a coin is imprinted with a character ordaining it for use in commerce. Analagously, just as a coin is moulded to the image of the reigning sovereign, so the Christian in Baptism is moulded to Christ, so that he bears the image or likeness of Christ".[15]

The definition of character used by St Albert the Great and quoted by St Thomas, throws further light on its significance. "Character", he says, "is a distinctive mark deriving from the eternal character and imprinted upon the rational soul, setting the seal of the Trinity which creates and re-creates upon the created trinity as an image of it and distinguishing the sealed from the non-sealed". St Thomas explains that the eternal character is Christ himself and he concludes by saying that the character is properly to be attributed to Christ".[16] He also explains that the way in which the image of the Trinity is made present in the soul is through its powers (memory, understanding and will).[17]

The character is also spoken of as a consecration. This is one reason given for the fact, which we have mentioned above, that the sacraments which impart a character may not be repeated. Consecrations are not repeated. Under this aspect the character is closely connected with the worship of God. The Dogmatic Constitution on the Church speaks of the faithful being consecrated by the baptismal character to exercise the cult of the Christian religion,[18] and the Constitution on the Sacred Liturgy makes it clear that by reason of their Baptism Christians have a right and duty to full, conscious and active participation in liturgical celebrations. These also include the sacraments.[19] "They become true adorers such as the Father seeks".[20]

It is not surprising then to find that according to St Thomas "the sacramental character consists in a certain participation in Christ's priesthood present in his faithful. It is present in the sense that just as Christ has the full power of a spiritual priesthood, so his faithful are brought into configuration with him in that they share in a spiritual power relating to the sacraments and what belongs to divine worship".[21] In another place he says that "each member of the faithful is deputed to receive or hand on to others those things which pertain to the worship of God, and it is for this, properly speaking, that the sacramental character is ordained. The rites of the Christian religion, taken as a whole, are derived from the priesthood of Christ, and hence it is clear that the sacramental character is specifically the character of Christ, seeing that a configuration to his priesthood is imparted to the faithful through sacramental characters which are nothing else than a kind of participation in the priesthood of Christ deriving from Christ himself".[22]

This sharing in the priesthood is brought out in the baptismal ceremony by the anointing with chrism. This also signifies that the character is a spiritual anointing and an interior consecration. The words which accompany the anointing are: "He (God the Father) anoints you with the chrism of salvation. As Christ was anointed Priest, Prophet and King (cf. also c.204 n.1), so may you live always as members of his body, sharing everlasting life". Priests are anointed at their consecration and Catholic kings are anointed at their coronation.

Canon 204 n.1 of the Code of Canon Law speaks of the faithful through Baptism being made sharers each in his own way in the priestly, prophetic and kingly office of Christ.

In his Encyclical Letter 'Redemptor Hominis', Pope John Paul II shows that prophetic mission is connected with the truths divinely committed to the Church to be communicated to all men and states that "the Church's responsibility for divine truth must be increasingly shared in various ways by all". Of catechesis, which is linked with this prophetic mission, Pope John Paul II says: "Catechesis certainly constitutes a permanent and also fundamental form of activity by the Church, one in which her prophetic charism is manifested"; and he speaks of the "universal sharing of the whole of the people of God in the prophetic office of Christ".[25]

With regard to the kingly office of Christ in which all Christians share, Pope John Paul II in the same Encyclical points out that " the sharing in Christ's kingly mission, that is to say the fact of rediscovering in oneself and others the special dignity of our vocation that can be described as 'kingship', is expressed in readiness to serve, in keeping with the example of Christ, who 'came not to be served but to serve' . . . In order to be able to serve others worthily and effectively we must be able to master ourselves and possess the virtues that make this mastery possible".[24]

4. *Baptism incorporates the faithful into the Church making them members of the People of God* (cf. c.849 and c.204 n.1).

5. *A bond of unity:* This effect of Baptism is mentioned at least three times in the documents of the Second Vatican Council. We read that "Baptism constitutes the sacramental bond of unity among all who through it are reborn",[25] and that "the Church knows that she is joined in many ways to the baptised who are honoured by the name of Christian, but who do not however profess the Catholic faith in its entirety or have not preserved unity or communion under the successor of Peter".[26] In the light of these statements "the ecumenical spirit should be nourished among the newly-baptised; they must appreciate that their brothers who believe in Christ are disciples of Christ, and having been reborn in Baptism share in many of the blessings of the people of God".[27]

The following quotation shows us how the Church today views the position of our separated brethren: "One cannot charge with the sin of separation those who at present are born into these communities and in them are brought up in the faith of Christ, and the Catholic Church accepts them with respect and affection as brothers. For men who believe in Christ and have been properly baptised are put in some, though imperfect, communion with the Catholic Church".[28]

Baptism is but a beginning

The Second Vatican Council reminds us that "Baptism itself is only a beginning, a point of departure, for it is wholly directed towards the acquiring of fullness of life in Christ. Baptism is thus ordained towards a complete profession of faith, a complete incorporation into the system of salvation such as Christ himself willed it to be, and finally, towards a complete integration into eucharistic communion".

The minister of Baptism

The ordinary minister of Baptism is a bishop, priest or deacon (c.861).

Cases of danger of death have already been dealt with when we spoke of the minister of the sacraments.

Responsibilities connected with Baptism

Other responsibilities in addition to those we have seen with regard to the sacraments in general, are incurred by those involved in the sacrament of Baptism, namely, the priest, the parents and the god-parents.

Before the Baptism of infants

Parish priests should personally or through their assistants see that parents are prepared for the Baptism of their children by pastoral counsel and by common prayer. With this in view he should visit groups of families whenever possible (cf. c.851 n.2).

Priests with the care of souls, especially the parish priest, should teach the faithful the proper way to baptise (c.861 n.2).

Parents are bound to see that their children are baptised in the first weeks after their birth. They should go to the parish priest as soon as possible after the birth, or even before it, to arrange for the Baptism of the child and to be prepared for it (c.867 n.1).

Parents and god-parents should be taught the meaning of the sacrament of Baptism and the obligations arising from it (c.851 n.1)

Before the Baptism of adults

An adult who intends to receive Baptism should be admitted to the catechumenate and, in so far as is possible, should go through the various stages of sacramental initiation (c.851 n.1). He must ask for Baptism, be sufficiently instructed in the truths and obligations of the Christian faith and have had experience of the Christian way of life through the catechumate. He should be sorry for his sins (c.865 n.1). It is left to the Episcopal Conference to decide on a suitable form of catechesis and to issue special guidelines about this (c.851 n.1). The bishop of the Diocese should see that a catechumenate for admitting adults to the sacraments of initiation is set up and observed throughout the diocese according to the guidelines given by the competent Church authority (cf. Directorium de Pastorali Ministerio Episcoporum, Vatican Press, n.72, p.75).

Without using the actual word catechumenate Pope John Paul II refers to something akin to it when he states that "in the course of the centuries an important element of catechesis was constituted by the *traditio Symboli* (the transmission of the summary of the faith), followed by the transmission of the Lord's Prayer. This

C

expressive rite has in our time been reintroduced into the initiation of catechumens. Should not greater use be made of an adapted form of it to mark that most important stage at which a new disciple of Christ accepts with full awareness and courage the content of what will from then on be the object of his earnest study?"[29]

After the Baptism of adults

When an adult is baptised he should be confirmed immediately afterwards and participate in the celebration of the Eucharist by receiving Holy Communion, unless there is a grave reason to the contrary (c.866).

God-parents

The law of the Church requires that there be a god-parent for those who are to be baptised in so far as this is possible. At most the law allows for two god-parents — a god-father and a god-mother, but one is sufficient (cc.872–3).

At the Baptism of infants the god-parent together with the parents is to present the child for Baptism (c.872).

The god-parents, who should be chosen either by the person to be baptised, or by his/her parents or by those who are acting in the place of the parents, and, failing these, by the parish priest or minister of the sacrament, must be capable of and willing to take on this duty (c.874 n.1,1°).

The god-parent must have completed the sixteenth year of his age, unless the diocesan bishop allows for a different age, or there is a just reason for making an exception in the opinion of the parish priest or the minister of the sacrament (c.874 n.1,2°).

The god-parent must be a Catholic who has been confirmed and has been admitted to Holy Communion and leads a life in keeping with the faith and the duty he is undertaking (c.874 n.1,3°).

He must not be under a canonical penalty which has been lawfully imposed or declared (c.874 n.1,4°).

The god-parent must be neither the father or the mother of the one to be baptised.

After the Baptism of infants

Together with the parents the god-parent is to see that the child leads a Christian life and faithfully fulfils the obligations attaching to his/her Baptism (c.872).

After the Baptism of adults

The god-parent has the duty of helping the baptised in his Christian initiation.

These prescriptions of law make it clear that the function of a god-parent is not just a formality.

The new Code of Canon Law has abolished the 'spiritual relationship' which in the 1917 Code arose between the person baptised, the one baptising and the god-parent(s) and constituted an impediment to marriage between the baptised person and these two.

May a non-Catholic be a god-parent at a Catholic Baptism?

A person who is baptised but belonging to a non-Catholic ecclesial community should be admitted only as a witness of the Baptism together with a Catholic god-parent (c.874 n.2).

The duty of education

With regard to the profession of their faith and living the Christian life, Baptism does not automatically make people good Christians. For this they require education.

We have already seen that the faithful have the right to acquire the requisite knowledge to enable them to live the Christian life as they should.

Parents have a very serious obligation and also the right to educate their children. It is their duty especially to see that their children are educated according to the teaching of the Church (c.226 n.2).

It is for the Episcopal Conference to decide on an adequate form of catechesis for children, adolescents, young people and adults who have been baptised in infancy in such a way that they can follow a definite form of catechumenate to gradually reach Christian maturity corresponding to that required by the sacraments of Penance, the Eucharist, Confirmation and Marriage. (Directory on the Pastoral Ministry of Bishops issued by the Sacred Congregation for Bishops, 1973, n.73).

Pope John Paul II has this duty of parents in mind when he writes: "One moment that is often decisive is the one at which the very young child receives the first elements of catechesis from its parents and the family surroundings. These elements will perhaps be no more than a simple revelation of a good and provident Father in heaven to whom the child learns to turn its heart. The very short prayers that the child learns to lisp will be the start of a loving dialogue with the hidden God whose word it will then begin to hear. I cannot insist too strongly on this early initiation by Christian parents in which the child's faculties are integrated into a living relationship with God. It is a work of prime importance. It demands great love and profound respect for the child who has a right to a simple and true presentation of the Christian faith".[30]

Pope John Paul II also speaks of the catechesis of children by their parents as the 'fundamental field' of catechesis.[31]

Finally, Pope John Paul II states that "Family catechesis precedes, accompanies and enriches all other forms of catechesis". He goes on to say that "there cannot be too great an effort on the part of Christian parents to prepare for this ministry of being their own children's catechists and to carry it out with tireless zeal".[32]

Speaking two years before Pope John Paul II issued his Encyclical 'Catechesi Tradendae', the Bishops of England and Wales referred to the educational role of the parents in the following words: "Catholic education means more than just sending the child to a Catholic school. What the child learns from its parents at home, and that from his earliest years, is an even more important part of his education".[33]

A number of the points already incorporated into the new Code of Canon Law are to be found in the Introduction to the new Rite for the Baptism of Children. One of the points this Introduction makes in connection with Baptism is that normally it is for the priest to recommend suitable literature for the parents and godparents because they will need publications which have been written for families.[34]

When the child reaches school age the parents should send him to a Catholic school. If this is not possible, they are bound to see that their children are given the necessary Catholic instruction outside school hours (cf. c.788).

The kind of education which the Church has in mind is true

education which embraces the complete formation of the human person, taking account of his final end and of the common good of society. Children and young people should be educated in such a way that they can develop their physical, moral and intellectual endowments in harmony, that they may acquire a more mature sense of responsibility and a correct use of freedom and are enabled to participate actively in the life of the society in which they live (cf. c.795).

Baptism and the children of non-practising Catholics

This is a very difficult question in view of what has been said about the obligation of the parents to bring up their children as Catholics. The difficulty arises from the fact that if the parents are not practising or lapsed Catholics the children will have imposed on them obligations which they will be unable to fulfil because they will not receive the necessary Christian formation in the home nor the Catholic education they will need once they reach school age. In these circumstances the god-parent(s) will not be able to exercise any useful influence with regard to the Catholic upbringing of such children.

The law of the Church states that for a child to be lawfully baptised there must be a well-founded hope that he will be educated in the Catholic religion. If these grounds are lacking, the Baptism should be delayed in accordance with the requirements of particular law, and the parents should be told why (cf. c.868 n.1,2°). It is to be hoped that by deferring the Baptism the parents themselves can be persuaded to receive instruction and return to the practice of their faith. Asking for such instruction could be a sign of their good faith.

This ruling should impress on Catholic parents the serious implications of the sacrament of Baptism. It is not just a meaningless family tradition, a ceremony without any moral or religious consequences, a celebration of the birth of the child which gives an opportunity for a family party, or a social convention. The uninstructed can also be motivated by some superstitious belief that Baptism will ward off evil from the child they love.

The mutual recognition of Baptism

In September 1971 the following statement was issued by the Bishops of England and Wales about the mutual recognition of

Baptisms performed by ministers of other Christian faiths.

"In the past a certain doubt was felt regarding the valid administration of Christian Baptism by non-Catholic ministers. This led to the prudent practice of conditional Baptism, especially in the case of the reception of converts.

This practice was never meant to impugn the unity of the one Baptism of Christ. Hence the Hierarchy of England and Wales were happy to recognise that the more stringent practice of the past should be re-considered.

Following upon the publication of the 'Enquiry into Baptismal Practice' undertaken, with Catholic participation, by the British Council of Churches, the bishops issued the following directives:

1. The Catholic Church in this Country accepts in principle the Baptism of non-Catholic Churches whose baptismal *rite* is recognised as valid (i.e. the 15 Churches of the BCC Report) unless there is prudent doubt to the contrary in a particular case.

   In all the Churches here listed Baptism is administered with the application of water in the name of the Father and of the Son and of the Holy Spirit:

Anglican Communion:	Church of England, Church in Wales, Church in Ireland, Episcopal Church in Scotland.
Methodist Church	
Presbyterian Churches:	Church of Scotland, United Free Church of Scotland, Presbyterian Church of England, Presbyterian Church in Ireland, Presbyterian Church of Wales.
Lutheran Church	
Congregational Church:	In England and Wales: Countess of Huntingdon's Connexion: Union of Welsh Independents.
Moravian Church	

   The validity of these baptismal rites administered elsewhere than in England and Wales must be judged according to the enactments of the local Conference.

2. A Certificate from these Churches that attests that a person has been baptised with water in the name of the Father and of the Son and of the Holy Spirit should normally be accepted as the

evidence required by the *Directory* (1,13,a) for the *fact* of valid Baptism.

It will be noted that the validity of the baptismal rite does not of itself dispel prudent doubt. In accordance, therefore, with the prescriptions of the *Directory on Ecumenism*, the fact of Christian Baptism must be known and sufficient evidence of this is given by a certificate issued by one of these Churches according to the terms of the directive".

When a convert is received into the Church a record of the date of his already valid Baptism should always be made in the parochial register.

All that has been said above is in accordance with the latest law of the Church on the subject where it is stated that:

If there is a doubt as to whether somebody has been baptised or whether the Baptism was validly administered, and after serious investigation the doubt remains, Baptism should be administered conditionally (cf. c.869 n.1).

Those who have been baptised in a non-Catholic ecclesial community are not to be baptised conditionally, except after having examined the matter and the form of words used in the administration of the Baptism and the intention both of the adult who has been baptised and that of the minister baptising, there remains a serious reason for doubting the validity of the Baptism (cf. c.869 n.2).

If in the cases mentioned above the administration or the validity of the Baptism remains doubtful, Baptism should not be administered except, if it is question of an adult, after having explained the teaching of the Church concerning the sacrament of Baptism. If it is question of a child, the reasons for doubting the validity of the Baptism which has already taken place should be made known to the parents (cf. c.869 n.3).

References

1. St Thomas Aquinas, op. cit., Vol. 57, p.33 (3a.66.8).
2. Dogmatic Constitution on the Church, n.17., Walter M. Abbott, S.J., p.36.
3. Decree on the Church's Missionary Activity, n.15, Walter M. Abbott, p.601.
4. Constitution on the Sacred Liturgy, n.6, Walter M. Abbott, op. cit., p.140.
5. Sacred Congregation of Rites, 'Instruction on Putting into Effect the Constitution on the Sacred Liturgy', C.T.S., Do.348 n.6, p.6.
6. St Thomas Aquinas, op. cit., Vol. 57, p.105 (3a.68.8).
7. ibid., Vol. 53, p.35 (3a.39.5).
8. ibid., Vol. 57, pp. 109 and 111 (3a.66.9).

9. Walter M. Abbott, op. cit., n.14, p.32.
10. Dogmatic Constitution on the Church, n.17, Walter M. Abbott, op. cit., p.36.
11. Declaration on Christian Education, n.2, Walter M. Abbott, op. cit., p.64.
12. Constitution on the Sacred Liturgy, n.6, Walter M. Abbott, op. cit., p.140.
13. Decree on the Church's Missionary Activity, n.21, Walter M. Abbott, p.611.
14. Dogmatic Constitution on the Church, n.7, Walter M. Abbott, op. cit., p.20.
15. St Thomas Aquinas, op. cit., Vol. 56, p.85 (3a.63.3).
16. ibid., Vol. 56, p.79 (3a.63.1).
17. ibid., Vol. 56, p.89 (3a.63.4).
18. Dogmatic Constitution on the Church, n.11, Walter M. Abbott, op. cit., p.28.
19. Constitution on the Sacred Liturgy, n.14, Walter M. Abbott, op. cit., p.144.
20. ibid., n.6, Walter M. Abbott, op. cit., p.166.
21. St Thomas Aquinas, op. cit., Vol. 56, p.93 (3a.63.5).
22. ibid, Vol. 56, p.87 (3a.63.3).
23. Pope John Paul II, Encyclical Letter 'Redemptor Hominis', 4.3.79, n.19, L'Osservatore Romano (English Edition), 19.3.79, p.11.
24. ibid., n.21, L'Osservatore Romano (English Edition), 19.3.79, p.12.
25. Decree on Ecumenism, n.22, Walter M. Abbott, op. cit., p. 364.
26. Dogmatic Constitution on the Church, n.15, Walter M. Abbott, pp.33–4.
27. Decree on the Missionary Activity of the Church, n.15, Walter M. Abbott, op. cit., p.602.
28. Decree on Ecumenism, n.3, Walter M. Abbott, op. cit., p.345.
29. Pope John Paul II, Apostolic Exhortation 'Catechesi Tradendae', 16.10.79, n.28, L'Osservatore Romano (English Edition), 12.11.79, p.4.
30. ibid., n.36, L'Osservatore Romano (English Edition), 12.11.79, p.6.
31. Pope John Paul II, Encyclical Letter 'Redemptor Hominis', 4.3.79, n.19, L'Osservatore Romano (English Edition), 19.3.79, p.11.
32. Pope John Paul II, Apostolic Exhortation 'Catechesi Tradendae', 16.10.79, n.68, L'Osservatore Romano (English Edition), 12.11.79, p.10.
33. Revised Directory (1977) by the Bishops Conference of England and Wales based upon the Apostolic Letter Motu Proprio of Pope Paul VI, 'Matrimonia Mixta', 31.3.70, n.13.
34. *The Rite of Baptism for Children* (Geoffrey Chapman, London), General Introduction — Christian Initiation.

3

CONFIRMATION

Scriptural background

In the Apostolic Constitution 'Divinae Consortium Naturae', Pope Paul VI first of all shows how the Holy Spirit assisted Christ in fulfilling his messianic mission.

In the New Testament we read that on receiving the baptism of John, Jesus saw the Spirit descending on himself. "And when he came out of the water, immediately he saw the heavens opened and the Spirit descending upon him like a dove" (cf. Mk 1:10). The Spirit also remained with him. St John tells us: "And John bore witness: 'I saw the Spirit descend as a dove from heaven and it remained on him'" (cf. Jn 1:32).

We are also told that Jesus was impelled by the Spirit to undertake his public ministry as the Messiah, relying on the Spirit's presence and assistance. When teaching the people of Nazareth in the synagogue he insinuated by what he said that the words of Isaiah "the Spirit of the Lord has been given to me" referred to himself. "He opened the book and found the place where it is written: 'The Spirit of the Lord is upon me because he has anointed me to preach the good news to the poor. He has sent me to proclaim release to the captives and recovering of sight to the blind, to set at liberty those who are oppressed, to proclaim the acceptable year of the Lord'. And he closed the book, and gave it back to the attendant, and sat down; and the eyes of all in the synagogue were fixed on him. And he began to say to them, 'Today this Scripture has been fulfilled in your hearing'" (cf. Lk 4:17–21).

The Holy Spirit was also with his disciples in carrying out their mission. Christ promised them that the Spirit would help them to bear fearless witness to their faith even in the face of persecution. "Do not be anxious how or what you are to answer for the Holy Spirit will teach you in that very hour what you ought to say" (cf. Lk 12:12). The day before he suffered he assured his apostles that he would send the Spirit of truth from his Father. "But when the Counsellor comes, whom I shall send you from the Father, even the Spirit of truth who proceeds from the Father, he will

bear witness to me; and you also are witnesses, because you have
been with me from the beginning" (cf. Jn 15 : 26–27). Finally after
his resurrection he promised that the Spirit would come to them.
"You will receive power when the Holy Spirit comes upon you and
then you will be my witnesses" (cf. Lk 24 : 49; Acts 1 : 8).

We know that on the feast of Pentecost the Holy Spirit came
down in an extraordinary way on the apostles together in the upper
room and they were so "filled with the Holy Spirit" that by divine
inspiration they began to proclaim 'the mighty works of God' (cf.
Acts ch.2).

From then onwards in fulfilment of Christ's wish they imparted the gift of the Holy Spirit by the laying on of hands to
complete the grace of Baptism.

Pope Paul VI observes that "the sacrament of Confirmation in
a certain way perpetuates in the Church the grace of Pentecost".[1]

Spiritual maturity

For St Thomas Aquinas Confirmation is related to Baptism as
growth is related to generation. Just as "Baptism is a spiritual
generation into the Christian life", so "Confirmation is spiritual
growth bringing man to spiritual maturity".[2] He also tells us that
"Confirmation is given for the purpose of attaining the fullness of
the Holy Spirit who works in manifold ways",[3] and, "in Confirmation man receives maturity in the life of the Spirit".[4] In the context
of regeneration and growth St Thomas makes a further comment.
He states that: "The sacrament of Baptism is a spiritual generation
which is change from non-being into being. But Confirmation is
more effective with regard to progress in good, because it involves
spiritual growth from imperfect to perfect being".[5] This means that
the being of the baptised as a Christian has attained a further degree
of perfection which he did not have before receiving Confirmation.

Confirmation therefore enables Christians to reach spiritual
maturity. St Thomas also uses the phrase 'spiritual coming of age'.

There are difficulties to be met with in reaching both physical
and psychological maturity. There are also difficulties to be met
with in developing as a mature Christian. All followers of Christ
have a duty to direct their affections rightly and to use this world's
good in accordance with the spirit of the Gospel. St Paul reminds
the Corinthians that "We have received not the spirit of this world
but the spirit which is from God that we might understand the
gifts bestowed on us by God" (cf. 1 Cor 2 : 12).

Signs of spiritual maturity

Spiritual maturity is shown by serious spiritual activity springing from sincere convictions and a deep knowledge of God himself, the Church and the world.

A Christian who is spiritually mature is able to evaluate the things and affairs of this world at their proper worth in relation to the Christian life.

Spiritual maturity enables us to discover our proper place in the life of the Church and the duties that go with it. We are made aware of our personal and social responsibilities as members of the Mystical Body of Christ.

Hand in hand with spiritual maturity goes the freedom to make a responsible choice, the wisdom to make the necessary adjustments that are called for in one's growth in the Christian life and a maturity of judgment.

St Thomas points out that "even in the years of childhood man can attain spiritual maturity. . . So it is that many children, because they received the strength given by the Holy Spirit, have bravely fought even to the shedding of their blood".[6]

In conclusion it can be said that there is not a complete parallel between natural growth and spiritual growth. There are people who have attained physical and psychological maturity whose faith is infantile and undeveloped.

The minister of Confirmation

According to the law of the Church the ordinary minister of Confirmation is a bishop. But a priest can validly administer this sacrament, if he has been given this faculty either in virtue of the common law or of a special concession on the part of the competent authority (cf. c.882).

In the eyes of the law a priest who, in virtue of his office, or of a mandate from the diocesan bishop, baptises someone who is no longer a child or receives a person, who has already been baptised, into full communion with the Catholic Church, has the faculty of administering Confirmation.

With regard to those who are in danger of death, the parish priest, or any priest, is empowered by law to administer Confirmation to such (cf. c.883, 2°, 3°).

Preparation for Confirmation

Outside cases where there is danger of death, it is required that if the candidate for Confirmation has the use of reason, he be properly prepared, rightly disposed and able to renew the baptismal promises (cf. c.889 n.2).

The age for Confirmation

The sacrament of Confirmation should be conferred on the faithful about the time of the age of discretion, unless the Episcopal Conference has decided on a different age, or there is danger of death, or in the judgment of the minister some grave reason counsels otherwise (c.891).

According to the 1917 Code the normal age for receiving Confirmation was the age of seven.

It will be noticed that in the text of the new Code of Canon Law the term 'age of discretion' is used. This is wider than 'the age of seven'. One of the conditions attached to the reception of Confirmation is that the candidate be able to renew the baptismal promises. This calls for a certain maturity so that the person to be confirmed can understand and appreciate the implication of these promises. One bishop is of the opinion that primary school children are seldom of sufficient maturity to be able to renew their baptismal promises with the understanding that the sacrament seems to demand and he goes on to say that "it is now more common than otherwise for youngsters to be presented for Confirmation early in their secondary school career".[7]

So that the reception of this sacrament may be more fruitful pastorally, the new Code of Canon Law leaves it to the judgment of the Episcopal Conferences and the customs of different places to fix the age for receiving Confirmation in accordance with the spirit of the Second Vatican Council.

Parents, pastors of souls, especially parish priests, should see to it that the faithful are properly prepared for the reception of this sacrament and that they should receive it at a suitable time (cf. c.890).

The faithful are bound to receive this sacrament in good time [*tempestive*] (cf. c.890).

The effects of Confirmation

1. *A further share in the priesthood of Christ:* Confirmation imprints a character. We have already seen that the character gives us a share in the priesthood of Christ.

In the Apostolic Constitution 'Divinae Consortium Naturae', introducing the new Rite of Confirmation, Pope Paul VI says: "In Baptism neophytes receive forgiveness of sins, adoption as sons of God and the character of Christ whereby they are made members of the Church and given *a first sharing* in the priesthood of their Saviour".[8] This reference to a first sharing in the priesthood implies that there are other sharings. The second sharing is given in Confirmation. One normally associates the priesthood of Christ with the worship of God. The fact is that the public profession and defence of the Christian faith, which is one of the obligations attaching to Confirmation, are said to be sacred actions and expressions of divine worship in that they represent the natural extension or continuation and necessary completion in real life of the profession of faith which the Christian has made in the liturgical functions. This is endorsed by what is said in the Decree on the Apostolate of the Laity, where we read that: "If they are consecrated a kingly priesthood and a holy nation (cf. 1 Pet 2:4–10), it is in order that they may in all their actions offer spiritual sacrifices and bear witness to Christ all the world over".[9]

2. *More perfectly conformed to Christ:* This likeness to Christ is also related to sacramental character. The *Ordo Confirmationis* tells us in the Introduction that "by the gift of the Holy Spirit the faithful are more perfectly conformed to Christ",[10] and in the homily given in the rite itself the minister of the sacrament tells the candidate(s): "You are about to receive the gift of the Holy Spirit which is for you a spiritual marking, uniting you more closely with Christ and making you more perfect members of his Church".[11]

3. *Strengthened by the Holy Spirit:* To appreciate the power of the Holy Spirit we have only to look at the change that came over the apostles at Pentecost. Christ had told them that he was entrusting to the Holy Spirit the work of enlightening their minds. "But the Counsellor, the Holy Spirit, whom the Father will send in my name, he will teach you all things, and bring to your remembrance all that I have said to you" (cf. Jn 14:26).

The apostles were not able to stand the test of Christ's passion and death. They had been with him for three years and for the most part they abandoned him in his passion. Even Peter, who did enter the court room, perjured himself before leaving. Jesus had foreseen this and, as we have seen, told them that he would send his Spirit to strengthen them in their faith and in their convictions. This is what exactly happened at the coming of the Holy Spirit. They understood through the enlightenment they had received from above what Jesus had revealed to them. They were fired with a love which showed itself in zeal and courage to the extent of eventually giving the supreme proof of their fidelity to Jesus with martyrdom.

4. *Strengthened to bear witness to Christ:* The purpose of bearing witness to Christ is, as stated in the Introduction to the *Ordo Confirmationis,* that his body may be built up in faith and charity".[12]

The reference to charity reminds us of the mission of Christ himself which is recalled in the words of the homily given in the course of the rite itself: "Christ himself, anointed by the Holy Spirit when John baptised him, was sent forth to the work of his ministry which was the enkindling on earth of the flame of that same Holy Spirit".[13]

Responsibilities arising from Confirmation

The sacrament of Confirmation is given with a view to a mission — the mission to be a prophet of the New Law. Prophecy here has nothing to do with foretelling the future. It refers to being a witness to Christ, a bearer of the good news of the Gospel, bringing the faith to others. The new Code of Canon Law reminds us that through Confirmation as witnesses to Christ we are more strictly obliged to spread and defend the faith in word and deed (cf. c.879).

The sign of the cross which the minister traces on the candidate's forehead is the sign of Christ's victory. It is traced on the forehead to remind us that we must not hide from anyone the fact that we belong to Christ. We do this by following and imitating Christ. Nor must we be afraid of professing publicly that we do belong to Christ. This requires us to act as Christ did, that is with courage and conviction, yet with meekness and gentleness. The gift of fortitude associated with Confirmation is given precisely for this. The author of the Letter to the Hebrews (cf. 12 : 1–3) reminds us that the Christian needs courage and endurance.

The following quotation from the Decree on the Missionary Activity of the Church spells out in greater detail what is involved in receiving Confirmation. "All Christians by the example of their lives and the witness of the word, wherever they live, have an obligation to manifest the new man which they put on in Baptism and to reveal the power of the Holy Spirit by whom they were strengthened at Confirmation so that others seeing their good works might glorify the Father (cf. Mt 5 : 16) and more perfectly perceive the true meaning of human life and the universal solidarity of mankind".[14]

The grace of the sacrament of Confirmation

The Introduction to the Rite of Confirmation speaks of the sacrament conferring grace on the person confirmed in order to spread among men the sweet fragrance of Christ.[15]

Commenting on Psalm 140 : 4–6, St Augustine says : "There is no scent more fragrant than that of the Lord. All who believe must possess this perfume". St Paul writing to the Corinthians says : "But thanks be to God, who in Christ always leads us in triumph, and through us spreads the fragrance of the knowledge of him everywhere. For we are the aroma of Christ to God among those who are being saved".

Man's co-operation with the grace of the Holy Spirit will enable him to spread among men this sweet fragrance of Christ.

God-parents

The law of the Church requires that the person being confirmed should have a god-parent if this is possible (cf. c.892).

The 1917 Code as a general rule required that the god-parent at Confirmation be different from the one at the Baptism of the person being confirmed.

The new Code of Canon Law recommends that the god-parent at Confirmation should be the same as the one for the Baptism (cf. c.893 n.2).

The conditions for acting as a god-parent at Confirmation are the same as those relating to the god-parent(s) at Baptism (cf. c.893 n.1).

The duty of the god-parent is to see that the one confirmed conducts him/herself as a true witness of Christ and that he/she fulfils faithfully the obligations attaching to the sacrament of Confirmation.

References

1. Pope Paul VI, Apostolic Constitution 'Divinae Consortium Naturae', 15.8.71, L'Osservatore Romano (English Edition), 23.9.71, pp.4–5.
2. St Thomas Aquinas, op. cit., Vol. 57, p.205 (3a.72.5).
3. ibid., Vol. 57, p.195 (3a.72.3).
4. ibid., Vol. 57, p.189 (3a.72.1).

5. ibid., Vol. 57, p.225 (3a.72.12).

6. ibid., Vol. 57, p.215 (3a.72.9).

7. Bishop D. Konstant, Letter to the Clergy of the Central London Area, Westminster 'Ad Clerum', Area Letters, February, 1980.

8. Pope Paul VI, Apostolic Constitution 'Divinae Consortium Naturae', 15.8.71, L'Osservatore Romano (English Edition), 23.9.71, pp.4–5.

9. Decree on the Apostolate of the Laity, n.3, Walter M. Abbott, op. cit., p.492.

10. *Ordo Confirmationis*, (Libreria Editrice Vaticana), Praenotanda, n.2, p.16.

11. The Rite of Confirmation, C.T.S., Do.482, p.4.

12. *Ordo Confirmationis*, (Liberia Editrice Vaticana), Praenotanda, n.2, p.16.

13. The Rite of Confirmation, C.T.S., Do.482, p..4.

14. Decree of the Church's Missionary Activity, n.11, Walter M. Abbott, op. cit., p.597.

15. *Ordo Confirmationis*, (Libreria Editrice Vaticana), Praenotanda, n.9, p.19.

4

THE EUCHARIST

The Eucharist gets its name from the central Eucharistic prayer — the Mass — which is a prayer of thanksgiving and praise to God for what he has done for the salvation of mankind. "The Church, especially in the great Eucharistic Prayer, together with Christ gives thanks to the Father in the Holy Spirit for all the blessings which he gives to men in creation and especially in the Paschal Mystery, and prays to him for the coming of his kingdom".[1]

In the new Code of Canon Law there is an excellent summary of the teaching of the Church on this sacrament in the first canon introducing the section on the Eucharist. It tells us that the most august sacrament is the Holy Eucharist. In it Christ the Lord is contained, offered and received. The Church lives and grows through it. The Eucharistic sacrifice, the memorial of the death and resurrection of the Lord in which the Sacrifice of the cross is perpetuated through the ages, is the crown and source of the whole worship and of the Christian life. By it the unity of the people of God is signified and brought about and the building up of the Body of Christ is achieved. The other sacraments and all the apostolic works in the Church are linked with it and directed towards it (cf. c.899).

The three aspects of the Eucharist

Speaking of the magnitude and essential meaning of this most holy sacrament in his Encyclical Letter 'Redemptor Hominis', Pope John Paul II refers to the three aspects of the Eucharist in the following terms: "It is at one and the same time a Sacrifice-Sacrament, a Communion-Sacrament and a Presence-Sacrament".[2]

The Instruction on the Worship of the Eucharistic Mystery also points out that "it is important that the mystery of the Eucharist should shine out before the eyes of the faithful in its true light. It should be considered in all its different aspects, and the real relationships which, as the Church teaches, are known to exist

D

between these various aspects of the mystery, should be so understood by the faithful as to be reflected in their lives".[3]

Although these aspects are interconnected, it will be more practical to discuss them individually. There is also an interesting parallel to be drawn between this mystery and similar aspects of God's dealings with the chosen people in the Old Testament.

Sacrifice — Biblical background

When Christ instituted the Eucharist he did so in the context of a covenant. In Matthew 26:27–28, we read: "All of you drink this; for this is my Blood of the Covenant which is being shed for many unto the forgiveness of sins". Here Christ is definitely contrasting the New Covenant or Alliance with the Old Alliance which foreshadowed it. With the notion of Covenant we are at the centre of God's plan for salvation. The whole history of salvation is, in effect, the gratuitous action of God calling mankind back to that *communion of life* with him which man had enjoyed before the fall, a communion of life which will be perfectly realised in the happiness of heaven when we see God face to face.

The Old Testament was a long preparation for the coming of the Redeemer and it was dominated throughout by the Alliance made by God on Mount Sinai, the account of which is given in Exodus 19–24. This Alliance between God himself and a people he had just delivered from the slavery of Egypt was inaugurated by Moses through the offering of a sacrifice. On this occasion Moses sprinkled the blood of the sacrificed victims on the altar (symbolising God) and then on the people, saying to them: "This is the blood of the Alliance which Yahweh has made with you. . .". The blood of the *same* victim sprinkled on the altar (God) and on the people symbolised the *union* between God and mankind (the chosen people).

The New Covenant

Coming now to the New Testament we find that the realities of the Old are paralleled in the New, but on a more sublime level. The New Covenant of which Christ spoke when he instituted the Eucharist is to be established by a *sacrifice*, the sacrifice which Christ himself will offer by the shedding of his blood the day after the Last Supper; a sacrifice which he enacts sacramentally at the Last Supper. On Holy Thursday night the first Mass was said.

There is a clear reference in the words of institution to sacrifice. "This is my Body which is being given *for* you". "This is my Blood of the New Covenant which is being shed for many" (equivalent to 'all' in Hebrew). When Jesus refers to his Blood of the Covenant he is clearly alluding to the sacrificial establishing of the Old Covenant under Moses and is implying that at the Supper he is now establishing the New Covenant in the sacrifice of his own blood. The next day on Calvary he will make the offering of himself in a bloody manner.

Sacrifice is a well-known manifestation of religion. It is man's acknowledgment and expresses his adoration of God as his Creator and Lord. It is also a recognition that he is Lord of every material and spiritual reality. Christ sacrificed himself not simply for the sake of doing so but to give glory to his Father by fulfilling his will.

Man's response

The sacrificial aspect of the Eucharist calls for a response on the part of man as indeed do the other aspects which we have still to consider. The words "Do this in remembrance of me" used by Christ at the Last Supper are seen by the Church as a *command* to the apostles and their successors to do just what Christ had done — to offer the sacrifice of the Mass. Commenting on these words of Christ, Pope Paul VI says: "When he instructed the apostles to do this in remembrance of him, it was his wish that it should be capable of constant renewal. The members of the early Church were loyal in carrying out this command, devoting themselves to the apostles' teaching and assembling for the celebration of the Eucharistic sacrifice".[4]

The kind of response to be given by the faithful and what this involves is clearly stated in the documents of the Second Vatican Council and in the teaching of the Magisterium of the Church that has followed these. It hardly needs saying that all the members of the Church are deeply involved in the Eucharistic sacrifice.

The response that is called for from priests and people is summed up in the word 'offering'. "The celebration of the Eucharist which takes place at Mass is the action not only of Christ, but also of the Church. For in it Christ perpetuates in an unbloody manner the sacrifice offered on the cross, offering himself to the Father for the world's salvation through the ministry of priests. The Church, the spouse and minister of Christ, performs together with him the role of priest and victim, offers him to the Father and at the same time makes a total offering of herself together with him".[5]

In the Decree on the Ministry and Life of Priests, the Fathers of the Second Vatican Council point out that the "priests teach the faithful to offer the divine victim to God the Father in the sacrifice of the Mass and with the victim to make an offering of their whole life".[6] A later document speaks of the faithful being "invited and led on to offer themselves, their labours and all created things together with him". The Dogmatic Constitution on the Church is even more specific when it says that "All their works, prayers and apostolic undertakings, family and married life, daily work, relaxation of mind and body, if they are accomplished in the Spirit, and even the hardships of life, if patiently borne — all these become spiritual sacrifices acceptable to God through Jesus Christ (cf. 1 Pet 2 : 5). In the celebration of the Eucharist these may most fittingly be offered to the Father along with the Body of the Lord. Thus, as worshippers whose every deed is holy, the laity consecrate the world itself to God".[8]

One writer has aptly said that if the faithful know how to offer their whole life to God, they do not go to Mass with empty hands. "People must offer themselves as they are and not in a vacuum. They must offer themselves in their concrete situation with their joys and sorrows, friends and enemies, as members playing a particular part in the civic and religious community. They should present themselves to Jesus in all simplicity, with their good qualities and also with their defects. No one is such a sinner that he has not some good quality, something deserving of merit to offer. No one is so holy that he has no defects, limitations and weaknesses from which he wants to be relieved, but for which he also asks forgiveness together with his brothers and sisters who are united with him at the altar. The Mass is the most living expression of the community of the faithful bound together by the same faith, the same love, the same grace and by a common destiny. At the same time no one surrenders what is characteristic of himself — his individuality, his personality".

"If the faithful are properly instructed they will realise that the Mass is not just a half or three quarters of an hour given to God once a week. It's influence should extend throughout the whole of one's personal, private, professional, family, social and public life by the faithful fulfilment especially of justice and charity which are a concrete expression of our Christian morality".[9] This reminds us of what was said when we were speaking of our sharing in Christ's priesthood through the sacramental character of Confirmation.

"The Christian who understands the place of the Mass in the Christian life will see it not as a religious interlude in his weekly programme but as a focal point around which his religious and moral life is organized and towards which everything is orientated".[10]

The priesthood of the laity

Without wishing to anticipate what will be said in connection with the sacrament of Holy Orders, it is necessary here to say something about the priesthood of the laity.

The participation in the Mass about which we have been speaking reflects what was said when we spoke of the sacramental character of Baptism in connection with the liturgy in general and applies with even greater force when it is question of participation in the Mass. The quotation from the Constitution on the Sacred Liturgy used then bears repeating here, namely, that "Mother Church earnestly desires that all the faithful should be led to that full, conscious and active participation in liturgical celebrations which is demanded by the very nature of the liturgy, and to which the Christian people, 'a chosen race, a royal priesthood, a holy nation, a redeemed people' (1 Pet 2:9) have a right and obligation by reason of their Baptism".[11] One must not confuse *active* participation with merely *vocal* participation. True participation must spring from the heart.

The Dogmatic Constitution on the Church not only states that "the faithful, indeed, by virtue of their royal priesthood participate in the offering of the Eucharist", but it also refers to the difference between the priesthood of the laity and the ministerial priesthood when it says: "Though they differ essentially and not only in degree, the common priesthood of the faithful and the ministerial or hierarchical priesthood are none the less ordered to one another; each in its own proper way shares in the one priesthood of Christ. The ministerial priest, by the sacred power he has, forms and rules the priestly people; in the person of Christ he effects the Eucharistic sacrifice and offers it to God in the name of all the people. . . . The faithful exercise that priesthood, too, by the reception of the sacraments, prayer and thanksgiving, the witness of a holy life, abnegation and active charity".[12]

The difference between the priesthood of the laity and the ministerial priesthood becomes clear when we consider the different ways in which the priest and the people are said to participate in the Mass. The faithful are said to offer *in their own name* and *with* the Church. The priest offers *in the name and on behalf of* the Church. Thus we read: "Through the ministry of priests the spiritual sacrifice of the faithful is completed in union with the sacrifice of Christ the only mediator, which in the Eucharist is offered through the priests' hands in the name of the whole Church in an unbloody and sacramental manner until the Lord himself returns".[13]

The ends for which the Mass is offered

The Eucharistic sacrifice is also said to be the sacrament of thanksgiving, propitiation, petition and praise.[14] This being so the Mass fulfils in a special and most efficacious way the four reasons for which we should worship God. The faithful are not just on-lookers when they participate in the Mass. When they offer Christ in the Mass they offer to God the best gift they have — the Son of God himself, "the beloved Son with whom the Father is well pleased" (Mt 3:17). By uniting themselves with Jesus the faithful share in his thanksgiving for his brothers and sisters, by grace in his atonement for their sins, in his pleading for all their needs of body and soul and especially in the all-perfect adoration and praise which he gives as man to the Father. Of themselves they could perform none of these duties in a way that is worthy of the Divine Majesty, they are enabled to do this through Jesus Christ. He alone can give adequate glory to the Father and the faithful at Mass glorify the Father through Christ and with Christ.

Devotion

The benefit to be derived from the Mass will depend on the devotion of those who are present. The Instruction on the Worship of the Eucharistic Mystery points out that "Like the passion of Christ itself, this sacrifice, though offered for all, 'has no effect except in those united to the passion of Christ by faith and charity. . . . To these it brings greater or less benefit in proportion to their devotion'".[15]

Devotion is defined as "the disposition of the will which renders it ready for the service and worship of God".[16] St Thomas Aquinas speaks of devotion as the will to do promptly what belongs to the service of God. The official expression of the devotion of the Church is to be found above all in the celebration of the liturgy.

The Mass is the form of worship laid down by Christ for his followers when he commanded the apostles (and their successors) to "do this in commemoration of me". Devotion consists in 'doing' and not necessarily in 'feeling'. If we do what God wills we can say that we are devout. So much the better if the emotions are involved. But this is not always possible. Nor must emotion be mistaken for true devotion. St Francis de Sales tells us that devotion is a kind of charity by which we not only do good, but do it carefully, frequently and promptly. Frequently is taken to mean as often as required. The qualities proper of true devotion throw light on the nature of the participation in the Mass on the part of the faithful.

True devotion should come from within, from the heart. It should spring from the love and esteem that we have for God. It should be holy, that is, it should inspire us to be determined to avoid sin and to do what is pleasing to God. It should be constant. This means that we are ready to do what is pleasing to God at all times in spite of what happens to us. Solid devotion does not depend on whims or moods. Finally, to be true our devotion must be disinterested. In other words we must worship God by participating in the Mass not only when we want something from him; not only for what we get out of it, but simply to please him. Devotion with these qualities will certainly help us to take a meaningful and profitable participation in the Mass because it will lead to imitation, especially imitation of the dispositions of Christ which are made clear in the Eucharistic sacrifice. St Augustine tells us that to imitate what we worship is true devotion indeed.

The obligation of Sunday Mass

1. *Man's duty to worship God:* Man's chief duty in life is to serve his Creator. As part of this service of God man has a duty to give him the worship that is his due and to do his will faithfully. Hence it is that the moral law obliges all men to obey the dictates of reason and to devote some part of their time exclusively to the worship of God their Creator.

Pope John XXIII points out that "To safeguard man's dignity as a creature of God, the Church has always demanded a diligent observance of the third Commandment: 'Remember that thou keep holy the Sabbath day'. God has a right to command man to devote one day a week to his duty of worshipping the eternal Majesty. Free from mundane cares, he should lift up his mind to the things of heaven, and look into the depths of his conscience, to see how he stands with God in respect of those necessary and inviolable relationships which must exist between the creature and his Creator".[17]

The duty to worship concerns men primarily as individuals but man's nature is social and his call is social and the whole community of mankind is joined together by social bonds. As a community it is also dependent on God's supreme authority. Therefore the whole community has the same duty to worship God as a community. This is a duty for human society and not only for the individuals who make up that society. Thus it is that man has a duty to give give social and public worship to God. The exact manner in which this worship is to be given is a matter to be determined by positive law. In the case of Catholics this means the law of the Church.

2. *The Jewish Sabbath:* The Jewish Sabbath was regulated by the Sabbath Law which God gave to the chosen people (cf. Exod 20:8–11; 21:13–17; Deut 5:12–15). The command to keep holy the Sabbath, as given in Exodus 20:8, is a permanent obligation in so far as it is an expression of the natural law which obliges man to devote some part of his time to the worship of God. The enactments of the Jewish Law determining the time and other details of this worship in the Old Testament pertain to a ceremonial law which ceased to have any binding force with the passing of the period of the Old Testament.

3. *The Christian Sunday:* With the coming of Christianity there could be no question of the Church abrogating the natural law obligation to worship God, but it could and did change both the day and the manner in which this obligation was to be fulfilled. The apostles under the guidance of the Holy Spirit changed the day from the last day of the week, the Jewish Sabbath Day, to the first day of the week, the Christian Sunday. Sunday was henceforth to be a joyful commemoration of the resurrection. Both St Paul (cf. Acts 20:7; 1 Cor 16:2) and St John (Apoc 1:10) call the first day of the week the Lord's Day.

At first a general custom arose for the early Christians to meet together for public worship on Sundays. In the course of time this custom gave rise to an obligation which was expressed in the law of the Church. This law is enshrined in the new Code of Canon Law (c.1247). There it is stated that on Sunday and other Days of Precept the faithful are bound to participate in the Mass.

The obligation to participate in the Mass on Sundays and Holydays of obligation is said to be a grave one. This obligation is satisfied by participating in the Mass wherever it is celebrated in a

Catholic rite either on the day itself or on the preceding evening (cf. c.1248 n.1).

Although the members of the Pontifical Commission for the Revision of the Code of Canon Law recommended that there should be just two holydays of obligation throughout the Church, namely Christmas and one of the major feasts of Our Lady at the discretion of the Episcopal Conference, Pope John Paul II retained the list of holydays of obligation which were contained in the 1917 Code, namely, Christmas, Epiphany, the Ascension, Corpus Christi, the Solemnity of Mary, Mother of God, her Immaculate Conception and Assumption, the feasts of St Joseph, Saints Peter and Paul and that of All Saints (cf. c.1246 n.1).

With the approval of the Holy See, the Episcopal Conference can abolish some of these holydays of obligation or transfer them to the Sunday (cf. c.1246 n.2). The Instruction on the Worship of the Eucharistic Mystery speaks of fulfilling a precept and an obligation with regard to Mass on Sundays and holydays of obligation.[18]

In the past moralists indulged in all sorts of casuistry in their attempt to decide when a person who came late for Mass actually missed Mass. This gave rise to a legalistic approach to the obligation of participating in the Mass with the result that certain types of people were content with doing the minimum to avoid committing grave sin. The documents of the Church stress the importance of being present for the whole of the Mass and the Instruction on the Worship of the Eucharistic Mystery exhorts pastors to "carefully teach the faithful to participate in the whole Mass, showing the close connection between the liturgy of the Word and the celebration of the Lord's Supper, so that they can see clearly how the two constitute a single act of worship. For the preaching of the Word is necessary for the very administration of the sacraments, in as much as they are sacraments of faith, which is born of the Word and fed by it. This is especially true of the celebration of Mass, in which it is the purpose of the liturgy of the Word to develop the close connection between the preaching and hearing the Word of God and the Eucharistic Mystery".[19] The Constitution on the Sacred Liturgy also points out that "The two parts which in a sense go to make up the Mass, viz., the liturgy of the Word and the Eucharistic liturgy, are so closely connected with each other that they form but one single act of worship. Accordingly this Sacred Synod strongly urges pastors of souls that, when instructing the faithful, they insistently teach them to take part in the entire Mass on Sundays and holydays of obligation".[20]

Actual presence of the faithful at Mass is required for the fulfilment of the precept to participate in the Mass on Sundays and Holydays of obligation. "Hearing" Mass over the Radio or on TV does not fulfil this obligation.[21]

According to the Ecumenical Directory (Part I) it is possible for a Catholic to fulfil the obligation to participate in the Mass by attending the Liturgy in an Orthodox Church on days of precept. The following quotation from the Ecumenical Directory gives the circumstances when this may be done: "A Catholic who occasionally, for reasons set out below, attends the Holy Liturgy (Mass) on a Sunday or Holyday of obligation in an Orthodox church is not then bound to assist at Mass in a Catholic church. It is likewise a good thing if on such days Catholics, who for just reasons cannot go to Mass in their own church, attend the Holy Liturgy of their separated Eastern brethren, if this is possible". The reasonable grounds mentioned above are, for example, those arising out of a public office or function, blood relationships, friendships, desire to be better informed, etc. In such cases there is nothing against their taking part in the common responses, hymns and actions of the Church in which they are guests".[22] The reception of Holy Communion is governed by what has been said in Chapter I about Catholics receiving the sacraments from non-Catholic ministers.

Participating in Mass on Sundays and days of precept gives the faithful an opportunity to complete their formation as Christians. It also enables them to fight against the spirit of the age which is one of materialism and to increase their hope in the future life.

The fact that by law the faithful can now fulfil this obligation by assisting at Mass on the previous evening should make it easier for the faithful to fulfil this obligation which is binding on all those who have been baptised in the Catholic Church or received into full communion with it provided they have sufficient use of reason and have reached the age of seven years (cf. c.11).

Writing in the *Dizionario Enciclopedico di Teologia Morale*, F. Appendino puts forward the view that it is better to present the duty of participating in the Mass on Sundays and other days of precept as the culminating point in the process of evangelisation and as a duty of love for Christ and one's brothers rather than as a precept to be fulfilled in order to avoid sin.[23]

Dispensations and excusing causes

For a just reason and in accordance with the directives of the

Diocesan Bishop, the parish priest can grant a dispensation from the obligation of observing a day of precept in individual cases. He can also commute this obligation into some other charitable work (cf. c.1245).

In the past, moralists gave a list of reasons excusing the faithful from the obligation of participating in the Mass on Sundays. D. Prummer, O.P., quotes St Alphonsus as saying that "any reason which is moderately grave excuses from the precept of participating in the Mass on Sundays and Holydays of obligation — namely, any reason which involves some notable inconvenience or harm to mind or body of oneself or of another".[24]

F. Appendino takes the view that if a person who habitually goes to Mass has a reasonable motive for not attending on a particular occasion he cannot be said to be guilty of grave sin".[25]

Work that is forbidden on Sundays

The term 'servile work' which was used in the 1917 Code does not appear in the new Code of Canon Law. There it is stated that the faithful should abstain from those works and occupations which interfere with the worship of God, with the joy which is proper of the Lord's Day and with the due relaxation of mind and body. One must therefore see if the work that is contemplated on a Sunday is of the type mentioned above. Much seems to be left to the conscience of the individual and the custom of Christian people.

The principle given by Canon E. J. Mahoney, a moralist of repute in the English speaking world in the first half of this century, is still valid today. He used to say that "We are bound to abstain from those works which in the sound judgment and custom of Christians are opposed to the purpose of the precept of Sunday observance, which is to secure a weekly rest in order the better to serve God".

Pope John XXIII expressed himself on this subject as follows: "Man has a right to rest a while from work, and indeed a need to do so if he is to renew his bodily strength and to refresh his spirit by suitable recreation. He has also to think of his family, the unity of which depends so much on frequent contact and the peaceful living together of all its members. Thus religion and moral and physical well-being are one in demanding this periodic rest, and for many centuries now the Church has set aside Sunday as a special day of rest for the faithful, on which they participate in the Holy Sacrifice of the Mass, the memorial and application of

Christ's redemptive work for souls. Heavy in heart, we cannot but deplore the growing tendency in certain quarters to disregard this sacred law, if not to reject it outright. This attitude must inevitably impair the bodily and spiritual health of workers, whose welfare We have much at heart".[26] The Second Vatican Council reminds us that "the Lord's Day is the original feast-day, and it should be proposed to the piety of the faithful and taught to them so that it may become in fact a day of joy and freedom from work".[27]

By universal custom throughout the Church it is agreed that such things as travelling, preparing food and doing other domestic work, which cannot be omitted altogether without serious inconvenience, do not violate the precept of Sunday rest. In many places custom allows hobbies or pastimes such as knitting which is not done for profit, gardening and in general light work which is done for exercise or recreation.

It is not forbidden to spend some time in harmless amusements and recreation on Sundays. What is forbidden is the excessive pursuit of amusement because it goes against the purpose of Sunday observance. It is wrong to give oneself up to amusement to the extent that Sunday becomes indistinguishable from a profane holiday.

Communion — Biblical background

In the context of the Eucharist as Communion we return to the parallel in Scripture between the Old Covenant and the New. In another powerful symbol of unity, the Alliance between God and his people was expressed by the *sacred meal*, in which the people *shared in*, communicated, the *victim of the sacrifice* which was frequently offered in the Old Testament to signify the continuance of the Alliance which God had once made on Mount Sinai. For example, every year the chosen people celebrated the Feast of the Passover in memory of the first conclusion of the Alliance. They sacrificed a lamb, and, gathered together, they *partook of the victim*, showing their union among themselves and with the God of the Covenant. Furthermore, one of the most frequent sacrifices of the Old Law was the so-called *sacrifice of communion* in which the people, as well as the priests, shared the victim of the sacrifice in a sacred repast. Sharing in the meal meant sharing in the sacrifice and thus in the Alliance itself. In other words, by eating the *sacrificial meal* they were brought into closer union with God.

The words used by Christ at the Last Supper: 'Take ye and

eat', 'All of you drink of this', indicate that the Eucharist is also a sacred meal, by which the people of the new Alliance partake of the victim of the new sacrifice, namely, Christ's own Body and Blood.

The Instruction on the Worship of the Eucharistic Mystery tells us that "the faithful participate more fully in this sacrament when they receive this same victim sacramentally",[28] and, "through sacramental communion the faithful take part more perfectly in the celebration of the Eucharist. It is strongly recommended that they should normally receive communion during the Mass".[29] It also states that "In the sacrifice of the Mass our Lord is immolated, when 'he begins to be present sacramentally as the *spiritual food* of the faithful under the appearances of bread and wine'. It was for this purpose that Christ entrusted this sacrifice to the Church, that the faithful might share in it both spiritually by faith and charity, and sacramentally through the banquet of holy communion. Participation in the Lord's Supper is always communion with Christ offering himself for us as a sacrifice to the Father".[30]

Frequent Communion

In the early Church the faithful who took part in the Eucharistic sacrifice also received Communion. This custom of receiving Communion declined in the course of time. The Jansenists contended that receiving Holy Communion at Mass was an abuse that had to be corrected. They were motivated by the false theory that Holy Communion was a reward for exceptionally holy people. In her day St Thérèse of Lisieux lamented the fact that she could not receive Holy Communion daily. St Pius X revived the practice of frequent Communion in the Church in the year 1905. He issued a Decree 'On Receiving the Most Holy Eucharist Daily' (*Sacra Tridentina Synodus*) on December 20, 1905. The practice has been given greater impetus in our own day through the modification of the Eucharistic fast. Because certain abuses arose on account of a false application of the teaching given in the Decree of St Pius X, a later Decree, 'Quam Singulari', dated August 8, 1910, and issued by the Sacred Congregation for the Sacraments, emphasised the fact that frequent Communion is not a *command* but an *invitation*.

The conditions

The two conditions for frequent or daily Communion are:

1) A right intention. This means that the communicant should desire to please God and to be more closely united to him by charity in availing of this practice. The faithful should not receive Holy Communion merely out of routine, or because they see others doing it, or out of vainglory or human respect. A suspicion that a person is not receiving Holy Communion with the proper motive would arise if he seems to show no progress in living the Christian life.

2) A state of grace. This means that the communicant should not be conscious of having committed grave sin which has not been remitted in the sacrament of Penance. Whilst freedom from venial sin and the attachment thereto is most desirable, this is seen as a fruit of frequent Communion rather than as a condition for receiving it.

The Instruction on the Worship of the Eucharistic Mystery reminds us that the precept "Let a man examine himself" (1 Cor 11:28) should be called to mind by those who wish to receive Communion. The custom of the Church declares this to be necessary so that no one who is conscious of having committed grave sin, even if he believes himself to be contrite, may approach the Holy Eurcharist without first making a sacramental confession".[31]

The law of the Church states quite clearly that he who is conscious of having committed grave sin may not celebrate Mass or receive Holy Communion without having gone to confession, except he has a grave reason for doing so and there is no opportunity of going to confession. In such a case he should call to mind the obligation to make a perfect act of contrition which includes the intention of going to confession as soon as possible (cf. c.916).

A priest would be considered to have a grave reason for celebrating Mass if he has to say Mass for the people on a Sunday or Holyday of obligation; if he has to say Mass for a special occasion, e.g. marriage or some anniversary that is normally celebrated; if he has to say a Mass which has already been announced; if he cannot omit saying Mass without giving scandal or exposing himself to suspicions or unfavourable criticism; if he has to say Mass to provide Holy Communion for the dying, the sick or for someone else in need of the sacrament; to avoid giving offence to the person who asked for the Mass to be said.

A lay person would be considered to have a grave reason for receiving Holy Communion if he/she were in danger of death; if he/she would risk losing his/her good name if he/she did not receive Communion; if it is a question of fulfilling the precept of

Easter Communion; if he would give scandal by not receiving Communion.

One should never comment on the fact that someone has omitted to go to Communion. He/she may do so for a variety of valid reasons.

In the case of a priest the phrase 'as soon as possible' is taken to mean before he next celebrates Mass or within three days.

In the case of a lay person the phrase 'as soon as possible' is taken to mean before he next receives Holy Communion.

Authors are agreed that if someone remembers a grave sin which through no fault of his own, he forgot to mention at his last confession, the law we have been discussing does not apply to him. Nor does it apply to the case of doubtful sins. The Council of Trent from which the law originated speaks only of one who is 'conscious of grave sin'.

The Eucharistic fast

In recent years the law of the Church concerning the fast before Holy Communion has been simplified and is enshrined in the new Code of Canon Law. Those who are about to receive the Holy Eucharist should abstain for at least one hour before receiving the sacrament from every kind of food and drink with the exception of water and medicine (cf. c.919 n.1).

The elderly, the sick and those who take care of them can receive Holy Communion even though they have taken something within the hour preceding the reception of the sacrament (cf. c.919 n.3).

Priests who celebrate Mass twice or three times on the same day can take something before the second or third Mass even though it is within the hour before saying the Mass.

In the case of the elderly the observance of the Eucharistic fast which is binding on the generality of the faithful could be a real difficulty for them.

A member of the faithful to whom Viaticum is administered in danger of death is not bound by the law of the Eucharistic fast.

The purpose and effects of Holy Communion

These are so closely inter-related that it is difficult to discuss the one without involving the other. We have already seen that Holy Communion is not a reward for the exceptionally good. It is rather a remedy for human weakness. To communicate fruitfully it is not necessary to be perfect but to have the desire to keep striving after perfection. In inviting us to his Supper, Christ has not established us in a state of perfection already achieved. The apostles who received their first Holy Communion at the Last Supper were far from perfect. Living as people do today in an atmosphere of ever increasing materialism and an age of weakened faith, there is an even greater need to receive Holy Communion frequently, if our Christian life is to be reinvigorated. When we receive Holy Communion we are conscious of our unworthiness and our insufficiency, but we are also full of confidence in him "without whom we can do nothing".

The Second Vatican Council reminds us that "the sharing in the Body and Blood of Christ has no other effect than to accomplish our transformation into that which we receive".[32]

To be nourished by Christ means to become more like him. The process that takes place is just the opposite to that which happens when we eat ordinary food. In the latter case the food and drink is changed into the substance of *our* body. Christ comes to us in Holy Communion not so much to console us but to change our life. He does this by continuing and perfecting the conversion begun at our Baptism. This is a process that must continue throughout the whole of our life. The effect of the grace of the Eucharist is to help us to change our life by detaching us from material things and worldly affairs and inspiring us to love God and our neighbour and to do all the good that lies in our power.

Pope Paul VI stated that the basis of the desire to approach the Sacred Banquet every day is that the faithful "should be united to God by the sacrament and draw strength from it to restrain lust, to wash away the slight faults of daily occurrence and to take precautions against the more serious sins to which human frailty is liable".[33]

The Eucharist is also presented to the faithful as "a medicine by which we are freed from our daily faults and preserved from grave sin".[34]

The Decree of Pope St Pius X teaches us that Christ instituted the Eucharist above all for the purpose of nourishing, healing and sustaining us.

Finally the Eucharist is said to be "the sacrament of love, the sign of unity, the bond of charity, and the paschal banquet in which Christ is received, our mind and soul are filled with grace and a pledge is given us, of the glory to come".[35]

The obligation to receive Holy Communion

We have already seen that frequent Communion is an invitation and not a command. However, frequent Communion is highly recommended today.

Once they have made their first Communion all the faithful are bound to receive Holy Communion at least once a year (cf. c.920 n.1).

This precept should be fulfilled at Paschal time, unless there is a good reason for fulfilling it at another time during the year (cf. c.920 n.2).

In England and Wales the time for fulfilling this obligation begins on Ash Wednesday and ends on Trinity Sunday.

Viaticum

The faithful who are in danger of death from any cause should be refreshed with Holy Communion as Viaticum (cf. c.921 n.1).

Even though they have received Holy Communion on the same day, it is highly recommended that those who are in danger of death should communicate again (cf. c.921 n.2).

During the danger of death it is recommended that Holy Communion should be administered several times on different days (cf. c.921 n.3).

"Communion given as Viaticum should be considered as a special sign of participation in the mystery celebrated in the Mass, the mystery of the death of the Lord and his passage to the Father. By it, strengthened by the Body of Christ, the Christian is endowed with the pledge of the resurrection in his passage from this life".

"Pastors must ensure that the administration of this sacrament is not delayed, but that the faithful are nourished by it while still in full possession of their faculties".

Holy Communion twice in the same day

He who has already received Holy Communion can receive it again on the same day but only within the Eucharistic celebration at which he takes part. One must bear in mind what was said above about Viaticum (cf. c.917).

E

When may Holy Communion be given?

Although it is highly recommended that the faithful should receive Holy Communion during the Mass, nevertheless it should be given to those who request it for a just cause outside of Mass making sure that the liturgical rites for the celebration of Communion outside of Mass are observed (cf. c.918).

The celebration of Mass and the distribution of Holy Communion can take place on any day and at any time but one must bear in mind the rules pertaining to the last three days of Holy Week.

On Holy Thursday the sick can receive Holy Communion at any time but the faithful who are not sick can receive it only during the Eucharistic celebration.

On Good Friday the sick can receive Holy Communion at any time but the faithful who are not sick can receive it only during the celebration of the Passion of the Lord.

On Holy Saturday Holy Communion may be given only as Viaticum.

"It is indeed eminently fitting that those who are unable to assist at the celebration of the Eucharist should receive the spiritual nourishment of the Blessed Sacrament and in this way feel that they are united not only to the sacrifice of the Lord but also to the community, and are sustained by the charity of their brethren".

"It should be carefully explained to the faithful that even when they receive Holy Communion outside Mass they are intimately united with the sacrifice which is the perpetuation of the sacrifice of the cross, and that they participate in the sacred banquet in which the people of God by receiving the Body and Blood of the Lord share in the treasures of the paschal sacrifice, and prefigure and anticipate the heavenly banquet in the kingdom of the Father, proclaiming the death of the Lord until he comes again".[36]

First Holy Communion

The Decree 'Quam Singulari' dated August 8, 1910, to which we have already referred, points out that the reason for admitting children to Holy Communion is Christ's love for them.

In the early Church it was customary to give infants the Precious Blood. This custom died out in the 13th century and it is now forbidden to give Holy Communion to anyone who has not reached the age of reason. After the Decree 'Quam Singulari' was issued children began to be given Holy Communion at too early an age. Canon Law aimed at remedying this situation.

According to the new Code of Canon Law, in order that the Holy Eucharist may be administered to children it is required that they have sufficient knowledge and have been properly prepared so that they can according to their capacity understand the mystery of Christ and receive the Body of the Lord with faith and devotion (cf. c.913).

But Holy Communion can be administered to children who are in danger of death provided they can distinguish the Body of Christ from ordinary bread and receive it with devotion (cf. c.913 n.2).

It is felt that normally a child begins to use its reason about the seventh year. In some cases it may be earlier, in others it may be later. The full use of reason is not required.

Those concerned with the child's preparation for first Holy Communion

It is the duty especially of parents and those who act in their place, i.e. teachers, and the parish priest, to see that children who have reached the age of reason are properly prepared and as soon as possible, after having made their sacramental confession, are refreshed with this divine food. Parish priests have a duty to see that those children who have not reached the age of reason or whom they consider not to be sufficiently disposed, do not approach the Holy Table (cf. c.914).

The knowledge required

We have already seen that the law requires first communicants to be able to receive the Body of the Lord with faith and devotion. This then is the aim of the instruction prior to the reception of first Holy Communion.

Apart from danger of death, when the minimum is required, there must rightly be a much more detailed preparation. It is for the Bishop of the Diocese in consultation with the other members of the Regional or National Episcopal Conference to approve a syllabus of instruction for those preparing for their first Holy Communion (cf. Sacred Congregation for Bishops, *Directorium de Pastorali Ministerio Episcoporum*, Vatican Press, 1973, n.72, p.75).

Knowledge is required because devotion being an act of the

will — the will to do what is pleasing to God — calls for this. We can't have one without the other. Knowledge is the background. Devotion is the main thing. It would be a mistake to concentrate on pumping in information without aiming at arousing faith and devotion.

Parents, teachers and priests, especially parish priests, are all involved in preparing children for their first Holy Communion.

The new Rite of Baptism reminds parents that it is their responsibility after Baptism, in gratitude to God and in fidelity to the duty they have undertaken, to enable the child to know God, whose adopted child it has become, to receive Confirmation and to participate in the Holy Eucharist. In carrying out this duty they are to be helped by their parish priest. Pamphlets are available at reasonable prices which will help parents to prepare their children for the sacrament of Confirmation, the Eucharist and Penance. A greater involvement of the parents is called for today and they should work in conjunction with the teachers at school who are also engaged in this work for their children.

It is important to concentrate on arousing devotion in the child. This means appealing to the heart and to the personal relations of the child with Jesus. The child should be encouraged to develop a personal love for Jesus. He should be made to realise that the Lord's coming to him in Holy Communion is the greatest of blessings. Simple acts of faith and love correspond to the sentiments the child should have when he receives our Lord. The matter should be brought down to situations with which the child is familiar — relations of friendship, etc. The period of preparation should be accompanied by efforts at good behaviour.

The tendency today is for the parents, and indeed for the whole family, to receive Holy Communion with the child. It is normal for children to make their first Communion in their own parish. There is no law about this. Sometimes the children make their first Communion with the children attending the same school. This may involve making their first Communion in another parish church or in a convent chapel.

With regard to the role of the parish priest to see that there are no abuses, he is entitled to examine the child to see if he has the minimum knowledge and the proper dispositions. If he is satisfied that these conditions can be fulfilled, it is the duty of the parish priest to see that the child makes his first Communion. He should not require a fuller knowledge than the Church requires.

The parish priest's duty of vigilance requires him to see that parents carry out their natural mandate to see to the religious instruction and education of their children by making arrangements for those who have reached the age of reason to be prepared for first Holy Communion. The parish priest himself may instruct the child but he has not an exclusive right to do so. Normally children are prepared by their teachers, parents and school chaplains. In parishes where there is no Catholic school the work is often done by religious or by the lay people of the parish. It is an excellent form of the lay apostolate.

The question of first confession will be dealt with when we treat of the sacrament of Penance.

The minister of the sacrament

Because the Eucharist is a permanent sacrament one can distinguish between the minister for the celebration of the Eucharistic Sacrifice who effects the Eucharist and the minister for the distribution of the Eucharist.

Only a validly ordained priest can be the minister who in the person of Christ has power to effect the sacrament of the Eucharist (cf. c.900).

The ordinary minister for the distribution of Holy Communion is a bishop, priest or deacon. The extraordinary minister for the distribution of Holy Communion is an acolyte.

Where these ministers are not available and there is a need for people to give out Holy Communion, lay people can be deputed to be extraordinary ministers for the distribution of Holy Communion in accordance with the prescriptions of the law (cf. c.910 nn.1 and 2; c.230 n.3).

Presence — Biblical background

The third aspect of the Old Alliance, which was of great importance, was the fact that God dwelt in the midst of his people. God chose *to dwell continually* with his people in a mysterious but real manner. This very presence was to be the *sign* and *guarantee* that the Covenant still continued. This *divine presence*, which was called 'Shekinah' by the Hebrews, *was in no way static*, but represented rather the *active, dynamic* and *salvific presence* of a God who had decided on the salvation of his people. When he appeared to Moses in the burning bush it was to announce his intention of *mightily leading* them out of slavery; when they were finally on their way out of Egypt, God *actively* led them, going before them in the pillar of a cloud by day and the pillar of fire by night; on the burning mountain of Sinai, God appeared in the cloud to initiate the Alliance. During the subsequent wanderings of the Israelites in the desert, God accompanied them, *dwelling in a tent* like them — *the Tent of Reunion* (cf. Exod 33:7–11) where God spoke to his people through Moses. During the conquest of the Promised Land, God *led* the Israelite armies into battle by his presence over the Ark of the Covenant (cf. 1 Sam 4). Later, when the people were established in the kingdom under David and Solomon, God still dwelt with the people of the kingdom in the new Temple of Jerusalem built by Solomon. From this Temple on Sion God continued to pursue *actively* and *dynamically* and *efficaciously* his designs for his people. God's presence always had as its object the drawing of men into greater union with him. To forget this is to misunderstand the nature of his presence among us.

When Christ said at the Last Supper: "This is my body; this is my blood", he was affirming in an absolute way, that is, without any conditions, the *Real Presence of his Body and Blood* under the sacramental species, indeed the presence of his whole Person. His words give no foundation for the view that the Mass is merely an external remembrance, that Christ is present only at the moment when he is received in Holy Communion or any other views which would set limits to his presence in the Eucharist. The Real Presence was already required by the sacrifice. Without the Real Presence of a victim there would be no sacrifice. Without the real presence of a victim there would be no Communion.

Furthermore, the Person of Christ was present at the Last Supper both in his natural mode of existence and under the appearances of bread and wine as the Redeemer of mankind actively engaged in carrying out God's designs for the redemption of all men. As in the Old Testament God not only acted on behalf of his people but also dwelt in their midst, so now he is actively present in the Person of his Son who has become man.

St John speaking of the Incarnation in the first chapter of his Gospel, says: "And the Word was made flesh, and pitched his tent among us". We are familiar with the phrase 'dwelt among us' but the literal translation given here shows that there is a definte allusion to the dwelling of God with his people in the Tent of Reunion in the desert.

Again in the second chapter of his Gospel St John refers to Christ's body as the new Temple. Here we have an allusion to the dwelling of God in the old Temple of Jerusalem. There is no doubt that for St John Jesus Christ himself is the Personal Divine Presence of the New Covenant, the sign of the New Covenant-relation between God and mankind. Jesus Christ, true God and true man, is now present under the appearance of bread in our tabernacles and in the monstrance, the perpetual pledge to men of the continuing regard of God for the human race.

Man's response

In instituting the Eucharist our Lord directly willed *all* its various aspects. The abiding presence is one of these aspects. This special presence of God to his people calls for a special response from his people. Just as the renewal of the sacrifice calls for active participation on the part of the people; just as the gift of Christ in Holy Communion demands a response from the communicant, so also does the permanent presence of Christ demand a recognition of that presence from the People of God. That response is precisely the cult of the Real Presence which down the centuries has developed in the life of the Church.

The documents of the Church leave no doubt about what our attitude should be towards the Real Presence outside Mass. Towards the end of the Second Vatican Council Pope Paul VI issued his Encyclical Letter 'Mysterium Fidei' in which among other things he stressed the importance of the Real Presence and the worship that is due to it outside Mass. In several places a later document speaks of the adoration due to the Real Presence. The following quotation will suffice: "It would be well to recall that the primary and original purpose of reserving the sacred species in Church outside Mass is the administration of the Viaticum. Secondary ends are the distribution of Communion outside Mass and the adoration of our Lord Jesus Christ concealed beneath these same species. For 'the reservation of the sacred species for the sick . . . led to the praiseworthy custom of adoring the heavenly food which is preserved in churches'. This practice of adoration has a valid and firm foundation, especially since belief in the Real Presence of the Lord has its natural consequence in the external and public manifestation of that belief".[37]

"When the faithful adore Christ present in the sacrament, they should remember that this presence derives from the Sacrifice and is directed towards both sacramental and spiritual communion. In consequence, devotion which leads the faithful to visit the Blessed Sacrament draws them into an ever deeper participation in the

Paschal Mystery. It leads them to respond gratefully to the gift of
him, who through his humanity constantly pours divine life into
the members of his body. Dwelling with Christ our Lord, they
enjoy his intimate friendship and pour out their hearts before him
for themselves and their dear ones, and pray for the peace and
salvation of the world. They offer their entire lives with Christ to
the Father in the Holy Spirit, and receive in this wonderful exchange an increase of faith, hope and charity. Thus they nourish
those right dispositions which enable them with all due devotion
to celebrate the memorial of the Lord and receive frequently the
bread given us by the Father. The faithful should therefore strive
to worship Christ our Lord in the Blessed Sacrament, in harmony
with their way of life. Pastors should exhort them to this, and set
them a good example".[38]

Speaking of the Blessed Sacrament Pope Paul VI says that "the
faithful should not fail to pay it an occasional visit. Such a visit is a
proof of gratitude, a pledge of love, an observance of the adoration
due to Christ the Lord present in the Blessed Sacrament".[39]

If one were asked to choose a text from the Gospels to serve
as Christ's invitation to men in connection with the Real Presence
in the Blessed Sacrament reserved in our churches, surely one
could not do better than to select the following: "Come to me, all
you who labour and are heavily laden, and I will give you rest"
(Mt 11 : 28).

Addressing itself to priests the Second Vatican Council says:
"That they may discharge their ministry with fidelity, they should
prize daily conversation with Christ the Lord in visits of personal
devotion to the Most Holy Eucharist".[40]

Some objections considered

At the time of the Second Vatican Council certain objections
were being raised about the devotion being paid to the Blessed
Sacrament. Since the closing of the Council no less than six documents have been issued by the Holy See on one aspect or another
of the Eucharistic Mystery, to say nothing of those concerning the
liturgy itself.

The relatively late development of the public adoration of the
Eucharist outside Mass and Holy Communion in the history of the
Church has caused some people to advocate a return to the practice
of the early Church when this form of devotion did not exist. To
do this would be to ignore the fact that the Church is a living

organism whose devotional life is subject to a certain development under the guidance of the Holy Spirit. In the Encyclical Letter 'Mediator Dei', of November 20, 1947, Pope Pius XII warned against a *mania* for restoring primitive usages in the liturgy. Karl Rahner's remarks are relevant to the point we are discussing. "What needs to be stressed", says Father Rahner, 'is the fact that there have been periods in which there was no actual Eucharistic devotion outside the Sacrifice of the Mass cannot be a valid argument against such devotions being genuinely Christian. It would be a severe loss to Catholic devotional life, if a false romanticism about the early Church led to the abandonment of what has developed in the course of the history of devotion. Christianity is history. A practice with a thousand years of history behind it has its rights, even if they are not the first thousand years".[41]

It should also be remembered that the revealed *fact* of the Real Presence has as a first consequence to make such cult of the Blessed Sacrament legitimate in accordance with the teaching of the Faith.

A living, dynamic presence

The abiding presence of Christ in the Eucharist has sometimes been referred to disparagingly as the *static* aspect of this mystery, in contrast to the dynamic aspect as shown forth in the Sacrifice of the Mass where Christ *offers* himself to his Father and *nourishes* us with his living, life-giving and glorified Body in Holy Communion. It is important to note that the word 'static' can only refer to the sacramental species, the appearance of bread and wine, under which Christ is present after the Consecration. It would be wrong to think of the presence of Christ in the Blessed Sacrament as a *thing*, it is the living, dynamic presence of a Person, the second Person of the Blessed Trinity. When we pray to Christ in church we are praying to a Person present among persons. Our relations with him are warm, personal relations. It is significant that Pope Pius XII in his address at the conclusion of the Liturgical Congress at Assisi on September 22, 1956, referred to the presence and *action* of Christ in the tabernacle. Present in the Eucharist, he is the same Christ who redeemed mankind on the cross, rose gloriously from the dead, and, in the words of St Paul, who is "always living to make intercession for us". In short, the Christ in the Host is the God-Man who redeemed man and who continues to apply this redemption to each one of us individually. Such a presence could never be static.

Not a substitute for frequent Communion

It is sometimes said that the cessation of the practice of frequent Communion in the past was due to the rise of devotion to the
Real Presence outside the Mass. Historically, it is more correct to
say that the real cause of this was an exaggerated reverence for the
Real Presence coupled with the unsettled conditions in the early
middle ages, from the sixth century onwards. This actual situation
then came to be supported by theological arguments against frequent Communion. Pope St Pius X finally rejected these arguments
when he restored the practice of frequent Communion throughout
the Church. The real truth is that when devotion to the Real Presence started it certainly did not become a substitute for frequent
Communion because the practice of frequent Communion had already died out. Such danger will be avoided today, if we foster a
properly orientated devotion to the Real Presence.

Devotion to the Real Presence unscriptural?

To the minds of some the reservation of the Blessed Sacrament
simply for the public and private adoration of the faithful is unscriptural because Christ did not mention this purpose in instituting the Eucharist. We have already seen that the primary purpose
of the Real Presence is that the Church should have in her hands a
Victim all-sufficient to offer to the Father and that the faithful
should be fed and nourished with the divine life by partaking of
the Victim offered in sacrifice. It is also true that since what *is*
reserved will eventually be eaten, the reservation of the Blessed
Sacrament on our altars still fulfils the purpose Christ had in wishing to be present under the appearance of bread, that is food. This
being so, the objection against reserving the Blessed Sacrament for
the adoration of the faithful loses its force.

*Devotion to the Real Presence in accord with the spirit of the
     liturgy*

It has been said that devotion to the Real Presence is contrary
to the spirit of the liturgy and that it ought to be played down in
this age of re-awakened liturgical piety. Pius XII answers this
objection in 'Mediator Dei' when he says: "These devotional practices have contributed greatly to increasing the faith and the supernatural life of the Church on earth. . . . They have their origin in

the spirit of the liturgy and, therefore, so long as they are conducted with due seemliness and with faith and devotion which are required by the sacred ritual and the instructions of the Church, they undoubtedly contribute greatly to the living of a liturgical life".[42]

In his address at the conclusion of the Liturgical Congress at Assisi, Pope Pius XII had this to say: "The most enthusiastic and convinced liturgist must be able to understand and appreciate what our Lord in the tabernacle means to the solidly pious faithful, be they unlearned or educated. He is their counsellor, their consoler, their strength and refuge, their hope in life and death. Not satisfied with simply letting the faithful come to their Lord in the tabernacle, the liturgical movement then will strive to draw them there even more".[43]

The Real Presence a means and not an end in itself

To some people visits to the Blessed Sacrament seem pointless. They argue that every soul in the state of grace enjoys a special manner of presence common to the Father, Son and Holy Spirit which is known as the indwelling of the Blessed Trinity in the soul. Surely, they say, I can talk to Christ present within me, I don't need to go before the Blessed Sacrament to do so. In a sense this is true. But the presence of Christ in the tabernacle is a means and not an end in itself. He is there to strengthen that union by grace, reminding us of his sacrificial action in the Mass and giving us a greater willingness to surrender ourselves through him to the Father. This is the one condition on which our deeper union with him depends. Our visits, then, provide the opportunity of renewing the sentiments we had in our hearts at Mass and during Holy Communion. We recall that we are united to Christ our Victim in order that we may sacrifice ourselves and offer ourselves with him by fighting sin and striving after self-sacrifice. We are united to Christ our food so that we may deepen our charity and love others more intensely in him and for him. In this way we renew in ourselves the effects of the Mass and Holy Communion and we share more fully in the fruits of the Redemption.

One can say whoever understands the Real Presence correctly will have an appreciation above the average of the real value of the Mass and Holy Communion.

Without using the terminology used by Pope John Paul II in his Encyclical Letter 'Redemptor Hominis', the new Code of Canon Law refers to these three aspects of the Eucharistic Mystery implicitly when it reminds the faithful that they should give the greatest honour to the Holy Eucharist, taking an active part in the celebration of the august Sacrifice, receiving this sacrament frequently with devotion and worshipping it with the greatest degree of adoration (cf. c.898).

Conclusion

We must not think of the Incarnation as an event that occurred two thousand years ago, the effects of which ceased when Christ ascended into heaven. On the contrary, when Christ became man a new relationship was established between man and God, a relationship which is eternal. It is necessary to recall that while Christ came on earth to do something, namely, to reveal the Father to us and to redeem us, he did this by permanently taking up his abode with us.

The period of history from the day Christ ascended into heaven until his Second Coming, is the continuation of the work which he performed during his time on earth. The sacramental system he instituted is not merely the 'application of the merits of Christ', it is Christ acting here and now and under sensible signs; it is Christ transcending the limitations of time and space to contact each succeeding generation directly. The Sacrifice of the Mass gives us *now* the possibility of being present to the Sacrifice of Christ. Holy Communion makes it possible for us to receive life directly from Christ by immediate contact with him *now*. But over and above this, the fact that Christ is really and permanently present, not only at the Sacrifice, or when we receive Holy Communion, but also in the tabernacle, has as its aim the strengthening of our union with him by reminding us of the sacrificial character of the Mass and enabling us to make a more complete surrender of ourselves to him.

Finally, the following words of Pope John Paul II form a fitting conclusion to this chapter: "The Eucharist is the ineffable Sacrament. The essential commitment and, above all, the visible grace and source of supernatural strength for the Church as the People of God is to persevere and advance constantly in Eucharistic life and Eucharistic piety in the climate of the Eucharist. With all the greater reason, then, it is not permissible for us, in thought, life or action, to take away from this truly most holy Sacrament its full magnitude and its essential meaning . . . Every member of the Church, especially bishops and priests, must be vigilant in seeing that this sacrament of love shall be at the centre of the life of the People of God, so that through all the manifestations of worship due to it Christ shall be given back 'love for love' and truly become 'the life of our souls' ".[44]

References

1. Instruction on the Worship of the Eucharistic Mystery, ch.I, A. Flannery, O.P., *Vatican Council II* (Dominican Publications, Dublin), p.103.
2. Pope John Paul II, Encyclical Letter 'Redemptor Hominis', 4.3.79, n.20, L'Osservatore Romano (English Edition), 19.3.79, p.11.
3. A. Flannery, op. cit., p.101.
4. Pope Paul VI, Encyclical Letter 'Mysterium Fidei', C.T.S., Do.355, n.28, p.13.
5. A. Flannery, op. cit., p.103.
6. Decree on the Ministry and Life of Priests, n.5, Walter M. Abbott, *Documents of Vatican II*, p.542.
7. Instruction on the Worship of the Eucharistic Mystery, A. Flannery, op. cit., p.106.
8. Dogmatic Constitution on the Church, n.34, Walter M. Abbott, op. cit., p.60.
9. F. Lambruschini, *I Sacramenti nella Teologia Morale e nella Vita Cristiana*, pp.148,143.
10. ibid., p.142.
11. Constitution on the Sacred Liturgy, n.14, Walter M. Abbott, op. cit., p.144.
12. Dogmatic Constitution on the Church, n.10, Walter M. Abbott, op. cit., p.27.
13. Decree on the Ministry and Life of Priests, n.2, Walter M. Abbott, op. cit., p.535.
14. Instruction on the Worship of the Eucharistic Mystery, A. Flannery, op. cit., p.104.
15. ibid., p.111.
16. *A Small Liturgical Dictionary* by Cardinal Lercaro (Burns & Oates, London), p.92.
17. Pope John XXIII, Encyclical Letter 'Mater et Magistra', C.T.S., S259, n.249., p.62.
18. Instruction on the Worship of the Eucharistic Mystery, A. Flannery, op. cit., p.119.
19. ibid., p.109.
20. Constitution on the Sacred Liturgy, n.56, Walter M. Abbott, op. cit., p.156.
21. Pope Pius XII, Allocutio, 6.6.54, *AAS* 46 (1954), p.369.
22. Secretariat for Promoting Christian Unity, Ecumenical Directory, Part One, nn.47 and 50, C.T.S., Do.391, pp.20–21.
23. L. Rossi and A. Valsecchi, *Dizionario Enciclopedico di Teologia Morale* (Edizioni Paoline, Roma, 1973), p.1106.
24. Prummer, O.P., *Handbook of Moral Theology*, n.425.
25. L. Rossi and A. Valsecchi, op. cit., p.1106.
26. Pope John XXIII, Encyclical Letter 'Mater et Magistra', C.T.S., S259, nn. 250–252, pp.62–63.
27. Constitution on the Sacred Liturgy, n.106, Walter M. Abbott, op. cit., p.169.
28. Instruction on the Worship of the Eucharistic Mystery, A. Flannery, op. cit., p.104.

29. ibid., p.120.
30. ibid., pp.102–103.
31. ibid., p.122.
32. Dogmatic Constitution on the Church, n.26, Walter M. Abbott, op. cit., p.50.
33. Pope Paul VI, Encyclical Letter 'Mysterium Fidei'. C.T.S., Do355, n.66, pp.27–8.
34. Instruction on the Worship of the Eucharistic Mystery, A. Flannery, op. cit., p.122.
35. Constitution on the Sacred Liturgy, n.37, Walter M. Abbott, op. cit., p.154.
36. Instruction on Holy Communion and the Worship of the Eucharist outside Mass, A. Flannery, op. cit., n.14, p.245.
37. ibid., n.5, p.243.
38. Instruction on the Worship of the Eucharistic Mystery, A. Flannery, op. cit., pp. 129–130.
39. Pope Paul VI, Encyclical Letter 'Mysterium Fidei', C.T.S., Do 355, n.66, p.28.
40. Decree on the Ministry and Life of Priests, n.18, Walter M. Abbott, op. cit., p.570.
41. Karl Rahner, *Mission and Grace*, Vol. I, p.304.
42. Pope Pius XII, Encyclical Letter 'Mediator Dei', C.T.S., Do270, n.141, p.54.
43. The Pope Speaks (Winter 1956–1957), p.284.
44. Pope John Paul II, Encyclical Letter 'Redemptor Hominis'. 4.3.1979, n.20, L'Osservatore Romano (English Edition), 19.3.79, p.11.

5

PENANCE OR RECONCILIATION

When in the sacrament of Penance the faithful confess their sins to a lawful minister, are sorry for them and have a firm purpose of amendment, they receive from God pardon for the sins which they have committed after Baptism through the absolution given them by the minister. At the same time they are reconciled with the Church they have harmed by their sins (cf. c.959).

The link between Penance and the Eucharist

Pope John Paul II speaks of the link between Penance and the Eucharist in these words: "If the first word of Christ's teaching, the first phrase of the Gospel Good News, was 'Repent, and believe in the Gospel', the sacrament of the Passion, Cross and Resurrection seems to strengthen and consolidate in an altogether special way this call in our souls. The Eucharist and Penance thus become in a sense two closely connected dimensions of authentic life in accordance with the spirit of the Gospel, of truly Christian life. The Christ who calls to the Eucharistic banquet is always the same Christ who exhorts us to penance and repeats his 'Repent'. Without this constant ever renewed endeavour for conversion, partaking of the Eucharist would lack its full redeeming effectiveness and there would be a loss or at least a weakening of the special readiness to offer God the spiritual sacrifice in which our sharing in the priesthood of Christ is expressed in an essential and universal manner. In Christ priesthood is linked with his Sacrifice, his self-giving to the Father; and precisely because it is without limit, that self-giving gives rise in us human beings, subject to numerous limitations, to the need to turn to God in an ever more mature way and with a constant, ever more profound, conversion".[1]

The meaning of conversion

The Greek word for conversion is 'metanoia'. The first conversion that takes place in the life of the Christian is brought about by faith and Baptism. This conversion is accompanied by repentance, which implies a detestation of sin, a turning away from sin and a turning to God. One of the best descriptions of 'metanoia' has been given by Pope Paul VI. " 'Metanoia' ", says the Pope, "means conversion, repentance, inner change. It means a change of outlook. And it is the latter that is the most important; to change one's thoughts, ideas, way of judging oneself, to change one's conscience, from false to true. This inner penitence is indispensable for us believers, for us Christians: because it means correcting our own logical and moral orientation in line with that truth which directs our lives to order, good, love and God. We who are fortunate to have this conception of our lives, destined by inborn vocation and insertion through Baptism in the plan of salvation, to communion with God, the heavenly Father, through Christ, in the Holy Spirit must continually be concerned with this generous and loving correction of course, as the pilot of a ship is continually aware of the need to adjust the helm to keep it on the pre-established route, from which it easily deviates by waves and winds . . . To change one's erroneous and faulty mentality calls for humility and courage to say to oneself: 'I have been wrong', requires considerable strength of character. The renunciation of certain fixed ideas one has, which seem to define one's personality . . . really calls for a spiritual revolution, possible only for one who sacrifices what is most personal in him, his own opinion or conviction to the truth. For those who are usually dominated by passionate instincts or by illicit interests, to change course in the direction of righteousness, virtue, religious spirit, is a very difficult and meritorious operation, an overwhelming attempt at renewal. To forgive an offence, for example, to overcome a capricious dislike, a point of honour, an opportunity to use violence, etc., can be an exercise of penitence, along the right line of Christian love".[2]

Christian repentance, penitence or penance is first of all a virtue — an interior force, a basic tendency in Christian existence which leads the sinner to detach himself from sin and destroy in himself the forces of evil. It is essential in the life of the Christian and forms an important part of his programme of life.

Pope John Paul II reminds us that "conversion to God always consists *in discovering his mercy*, that, is in discovering that love which is patient and kind (cf. 1 Cor 13 : 4) as only the Creator and Father can be".[3]

The sacrament of Penance

In the Decree of the Sacred Congregation for Divine Worship accompanying the revised Rite of Penance we read: "Through human frailty it happens that Christians abandon the love they had at first (cf. Rev 2 : 4) and the friendship that united them to God is broken through sin. Therefore the Lord instituted a special sacrament of Penance for the forgiveness of sins committed after Baptism (cf. Jn 20 : 21–23), which the Church has used throughout the centuries, in varying forms, but which in its essential elements is always the same".[4]

Confession in the early Church

As there are different views about the practice of confession as we know it in the early Church, it is necessary for us to say something about them at this point.

Referring to the controversy on the subject Pope Paul VI had this to say: "Let us choose for the present the main point, which is the place occupied by this sacrament in the plan of salvation. The question which has a distinct historical root in the third century and a later one in the Protestant controversy, is whether there exists in the economy of the Christian faith a sacrament of Penance, after Baptism".[5]

The Pope mentions the third century because the forms of penitential discipline in the Church are not clear in the documents until the third century. Before this only incidental remarks and scattered information are available to the inquirer. From the third century, however, a certain uniformity appears in the penitential discipline. The two recognised leaders in the controversy we are discussing are Paul Galtier, a former professor at the Gregorian University, Rome, and Bernard Poschmann. In a controversy with the latter Karl Adam championed confession is secret or private penance as it is sometimes called. Karl Adam called Galtier's work *L'Eglise et la remission des pechés* the decisive work on the subject.

Galtier has clarified the terms of the problem. The terms 'public' and 'private' in relation to penance refer to the satisfaction and not to the confession which was private in both disciplines; at the same time the element of reconciliation may well have been public in both disciplines. Public penance is that in which the sinner, after privately confessing his sins to the bishop (or his delegate), was relegated to the order of penitents, there to work out his 'official

F

penance'. Galtier maintains that alongside this there always existed a sacramental means of remission in which the sinner was not obliged to take his stand with the penitents. This was the normal procedure for intermediate sins. "Public penance", says Galtier, "must not be confused with public confession; the one did not necessarily imply the other. On the contrary, the confession preceding public penance was under ordinary circumstances secret and in private".[6]

Referring to the writings of Origen and St Cyprian, who was martyred in 258 AD, Galtier finds clear evidence of the practice of sacramental confession in the third century. He mentions the fact that the Council of Nicea (325 AD) commanded that Communion, and therefore absolution, shall be given to whosoever shall ask for penance on their death-bed; but that this shall not be done until after the case has been examined by the bishop". As further evidence of private confession in the fourth century Galtier quotes from a work probably attributed to St Basil; and for evidence of the practice in the fifth century he quotes Pope St Leo the Great.[7]

Relying on Poschmann alone, one Catholic liturgist makes the bald statement that "until the seventh century or so private confessions were unknown and earlier than that it was common practice to receive Holy Communion whenever a Christian attended the Eucharist".[8]

Theological premises to the revised Rite of Penance

Before discussing the structure of the sacrament of Penance and the part played by the priest and the penitent, it will be necessary to refer to the Introduction (*Praenotanda*) to the revised Rite of Penance which was issued by the Sacred Congregation for Divine Worship on December 2, 1973. In this Introduction we have the official statement of the Church's theological understanding of the sacrament of Penance or Reconciliation. This implicitly involves among other things the teaching on sin and the necessity of confession.

A new category of sin?

Although the document does not set out to resolve matters of theological debate, it is interesting to note that it does not reflect the threefold division of sins (mortal, serious — or, according to some, grave — and venial) which has been put forward in recent years by certain theologians. It is hardly likely that those responsible for the document were unaware of this new division of sins. In an area in which it is difficult enough for the ordinary Christian in practice, the introduction of yet another category of sins would simply serve to confuse the faithful. Only two types of sin with which the faithful are familiar are mentioned, namely, grave sin and venial sin (cf. n.7). Grave sin is defined as: "an offence against God which destroys friendship with him" (n.5). In the press release issued when the new rite was promulgated and in the address of Pope Paul VI at the General Audience on April 3, 1974, 'grave' sin is equated with 'mortal' sin. It is interesting to note that although the term 'mortal sin' appears in the 1917 Code, in the new Code of Canon Law the term used is 'grave' when applied to sins which must be confessed (cf. c.989).

With regard to venial sin, the traditional teaching has always distinguished between deliberate and semi-deliberate venial sin. The former represents some resistance to the Holy Spirit, and, if allowed to go unchecked, could give rise to a lax attitude of mind which would make it easier for the individual to contemplate committing grave sin. The criteria for judging the morality of a human act (consideration of the moral object of the act, the intention of the agent and the circumstances in which the act has been placed) and those for assessing both the gravity of and responsibility for an immoral act, namely, grave matter, full knowledge and full consent, when properly understood, and applied in the light of sound psychology, should be adequate for the purpose and cover the very limited number of cases for which the theory of the 'fundamental option', which is mentioned below, might be invoked.

The determinants of morality of a human act

The order in which the criteria for judging the morality of a human act is given is very important. The matter is fully discussed in the field of fundamental moral theology. Suffice it to say here that one must first look at the act not simply as a physical act but as a physical act in relation to its moral aspect, that is, its relation to the norm of reason and the order established by God for the behaviour of men. We call this the moral object of the act. The physical act of taking something which belongs to someone else considered from the moral angle may be perfectly justified and therefore a good moral act, or it may be an immoral act if it amounts to stealing, that is, taking something which belongs to another against the owner's reasonable wish. Some acts of their very nature are wrong and no amount of good intention will make them morally good, and therefore justifiable. Today there is a tendency for some Catholic moralists to neglect to give due consideration to this first guideline of the criteria and to concentrate rather on the motive or the intention of the agent. What the well-known Catholic moralist, Henry Davis, S.J., wrote some years ago still applies today because it concerns not only the non-Catholic approach but also the humanist approach to moral or ethical problems in our present society. Fr Davis writes: "The non-Catholic approach to moral teaching seems to imply that externals do not matter so much; what is of first importance is that the interior motive should be upright; there is no evil if one's motive be good. This may seem a travesty on sincere teaching but a study of the books of Anglican writers reveals the deep cleavage between Catholic and non-Catholic doctrine of the morality of the human act. Catholic teaching has always been that the motive is only one determinant of moral conduct; the other two determinants are the thing done and the circumstances in which it is done. If these three factors are not admitted, the consequences for morality do not bear thinking about. Catholic teaching pays great attention to external actions, bids us keep motives good and at the same time avoid external evil actions".[9]

The fundamental option

The new division of sins mentioned above is bound up with a modern theory known as the 'fundamental option'. This theory is clearly and concisely outlined by J. D. Crichton in *The Ministry of Reconciliation*, as follows: "For some time now theologians have been urging that the matter should be reconsidered and seem to be agreeing that there is a difference between mortal sin, that is, deadly sin, 'sin that is to death' and grave or serious sin. The terms are not of the highest importance. What is important is that these and other theologians distinguish between sin that is a complete turning away from God — and that is what the Bible seems to be thinking of when it speaks of sin — and the sort of sin that is by no means a rejection of God but rather a falling short of the fundamental direction of their life which is Godward. This has been called the 'fundamental option'. People whether consciously or not have chosen God and his demands but from time to time they fall away from that which is the fundamental direction of their lives.

There is a failure of response to the demands of God whom they have chosen and wish with all their heart to serve, and it is argued, the relationship with God is not broken".[10]

It should be pointed out that the distinction between 'sins unto death' and 'sins not unto death' mentioned above, does not concern the universality of forgiveness. Commentators tell us that the distinction is not the same as that between mortal and venial sin, since the sins not unto death include grave sin. The antithesis presented is between the sins against light and truth and the means of pardon offered to sinners. If these are rejected where else can one turn? (cf. Jn 5 : 15–17). The only sin mentioned specifically in the New Testament as not forgivable by God is 'blasphemy of the Spirit'.

Official clarification of the fundamental option

Commenting on the view we have been considering, the Sacred Congregation for the Doctrine of the Faith had this to say: "The observance of the moral law in the field of sexuality and the practice of chastity have been considerably endangered, especially among less fervent Christians, by the current tendency to minimize as far as possible, when not denying outright, the reality of grave sin, at least in people's actual lives".

"There are those who go as far as to affirm that mortal sin, which causes separation from God, only exists in the formal refusal directly opposed to God's call, or in that selfishness which completely and deliberately closes itself to the love of neighbour. They say that it is only then that there comes into play the fundamental option, that is to say the decision which totally commits the person and which is necessary if mortal sin is to exist; by this option the person, from the depths of the personality, takes up or ratifies a fundamental attitude towards God or people. On the contrary, so-called 'peripheral' actions (which, it is said, usually do not involve decisive choice) do not go so far as to change the fundamental option, the less so since they often come, as is observed, from habit. Thus such actions can weaken the fundamental option, but not to such a degree as to change it completely".

"In reality, it is precisely the fundamental option which in the last resort defines a person's moral disposition. But it can be completely changed by particular acts, especially when, as often happens, these have been prepared for by previous more superficial acts. Whatever the case, it is wrong to say that particular acts are not enough to constitute mortal sin".

"According to the Church's teaching mortal sin, which is opposed to God, does not consist only in formal and direct resistance to the commandment of charity. It is equally to be found in this opposition to authentic love which is included in every deliberate transgression, in serious matter, of each of the moral laws".

"Christ himself has indicated the double commandment of love as the basis of the moral life. But on this commandment depends 'the whole Law, and the Prophets also' (cf. Mt 22:38,40). It therefore includes the other particular precepts. In fact, to the young man who asked, 'What good deed must I do to possess eternal life?' Jesus replied: 'If you wish to enter into life, keep the commandments . . . You must not kill. You must not commit adultery. You must not bear false witness. Honour your father and mother, and 'You must love your neighbour as yourself' (cf. Mt 19:16–19)".

"A person therefore sins mortally not only when his action comes from direct contempt for love of God and neighbour, but also when he consciously and freely, for whatever reason, chooses something which is seriously disordered. For in this choice, as has been said above, there is already included contempt for the divine commandment: the person turns himself away from God and loses charity".[11]

The element of choice

As has been stated above an element of choice is involved in all mortal sin. It will also be helpful to quote Pope Paul VI on this subject.

Speaking of the subjective aspect of mortal sin Pope Paul VI had this to say: "The second reality (involved in the notion of sin) is a subjective reality, connected with our person, a metaphysico-moral reality; that is the inalienable relationship of our action with God, present, omniscient and examining our free choice. Every free and conscious action of ours has this value of choice in conformity or not with the law, with the love of God, and our 'yes' or 'no' is transcribed in him, so to speak, is recorded in him. This 'no' is sin. It is suicide".

"Since sin is not only a personal defect of ours, but an interpersonal offence, which begins with us and arrives at God, it is not merely a lack of legality in the human order, an offence against society, or against our inner moral logic; it is a fatal snapping of the vital objective bond that unites us with the one supreme source of life, which is God. With this first deadly consequence: that we, who are capable, in virtue of the gift of freedom, which makes man 'like to God', of perpetrating that offence, that break, and *with such facility* [italics mine] are no longer capable of putting it right by ourselves (cf. Jn 15:5). We are capable of ruining ourselves. This makes us mediate on the extent of our responsibility. The act becomes a state: a state of death".[12]

According to the theory of the fundamental option the state of mortal sin is reached only after a series of what are called serious or grave sins has been committed. It is to be noted that in the Pope's analysis there is no reference to such a series of sins being necessary before a person puts himself in a state of mortal sin. The words "the act becomes a state: a state of death" are of the greatest significance here.

Law and sin

Some writers in their desire to point out the faults of the past tend to make the same mistake themselves of bringing the law into disrepute by their manner of speaking. It is not that the law is at fault. The defect of the past lies rather in the impoverished way in which the teaching was presented and understood. The divine law is the law given to man by God to love himself. It calls man to the union of life in the Blessed Trinity. By his life on earth man is preparing for this union and refusal to love is sin. The moral law expresses the order of love and what is involved in the call of man in his life in relation to God and men. For St Thomas Aquinas law is the external means by which man is led to God; the internal means is grace. It is also important to realise that the moral order is the work of God and not of man.

Conscience alone is not enough

Pope Paul VI stresses the necessity of law when he says: "Conscience alone is not enough; even though it bears within it the fundamental precepts of the natural law (cf. Rom 2:2–16). The law indeed is necessary and the law that conscience offers by itself for the guidance of human life is not sufficient. Conscience must be educated and the law explained. It must be integrated with the external law both in the civil order — who does not know this? — and in the Christian order. Of this too everyone is aware. The Christian 'way' would not be known to us, with truth and with authority, if it had not been announced to us by the message of the external word, of the Gospel and of the Church. Anyone who thinks of emancipating himself from legitimate law and authority would have a moral sense that was silent on many difficult precepts which are important and, for a Christian, fundamental, such as charity and sacrifice; and he would end up by losing correct moral judgment, and by indulging in that elastic and permissive morality which seems unfortunately to prevail today".[13]

Law in the context of love

The Christian must view law in the context of love. His observance of it must be an act of loving obedience to God. The law of love is wider than the ten Commandments. They do not embrace in detail all the demands of love, just as they do not embrace all the Christian virtues. The Christian life consists in following and imitating Christ, and the more helpful approach is to see it in terms of living out the theological and moral virtues. But the ten Commandments have their place in such a scheme for the daily life of the Christian. From the words of Jesus himself their deliberate non-observance indicates a lack of love which will be serious or not according to the importance of the matter in question. They also serve to give us a sense of the concrete in our moral lives, and a proper understanding of their place in the Christian life will help to remove some of the moral uncertainty which is widespread today.

The social and ecclesial aspects of sin

The mention of the social and ecclesial aspects of sin in the documents of the Second Vatican Council, and the stress that is now rightly being put on them in the revised Rite of Penance, is simply a revival of something which has mainly been forgotten by the majority of Christians. This may cause people to look upon these aspects as new in the Church. In fact the first centuries of Christian experience had to face the fact of serious sin in the Church and the aspects of sin which we are considering go back to the time of the apostles as is clear from Galatians 16:1-2, 2 Timothy 2:24-25 and 4:2. Here St Paul shows that sin and repentance are the concern of the Church and that Christians have a duty of fraternal correction. In 2 Corinthians 2:5-11 St Paul refers to the punishment of the man, who had given offence to him or to his representative, being enough because the punishment has brought about his repentance and he must now be brought back into the community. In 1 Corinthians 5 : 1ff we read of the case of the incestuous man who was told to break off his association. He did not do so and he is handed over to Satan, that is, according to Tertullian, excommunicated. Exclusion from the community is intended to help the sinner to reach salvation. Once the punishment has been effective in achieving the repentance of the sinner, love demands that he be re-instated.

Pope Pius XII reflects the attitude of the early Church when he speaks of 'the danger of contagion' with reference to sin.[14] The prayers in the solemn rite for the reconciliation of sinners in the Pontificale Romanum (Part III) speak of some of the effects of sin on the community and on the Church. The traditional teaching about the importance of not giving scandal and bad example is intended to illustrate the same point.

Theologically every sin has a social aspect because the nature and call of man is social. The social aspect of sin and the ecclesial dimension are closely connected. Through Christ man's union with God is realised. Sin attacks the union of man in Christ. This union with Christ is brought about in the Church as the *institution* of salvation possessing faith and the sacraments, and also as the *community* of salvation in which men form one body in Christ. Every grave sin destroys the Christian life in the baptised. It signifies the loss of the love of God and of the life-giving union with Christ by a member of the Christian community. Deliberate venial sin indicates a love that is still imperfect and weak, a lack of vigilance and it too lowers the level of life and love in the Christian community.

It is true that not every sin has the effect of breaking the bonds that unite the faithful to the Church.[15] The sins which do break these bonds are those which are directly opposed to unity, such as schism, which breaks the bond of communion, heresy, which breaks the bond of faith, and apostasy, which attacks both of these relationships. Even if it does not directly affect the bonds of communion and faith, a sin committed by a member of the Mystical Body of Christ casts a cloud over the holiness of the Mystical Body, decreases the exercise of charity and lessens its effectiveness in the field of the apostolate. Every act which arrests the development of the divine life in us diminishes and damages the vitality of the Mystical Body itself.

When a Christian sins he renders himself guilty before the

Christian community because he besmirches the holiness of the Church. He deprives the Mystical Body of the contribution it has a right to expect from his co-operation. He casts a reflection on the intimate sacramental character of the Church because in him the Church ceases to be in a certain sense the sign and vehicle of grace and salvation. This is absolutely true when it is a question of grave sin. It is verified to a lesser degree in the case of venial sin which results in a lesser good for the members of the Mystical Body. The sins of the baptised represent wounds which in the words of the revised Rite of Penance "can take varied and multiple forms in the life of each member of the community" (n.7b), and at the same time do harm to the Church. It is not surprising then that these aspects are now given greater prominence in relation to the sacrament of Penance or Reconciliation, as it is more appropriately called; and the suggestion that whenever possible penances should be given which will bring home to the penitent these aspects of sin, is a step in the right direction.

The structure of the sacrament

Tradition presents the sacrament of Penance as a judgment, a tribunal. By using these terms the Church wants to stress two aspects of the sacrament in particular: a) the particular form of intervention by the Church and b) the part played by the personal effort of the sinner.

a) Ecclesial penance has always taken the form of a judicial process. It supposes a judgment of the repentant sinner. This demands the intervention of one who possesses the power of the keys.

The revised Rite of Penance states that "the Church exercises the ministry of Penance through her bishops and priests, who call the faithful to repentance by preaching the word of God to them, and declare their sins forgiven as they absolve them in the name of Christ and by the power of the Holy Spirit".

"In the exercise of this ministry, priests act in communion with their bishops, sharing in their office and power. The bishop directs his priests in all matters concerning the ministry of Penance".

"In order to be able to administer the sacrament of Penance, a priest must have the faculty to absolve according to Canon Law" (cf. also c.966). A priest, who has the faculty habitually of hearing confessions either by virtue of his office or from the bishop of the place where he has been incardinated or of the place where he lives, can use this faculty everywhere, unless the bishop in a particular case has revoked it (cf. c.967 n.2).

Any priest, even though he has no faculties to hear confessions, validly and lawfully absolves penitents who are in danger of death from all censures and sins even if a priest with faculties is present (cf. c.976).

The minister of the Church must judge not only the sin but also the repentance of the sinner. To receive the confession of a sinner presupposes a judicial power by which the sinner is reconciled to the Church as well as obtaining pardon from God. This pardon calls for the power of Orders because it comes from the Church's power to sanctify or make holy. Christian Penance requires sacramental power because it brings forgiveness. Thus for the valid administration of the sacrament one needs the power of Orders and that of jurisdiction, i.e. authority to exercise this power over the people. That this has been the constant teaching of the Church is shown from the way in which the ministry of Penance has always been exercised, that is, in dependence on the bishop. As penance became less public, this dependence was increasingly stressed and the rise of penitential theology in the 12th century was responsible for formulating the traditional conviction. To have the power of Orders is not enough, one must have received a pastoral charge or jurisdiction in regard to the penitent. In virtue of the sacrament of Orders, all priests of the New Testament receive from Christ, among other things, the power to retain or remit sins. Christ gave this power to the apostles — a power to be passed on to their successors. Priests are associated with the apostles through the bishops.

Penance is a judgment and a pardon. Judgment presupposes an accusation, and an expiation which leads to reconciliation and hence pardon. Pardon is signified by the absolution which also implies restoration to friendship with God. This reconciliation follows the acts of the penitent which have been imposed and consecrated by the Church. At the present time confession constitutes the principal satisfaction and penance imposed by the Church. The satisfaction is salutary because it is an expiation united to the passion of Christ.

b) With regard to the part played by the personal effort of the sinner, at first stress was placed on a long process of expiation and satisfaction under the control of the Church. When the emphasis was put on 'confession' as such, the basic idea remained. Confession is salutary satisfaction for the repentant sinner. St Thomas

Aquinas firmly upheld the essential necessity of personal effort as part of the sacrament. Tradition has always held that justification of free and responsible people always supposes a personal consent.

The acts of the penitent

The true nature of the sacrament of Penance involves the acts of the penitent and the intervention of the priest. These aspects form the reality of the Christian sacrament of Penance. The present rite of confession and absolution expresses the submission of the sinner to the minister of the Church, and the intervention of the Church. The acts of the penitent in this context are contrition, confession and satisfaction.

Contrition

The revised Rite of Penance describes contrition as follows: "It is of the first importance that the penitent should have contrition, which is 'the sorrow from the heart for sin', and detestation of the sin committed, together with the resolve to avoid the sin in future. We must make our way towards Christ's kingdom through *metanoia*, which, as we have seen, means a change of heart and way of life. The love and holiness of God, manifested in his Son and generously imparted to us, thus become the dominant influence in a Christian's life, and in all his thoughts and judgments (cf. Heb 1:2; Col 1:19 and throughout; Eph 1:23 and throughout). The reality of repentance depends on this heartfelt contrition. Conversion must affect a man inwardly if he is to be progressively enlightened and conformed to Christ" (n.6a).

The above description gives the essential elements of contrition, namely, interior sorrow, detestation of sin and a firm resolution not to sin again. Detestation for sin means such a hatred for the sin committed that the sinner wishes he had not committed it.

Perfect contrition

Theologians speak of perfect and imperfect contrition or attrition. This is a distinction which has been officially recognised by the Church. Contrition is said to be perfect when the motive from which it springs is perfect, namely, sorrow for sin because it has offended God who is infinitely good in himself — love of God for

his own sake. Perfect contrition can arise from the consideration
of the sufferings of Christ for our sins. The sinner is eventually
moved to love God and to detest his sins because they have offended
a God who is so good in himself. It can also arise from a consideration of God's blessings. The sinner loves God who is his greatest
benefactor. This causes him to realise that God is infinitely good
in himself. Perfect contrition effects immediate justification but it
must be followed by confession. This is the will of Christ. Also
since we cannot be sure of our dispositions confession gives us a
further degree of certitude.

Imperfect contrition or attrition

Imperfect contrition is given its name because it arises not
from the love of God for his own sake but from some other supernatural motive. The motive must be a supernatural one, that is, it
must have some reference to God. Such motives could be: 1) the
foulness of sin in so far as it is against a particular virtue God
wants us to practise, it deprives the sinner of grace, makes him a
slave of the devil and an enemy of God; 2) the fear of eternal
punishment; 3) the fear of punishment in this life. These motives
could eventually lead to the motive for perfect contrition. It is safe
teaching that imperfect contrition or attrition suffices for justification *in the sacrament*. Naturally one should aim at making an act
of perfect contrition.

Sorrow for sin because it has injured one's health, one's good
name, has deprived the sinner of some benefit, is not based on
supernatural motives.

The qualities of sorrow for sin

In addition to what has already been said true sorrow must be
an internal act of the will. It is not merely a matter of words. If a
penitent keeps coming back with the same sin, it *may* be an indication that his sorrow is not up to standard. In this case he should
look into the matter.

A person who has genuine sorrow looks upon sin as the greatest
of evils. The books say it should be '*summa appretiative*' as opposed to '*intensive*'. This means that it is an intellectual judgment
and not necessarily a feeling of the emotions. One may not commit
grave sin for one's father or mother, or anyone else for that matter.
We must not love father or mother more than Christ. Many people
would be intensely sorry if they were to lose a very dear friend in a

car accident. On the other hand they would look upon the death of a much needed head of State as a worse tragedy even though they might not feel it in the same way. If in addition to the intellectual judgment about the evil of sin one can shed tears of repentance, well and good. But not everyone can do this.

Genuine sorrow must embrace all grave sins that have not yet been remitted in the sacrament.

Finally the sorrow must have some relation to absolution. There must be some positive act by which the penitent truly and explicitly expresses his sorrow for past sins as distinct from an implicit act of sorrow which might be implied by doing an act of charity.

The purpose of amendment

The new Code of Canon Law reminds us that in order to benefit by the saving remedy of the sacrament, a member of the faithful must be so disposed that repudiating the sins he has committed and having a purpose of amendment he turns back to God (cf. c.987).

The real test of sorrow is the firm purpose of amendment — the resolve not to sin again. This serious intention to avoid sin in future is implied in the act of sorrow. In so far as venial sins are concerned the attitude of the penitent should be to improve or to do better.

The knowledge that one may fall again because of the weakness of one's nature is not an obstacle to making a firm purpose of amendment. The purpose of amendment is not an intellectual persuasion that the penitent will not sin again; nor is it that same as the fear of a relapse or distrust of oneself on account of one's past experience. The promise not to sin again is an act of the will. It is important to remember that in making this promise the penitent counts on the help of God's grace. Both man's co-operation and the help of God's grace are necessary. In making the promise the sinner does not consider himself impeccable.

The resolution includes making the necessary efforts, taking the steps that are necessary to ensure that one does not fall again. It doesn't mean that such efforts will always be crowned with success. God alone can secure a future of absolute fidelity. The firm purpose of amendment carries with it the moral obligation of not wanting to sin again; of avoiding the dangerous occasions of sin; taking steps to be faithful to God's law and relying on the help of God's grace rather than on one's own weak strength. If we are afraid that we will fall again, we should ask ourselves: "Do I want to fall again?" If the answer is "No", we should face the future with confidence, doing all that has been suggested above.

After he has made his confession and has been given whatever advice the confessor considers appropriate, the penitent should make his act of contrition and then listen to the words of absolution.

It is Christ who in the person of the priest says: "Go in peace and sin no more", as he said to the woman in adultery. The Gospel shows us that Jesus understands how imperfect we are. When St Peter asked Jesus if he should forgive someone who had offended him seven times a day, Jesus replied: "Not seven but seventy times seven". Peter thought he was showing mercy by pardoning seven times. But Jesus told him that he must be seventy times more merciful. Jesus is also God. He knows us better than we know ourselves. He will make allowances for us where we might not make allowances for ourselves.

Remorse

Sorrow for sin must not be confused with remorse. Alfred Wilson, C.P., brings out the difference between remorse and repentance when he says: "Judas said: 'I have sinned'; David said the same. Judas had remorse; David had repentance. David was contrite, Judas was not. Both were sad about sin, both regretted it, both did not have repentance. Judas made a public confession of sin: 'I have sinned in betraying innocent blood'; yet despite his remorse and confession and restitution of his foully-gotten gains, he did not have effective repentance. Remorse is a product of wishful-thinking and implies the wish to avoid sin; repentance implies the determined will to avoid it. Remorse is conditional; repentance is absolute. The remorseful would like to avoid sin if doing so did not entail so much effort and sacrifice; and if he had enough faith, hope and charity. Contrition admits neither 'ifs' nor 'buts', and does not recognize the sacrosanctity of ruts. The remorseful would like to undo his sin, but he has not the requisite determination to remove the occasions of sin and surmount the obstacles to reform".[16]

Confession

Individual and integral confession and absolution are the only ordinary means by which a member of the faithful who is conscious of having committed grave sin is reconciled with God and with the Church. Only physical or moral impossibility excuses from this kind of confession. In this case reconciliation can be had in other ways (cf. c.960).

When some people do wrong they instinctively want to tell someone else about it — to get it off their chest, as we say. Others don't want to tell anyone. Likewise some people find no difficulty in going to confession. Other people find it very difficult. What is needed here is a strong faith. Confession is an act of submission to the Church and through the Church to Christ who gave the apostles and their successors the power to forgive and to retain sins. As such it involves an act of faith.

The minister represents Christ and the Church and for this reason he is bound to secrecy. The information he receives is not his own. According to the teaching of the Council of Trent it has always been the practice in the Church to observe such secrecy.

The sacrament has been instituted in the form of a judgment but there is no parallel between this and what happens in civil processes. The penitent is his own accuser. He tells his sins in all simplicity and he is certain of receiving absolution provided he has the proper dispositions. There is no room for deception here because God cannot be deceived. Deception might mislead the confessor but it would not mislead God. This would be a failure to show proper respect for the sacrament to the point of committing sacrilege and cause harm only to the penitent himself.

Confession has not always been as specific as it is now. This depends also on the education of the faithful about the distinction of sins at a particular time and place. Even today in the East confession is more general in form than it is in the West.

The integrity of confession

The canon quoted above referred to the confession being integral. Another canon of the Code of Canon Law is more specific. It states that a member of the faithful has the obligation of confessing the number and species of all the grave sins he has committed after Baptism and which have not yet been directly remitted through the power of the keys of the Church nor accused in an individual confession. He comes to know of these through a careful examination of conscience (cf. c.988).

It will be noted that the reference is made to post-baptismal grave sins which have not yet been submitted to the power of the keys of the Church. This is what the theologians call necessary matter for confessions as opposed to free matter which applies to venial sins or grave sins which have already been remitted in the sacrament.

Integrity can be of two kinds: material and formal.

Material integrity is present when the penitent confesses *all* his post-baptismal grave sins which have not been confessed and absolved. He gives, in so far as he can, their number, species and the circumstances which change the species or malice of the act.

Formal integrity, on the other hand, is present when all mortal sins not yet remitted *which can and should be confessed here and now,* taking into account all the circumstances, are confessed. What this means will be explained later.

Number: If the penitent knows the exact number of times he has committed a particular sin, there is no problem. If he doesn't, an approximate number will do. If he cannot even arrive at an approximate number, the confessor will try to help him. This may happen when people have been away from confession for a long time. The penitent is only expected to do his best to give the confessor as accurate a picture as possible. Difficulty with regard to the number of times arises in connection with sins that are committed through habit. A thorough preparation will help here.

Species: In this context there are two types of species: the *theological* and the *moral* species.

The theological species refers to the gravity of the sin, i.e. whether it is light or grave.

The moral species refers to the virtue(s) against which the sin has offended, e.g. adultery is against the virtue of chastity, justice and charity. Penitents are not expected to be moral theologians but determining the species of their sins is useful for educating their consciences. A person may think that a sin he has committed is one against charity when at the same time it is also a sin against justice which may call for restitution. Educating the penitent's conscience will help him to mature as a Christian. At the same time there is no obligation to confess those sins again which through inadequate education were confessed inaccurately in a previous confession.

Circumstances which change the theological or moral species of the sin must be confessed, e.g. stealing even a small amount from a poor man could be a grave sin. A sin against chastity committed by a married man with someone who is not his wife would have the further malice of adultery. Hence the necessity also of mentioning the circumstances that one is married or single.

There is no obligation to mention other circumstances which do not come within the categories we have been considering.

The revised Rite of Penance recommends that "If the penitent is unknown to the confessor, he should explain his circumstances to the priest, and any difficulties he may have in leading the Christian life, and whatever else may be of use to the priest as a help to the administration of the sacrament. He should also tell the priest when he last went to confession" (n.16).

Causes excusing from material integrity

Material integrity as canon 960 implies may not always be possible. The penitent may have forgotten sins which in fact he should confess or may find himself, as we shall see below, unable to tell what normally should be told here and now. If he confesses all the necessary matter of which he is aware and can confess in the circumstances, his confession has formal integrity. Formal integrity is sufficient in the sacrament of Penance. When Christ instituted the sacrament he did not wish to oblige people to do what would be physically or morally impossible. The law concerning the material integrity of confession, like all positive laws, admits of excusing causes. A penitent is obliged only to make his confession as complete as he can in the circumstances.

Formal integrity, at least, is necessary because Christ instituted the sacrament in the form of a judgment. The confessor cannot pass a fair judgment unless he knows the facts of the case. He can only know the facts if the penitent makes them known to him.

Physical impossibility

a) *Ignorance or forgetfulness* is an excusing cause from material integrity. This applies especially to the sick and the aged. The rigid application of the teaching on integrity would prevent people from going to confession.

b) *Serious illness.* People who are seriously ill cannot confess fully because of their weak condition. They should not be worried unduly. The priest will be satisfied with whatever kind of confession they are able to make at the time. If they haven't been to confession for a long time a generic confession is all that may be possible accompanied by an act of contrition. If they recover they must make good the omission at their next confession. If the priest has a good bedside manner he will put people at their ease.

c) *The dumb*. If they can, they should confess fully by using deaf and dumb language with a confessor who can understand it. Otherwise it is enough for them to give some indication that they have sinned in order to be absolved. It is recommended by some that they should write down their sins but they are not bound to do this. Some do this. If they recover the use of speech, the law regarding integrity operates.

d) *The deaf and those who are hard of hearing*. A number of churches now have confessionals for those who are deaf. If not, they can make their confession in the sacristy, if they wish to do so. The difficulty about using the ordinary confessional for such people is that there is danger of them being overheard. If there is a danger of the seal of confession being violated, the confessor is excused from putting questions to such penitents, if this means that he will have to raise his voice. For the same reason the confessor is justified in giving a light penance even if serious sin has been confessed. Some deaf people are good lip readers. It will help them if they can see the confessor. Hearing aids may solve many difficulties for the deaf, but there are some who are not helped by them. When a priest gets to know a particular penitent who is deaf, he will be able to indicate the penance by some sign which the penitent will understand.

e) *Difficulty of language*. This applies when the penitent does not speak the same language as the confessor and cannot confess in a common language. Confessional cards which have the essentials in a number of foreign languages are available and can be very useful. No one is forbidden to confess by means of an interpreter provided this is not abused and there is no danger of scandal. The interpreter is bound by the seal of confession in the same way as the confessor is (cf. c.990). The penitent, however, is not bound to make use of an interpreter because this is looked upon as an extraordinary means. He can always be absolved on the strength of a generic confession and in this case he has a duty to make good the omission of the sins that he should have confessed when a confessor who speaks his language is available.

f) *Lack of time*. One thinks of soldiers going into battle, of people involved in a ship-wreck, in a fire, etc. If there is no time to absolve such people individually, they can be absolved collectively on confessing that they have sinned, showing that they are sorry and want absolution. If they survive the emergency they have an obligation to confess all post-baptismal grave sins which they could not then confess whenever the opportunity presents itself.

Moral impossibility

Moral impossibility would be present in this context when the penitent would suffer some *grave harm extrinsic to the confession* if he had to make a materially complete and full confession here and now. The grave harm in question can be serious spiritual or material harm to the penitent or to someone else. The people affected may be the penitent himself, the confessor or some third party.

By saying that the harm must be extrinsic to the confession we mean that it must be something that will make confession exceedingly difficult. There is a conflict here between the law concerning integrity and that of justice and charity. It must be noted that the difficulty or embarrassment inherent in confession itself does not excuse the penitent from omitting certain sins. Of its very nature confession can be distasteful; can cause the penitent to feel ashamed of having to accuse himself of certain sins and can cause him to lose his good name before the confessor. This was foreseen by Christ, yet he still made the sacrament, which includes confession, of obligation.

To justify a penitent considering himself excused from mentioning a certain sin or sins on the ground of moral impossibility two conditions must be fulfilled: a) there must be no other confessor available to whom the penitent can confess all his sins without the harm in question resulting; b) the confession must be necessary here and now. Confession would be considered necessary if a person is in danger of death, or if he has to comply with the precept of annual confession and Communion; if a penitent would find it hard to remain unabsolved until he could go to another confessor, etc.

Examples of moral impossibility

1) Danger of breaking the seal of confession. This could happen if a priest cannot confess fully to the confessor available without revealing at least indirectly sins which he heard in confession and the identity of the penitent who is known to the confessor. Another case could be where the penitent rightly fears that the confessor will be heard by those outside because he is accustomed

to speak in a loud voice. The confessor himself may be deaf.

2) The danger of losing one's good name or character before others (not the confessor). This applies especially to patients in hospital where the beds are so close that other patients will hear the sick person's sins.

3) Scrupulosity. Scrupulous people are not bound to repeat confessions although they feel they have omitted sins. A confessor who gets to know those who are scrupulous will be able to counsel them accordingly. Above all he will be very sympathetic to their condition whilst at the same time being firm when the occasion requires it. He will try not to aggravate their scruples and in some cases may have to refer them for medical advice or treatment.

4) The extraordinary embarrassment extrinsic to confession on account of the special relationship between the penitent and the confessor, e.g. if a sister of the confessor had to confess some shameful sin to him and he was the only confessor available at the time.

It is understood that only those sins or circumstances may be omitted which cannot be mentioned without the harm resulting which we have in mind.

If the penitent avails himself of one of the excusing causes mentioned above to justify his making a materially incomplete confession, the following guideline should be kept in mind. Whatever the excusing cause may be, a penitent is excused from making a complete confession only in so far as the excusing cause is verified and only for as long as it lasts. The obligation to confess the grave sin(s) justly omitted remains and must be fulfilled in the first confession after the cause has ceased to exist. As is implied, the excusing cause may be temporary or permanent. The sins in question have been remitted indirectly but they must be submitted directly to the power of the keys.

Normally the confession of one's sins will be sincere, verbal, secret and complete or integral.

Generic confession of sins

So far we have been speaking about the specific confession of sins where the penitent gives the number, species and the circumstances changing the species as already explained.

The phrase to confess one's sins 'only generically' is taken to mean a confession of sins which is expressed in general terms either by words or signs, e.g., "I have sinned" or by striking one's breast to indicate that one has sinned. There is no indication as to whether the person has sinned gravely or venially, how many times or against which virtue or commandment. When there is no time to do more than this, generic confession suffices. There is sufficient here for the essence of the sacrament or for making a judgment, even if an imperfect one, and giving absolution. The penitent shows that he is a sinner or that he has sinned and is sorry for what he has done. In the case of emergency the generic confession suffices.

This type of confession is mentioned in connection with general absolution. General absolution is regulated by the Code of Canon Law where it is stated that absolution for a number of penitents at the same time without previous individual confession cannot be given unless:

1° There is imminent danger of death and there is not sufficient time for the priest or priests to hear the confessions of the penitents individually.

2° A grave need is present, namely, when taking into account the number of penitents, the number of confessors available is not sufficient to duly hear the confession of each within a reasonable time, so that the penitents through no fault of theirs are compelled to go without sacramental grace or Holy Communion for a long time; the need is not considered to be sufficient when confessors cannot be at hand solely because of the great number of penitents as happens at the time of a great feast or pilgrimage.

It belongs to the Diocesan Bishop to decide whether the conditions mentioned above are present. He can decide on cases where he considers there is such a need after examining the criteria in consultation with the other members of the Episcopal Conference (cf. c.961 nn.1 and 2).

So that a member of the faithful may validly take advantage of the sacramental absolution given to others at the same time, it is required not only that he be properly disposed but also at the same time that he intends in due time to confess the grave sins one by one which he cannot then confess (cf. c.962 n.1).

It is argued that the sinner cannot be sincere, and therefore his sorrow is not up to standard, if he does not intend to use the means of pardon in the way laid down by Christ when this becomes possible, i.e. individual confession.

Therefore he whose grave sins have been remitted in a general absolution must go to confession when the first opportunity presents itself before he receives another general absolution, unless some good reason intervenes (cf. c.963).

The reason for this prescription of Canon Law lies in the fact that Christ willed that all grave sins should be submitted to the power of the keys, as we have already seen. The invalidity of a generic confession where the intention of going to confession individually later were lacking would arise from the defective dispositions of the penitent in so far as he is not willing to comply with the command of Christ.

On the occasion of receiving general absolution, in so far as is possible, the faithful should be instructed about being properly disposed for the sacrament and the need to make an individual confession later if they have grave sins to confess, even when there is danger of death, if time permits. They should be exhorted to see that each one makes an act of contrition before receiving the general absolution even in the case of danger of death if there is time.

The precept of confession

The divine law obliges all the faithful who are guilty of grave sin to receive the sacrament of Penance in danger of death.[17]

The law of the Church obliges all the faithful after they have reached the age of discretion to faithfully confess grave sins they have committed at least one a year (cf. c.989). Commentators tell us that the year can be reckoned from January 1 to December 31, from Easter to Easter, or from the day on which a person has committed grave sin.[18]

The official attitude of the Church concerning the hearing of confessions *during* Mass can be said to be one of discouragement. "The faithful are to be constantly encouraged to accustom themselves to going to confession outside the celebration of Mass, and especially at the prescribed times. In this way the sacrament of Penance will be administered calmly and with genuine profit, and will not interfere with participation in the Mass".[19]

Frequent confession of venial sins

According to the strict letter of the law Christians who have not committed grave sin are not bound by any law to go to confession. The new Code of Canon Law recommends the faithful to confess also their venial sins (cf. c.988 n.2).

The Sacred Congregation for the Doctrine of the Faith reminds priests that they "should be careful not to discourage the faithful from frequent or devotional confession". "It must be absolutely prevented", the document states, "that individual confession should be reserved for serious sins only, for this would deprive the faithful of the great benefit of confession and would injure the good name of those who approach the sacrament singly".[20]

Pope John Paul II points out that "the sacrament of confession is the irreplaceable means of conversion and spiritual progress. It leads to the restoration of the Covenant broken by sin".[21] Although the Pope has grave sins in mind, what he says applies equally to the confession of venial sins which do not break the Covenant in question.

The new Rite of Penance says that "a frequent and diligent use of this sacrament is also very useful for overcoming venial sins. It is not merely a ritualistic repetition, nor a psychological exercise but an assiduous effort towards the fulfilment of the grace of Baptism. 'We carry with us in our body the death of Jesus, so that the life of Jesus, too, may always be seen in our body' (cf. 2 Cor 4:10). In this type of confession, the penitent, while accusing himself of venial sins, should aim especially to be conformed to Christ, and to be obedient to the voice of the Spirit" (n.7b).

Bernard Häring, C.SS.R., tells us that "the pretext that the present practice of confession of devotion in the Church is contrary to the ideals of the early Church as shown by studies in early ecclesiastical history is utterly absurd. The early Church did far more than we are doing to maintain a lofty penitential ideal and a living spirit of penance among the faithful. It should also be borne in mind that there is a development of the rich treasure of the faith, not merely on the level of doctrine, but also in practice and discipline. One of the most significant domains of such development is precisely in the use of the sacraments".

"Not the confession of devotion as such, but the superficial and routine manner in the reception of the sacrament of Penance is a bar to the tremendous earnestness that should characterise our approach to the sacrament of conversion. Only too readily the practice of confession degenerates into mere habit or routine, because of the constant confession of venial sins without true sorrow. Such confession of venial sins to which one is still attached is not only mechanical and superficial, but even perilous to the spiritual life".[22]

The Instruction on the Worship of the Eucharistic Mystery points out that "those who receive Communion daily or very frequently, should be counselled to go to confession at times suitable to the individual case".[23]

Confession of devotion, as confession of venial sins is called, gives the Christian an opportunity to re-affirm the basic direction of his will and serves as a check in the matter of venial sin. Sacramental confession is a providential means for overcoming sin. This includes also venial sin. Man's conversion can always be perfected. The re-affirmation of one's will to love God does this and in the sacrament joins the sinner to the passion of Christ.

The benefits of frequent confession of venial sins are outlined by Pope Pius XII in the Encyclical Letter 'Mystici Corporis'. "For a constant and speedy advancement in the path of virtue", says the Pope, "we highly recommend the pious practice of frequent confession, introduced by the Church under the guidance of the Holy Spirit; for by this means we grow in true knowledge of ourselves and in Christian humility, bad habits are uprooted, spiritual negligence and apathy are prevented, the conscience is purified and the will strengthened, salutary spiritual direction obtained, and grace is increased by the efficacy of the sacrament itself. Therefore those among the young clergy who are diminishing esteem for frequent confession are to know that the enterprise upon which they have embarked is alien to the spirit of Christ and most detrimental to the Mystical Body of our Saviour".[24]

With regard to the frequency of this type of confession Bernard Häring, C.SS.R., states that "it is more beneficial to go twice a month and make a really serious confession with a thorough preparation, with a good purpose of amendment, than to go every week or every day with less earnestness".[25]

"A good practical guideline is to go once a month".[26]

General confession

The term 'general confession' is taken to mean the confession of all the sins of one's past life which have already been remitted in the sacrament of Penance. It must not be used as a substitute for the specific confession of sins which we have been discussing above. It is useful when there is some doubt about past confessions or when the penitent is about to enter a new state of life such as entering the religious life, embracing priesthood or getting married. It is not to be recommended to those who suffer from scruples. In general it is to be used sparingly.

Satisfaction

The revised Rite of Penance speaks of satisfaction as follows: "True conversion is made complete by satisfaction for the faults committed, amendment of life and reparation of any damage caused by sin. The measure of satisfaction required of the penitent must be proportionate to his sin. That order which has been harmed must be restored and the sickness responsible for the sin must be healed by means of a suitable remedy. The punishment of sin must be seen as a remedy, and a certain renewal must take place in the life of the penitent. Thus the penitent forgets the past (Phil 3 : 15) and strains ahead for what is still to come, as he finds himself taken up once more into the mystery of salvation" (n.6c).

Confession is at present the principal part of sacramental expiation. As efficacious contrition it obtains the remission of sins. But sacramental expiation does not necessarily or generally destroy all the consequences of sin. Conversion is not yet fully effective and liberation from sin is not yet fully realised. The Church teaches that all temporal punishment, i.e. the consequence of sin, is not necessarily remitted when the sinner is reconciled with God and the Church".[27]

Certainly sincere confession with effective conversion unites the sinner to God and there is no *eternal* punishment to expiate. But conversion must be fully realised in the expansion of charity. The consequence of sin brought about by works of penance, by the acceptance of sufferings, by making use of all the opportunities to develop the love of God and one's neighbour in this life. Any act which heals, weakens or puts right the consequences of sin which remain after the remission of guilt, remits what is called temporal punishment. It is in this general context of salutary satisfaction for sin that we must place the satisfaction imposed by the Church in the form of penance. The sacramental satisfaction imposed by the Church and freely accepted by the repentant sinner is aimed at the complete destruction of sin — the remission of guilt and healing the consequences of sin.

The sacramental penance

According to the quality and number of sins, and taking into account the condition of the penitent, the confessor should impose a salutary and suitable penance, which the penitent binds himself to fulfil (cf. c.981).

In a certain sense the present practice is an indulgent one. Instead of imposing a special expiation, a more or less lengthy type of penance, aimed at the complete destruction of sins, the Church, through the priest, prescribes some prayer or exercise of devotion. It is a token penance and implies the desire to live a life of penance. By this act faith and charity are made to come alive. This makes fruitful the penitential meaning and value of our daily life in Christ. The measure of the remission of temporal punishment by the Church through the sacramental satisfaction will be according to the degree of faith and charity in the penitent; and according to the sincerity of his detestation of sin. Present-day practice is intended to stress the relationship between the sacrament of Penance and the exercise of penance in our daily life. The penance imposed by the priest is meant to assume and consecrate our daily exercise of penance in a sign of faith and conversion.

The obligation on the priest to impose a penance is a grave one when serious sins have been confessed. This obligation ceases to exist if the penitent is unable to perform even a very light penance, e.g. when the penitent is unconscious or dying.

The minimum required for the valid reception of the sacrament is that the penitent must be willing to accept and carry out the penance imposed. In theory the penitent is entitled to dispute the penance, so it should be given before the absolution. The validity of the sacrament depends on the acceptance of the penance by the penitent. If he does not carry it out that is another matter. If the confessor forgets to give a penance, the penitent should ask for one. The principle is a grave penance for a grave sin; a heavier penance for a particularly heinous crime, and a light penance for a light sin. The penance should also be adapted to the physical and moral strength of the penitent. It should not be too long, too complicated or too difficult for him in his present circumstances. A penance, for example, which is spread over a long period could easily be forgotten or it might cause undue anxiety to the penitent. For the same reason it should not consist of many different works. Nor should it be such as to make confession odious. Assisting at Mass or saying five decades of the Rosary are classic examples of grave penances. These practices are imposed by the Church as of grave obligation in certain circumstances, e.g. assisting at Mass on days of precept or when the Church commutes the Divine Office by replacing the obligation to say it with five decades of the Rosary daily. The obligation to say the Divine Office for priests and others is a grave one. Custom considers the practice of making the Stations of the Cross to be an example of a grave penance. In particular cases prudence will suggest greater leniency.

St Antonine, who has been called the father of moral theology, says that the priest should give a penance which he thinks the penitent will perform. If a man who has committed grave sin declares that he is not able to undertake a severe penance, the confessor should impose a penance which he can persuade him to perform.

In view of the emphasis now being placed on the social and community aspects of sin penitents could well be asked as a penance to visit someone who is sick or lonely, or to perform some act of fraternal charity for his neighbour.

Reasons for lessening the sacramental penance

1) Bodily weakness: This justifies the giving of a light penance, e.g. when the penitent is sick. He should be advised to offer up the pains of his illness in union with the sufferings of Christ and in reparation for his sins. If he is too ill to do very much the confessor can recite some short prayer with him.

2) Spiritual weakness: This also justifies the giving of a light penance because in the penitent's present condition a heavier penance might turn him away from the sacraments.

3) The great sorrow shown by the penitent in some cases will justify a lighter penance that one might be tempted to give.

4) The indulgences attached to certain practices can also be taken into account in imposing a penance.

5) Vicarious satisfaction: After the example of St John Vianney the confessor may take it upon himself to make satisfaction for the penitent. This idea is based on the doctrine of the communion of saints.

If grave sin has been confessed there is a grave obligation to perform the penance imposed. If before receiving absolution, the penitent finds that the penance he has been given will be too difficult for him, he may ask for a lighter one. If the confessor refuses, the penitent is free to go out without receiving absolution and go to another confessor.

People are so used to being given some prayer to say as a penance that the confessor who wishes to impose something else should first of all get the consent of the penitent. Much will depend on the penitent's standard of education and his cultural background.

Almsgiving is recommended explicitly in the Scriptures as a means of repairing offence committed against God and our neighbour. But in addition to giving the needy some of one's money, one can also give him something of oneself, which he may need as much, if not more, namely, one's friendship.

Absolution

The new Rite of Penance reminds us that "when the sinner manifests his repentance to the Church's minister in sacramental confession, God's forgiveness is granted him by the sign of absolution, and thus the sacrament of Penance is completed. According to the plan by which 'the kindness and love of God our Saviour for mankind were revealed' God wishes to bring us salvation by means of visible signs, and renew the Covenant that we have broken. Through the sacrament of Penance, the Father welcomes the son who returns to him. Christ places the lost sheep on his shoulders and takes it back to the flock. The Holy Spirit sanctifies his temple anew, so that he may inhabit it more fully. All this is made evident by a renewed and more fervent participation in the Eucharist, and the Church rejoices in the return of each prodigal son" (n.6d).

Also in the revised Rite of Penance a new formula has been added to the essential words of absolution. This makes it more meaningful and relevant for both priest and penitent than the formula it replaces: "God, the Father of mercies, through the death and resurrection of his Son has reconciled the world to himself and sent the Holy Spirit among us for the forgiveness of sins; through the ministry of the Church may God give you pardon and peace, and I absolve you from your sins in the name of the Father, and of the Son, and of the Holy Spirit". The penitent answers "Amen" (n.46).

The traditional teaching of the Church, as well as its practice, is that the words of absolution must be spoken and for validity should be said over the penitent, i.e. while he is present. The penitent should be able to hear the words of absolution being said over him. Absolution by letter, telephone or telegraph is not permitted.

If the confessor has no doubt about the dispositions of the penitent who is asking for absolution, absolution may not be refused or deferred (cf. c.980).

If, on the other hand, the confessor finds that the dispositions of the penitent are not up to standard for a valid and fruitful reception of the sacrament, he should try to help him to attain the necessary dispositions by instruction and exhortation. A penitent who would be unwilling to give up a free occasion of sin would not be disposed to receive absolution. Even if the words of absolution were pronounced over him, they would have no effect.

The confessor will hardly ever be able to say with absolute certainty that the penitent is disposed because it is a question of interior dispositions; but there are certain external signs which indicate that the penitent is properly disposed such as a spontaneous confession, the penitent's own admission that he is sorry for his sins, the frank and humble way in which he makes his confession, the care he has taken to avoid the dangerous occasions of sin, his own request for help and advice and his sincere promise to make use of the remedies suggested for overcoming his sins.

If, after all the confessor's efforts to get the penitent properly disposed, his dispositions remain doubtful, absolution ought to be deferred unless circumstances would render this course inadvisable, dangerous or seriously harmful to the penitent. In such a case absolution should be given conditionally acting on the principle that, when one is in doubt, it is lawful to administer a sacrament conditionally as often as it would be exposed to nullity if given absolutely, or if the refusal of the sacrament would expose the person to spiritual harm.

Lack of preparation for the sacrament on the part of the penitent, neglect of the remedies suggested by the confessor to prevent future lapses, frequent relapses with no attempt to improve and a lack of humility in making one's confession could indicate that the dispositions of the penitent are doubtful.

Refusal on the part of the penitent to comply with a grave obligation, e.g. to make restitution of a grave amount which he has stolen, if and when he can, or neglecting to take the ordinary means to correct a serious fault, would show that his dispositions were not up to standard.

The examination of conscience

We have already quoted canon 988 which speaks of a careful examination of conscience to enable the penitent to discover his sins.

The examination of conscience is meant to be a personal, conscious and accurate preparation for the sacrament. One should ask the guidance of the Holy Spirit and put one's trust in God as a merciful Father. In examining their consciences penitents should give that amount of time and care which they would give to any matter of importance in life. The time needed will depend on the length of time the penitent has been away from confession and the type of life he/she has been leading. Extraordinary care is not necessary. The scrupulous are recommended not to spend too much time in examining their consciences.

In Appendix III to the revised Rite of Penance — an unofficial part of the document — alternative schemes are set out for the examination of conscience. Different schemes will appeal to different people. Some find it easier to review their life with the ten Commandments in view. Others prefer to take their duties towards God, the Church, their neighbour and themselves. Others base their examination of conscience on the theological and moral virtues. It might be advisable to change one's method from time to time. This will remove the danger of formalism and the mechanical accusation of one's sins. Formalism shows itself when people confess their sins as they did when they were children.

If properly made, the examination of conscience should help the penitent to purify his life and to make progress in the Christian life. Excessive preoccupation about the sins one has committed is almost as harmful as culpable negligence in hurrying over one's examination of conscience. When an adult Christian has reached maturity not only in age but also in his faith he should confess his sins in a manner which is in keeping with his spiritual growth. His confession will not longer be like that of a child but it will take account of his failure in his responsibilities as a Christian, in his professional duties, the duties of his state of life, in his relations with others, in the place he gives to his spiritual duties and the other interests in his life. If the examination of conscience is serving the purpose it should, it will help to educate the penitent's conscience according to his age and condition along the right lines and he should see a steady growth in his spiritual life. As persons, we don't change to the extent that we always have different sins to confess — there will always be a constant in our lives in this respect. But we should be able to notice a gradual improvement. A humble confession of sins which is the result of a thorough preparation is one of the best ways of continuing and gradually completing the conversion which began at Baptism and must continue until the end of our lives. The habitual state of detachment from serious sin should encourage the penitent to strive with the help of grace to get ever more close to what our Lord wants him to become.

It is not the confessor's business to examine the penitent's conscience for him. But there are occasions when he will need to help the penitent especially if he has been away from confession for a very long time. If a penitent comes unprepared the confessor will try and find out why he has not been able to make a suitable preparation. It may be necessary for the greater good of the penitent to ask him to go away and examine his conscience and then come to make his confession. Respect for the sacrament demands this. On the other hand, the confessor will not require the same standard from the sick which he would from a person in good health.

Occasions of sin

The teaching of moralists on the occasions of sin has the advantage of providing penitents with certain guidelines which they can apply to the concrete situations in which they find themselves.

An occasion of sin is some external circumstance which acts as an enticement or an allurement to sin with the consequent likelihood or danger of sinning. The likelihood or danger would not be present, or would be greatly diminished, if the external circumstance were avoided. The occasion of sin may be some person, place or thing, e.g. a public house, or a film. It is important to note that the occasion must be some *external* circumstance, something external to the person as distinct from the internal propensity to sin because of some inherent weakness. On the other hand, a circumstance which is deliberately chosen for the purpose of committing sin or as a means of committing it is not an occasion of sin in the generally accepted meaning of the term. The man who seeks out a particular person, place or thing, has already decided to commit sin and the person, place or thing has simply been chosen as a means to that end.

Remote occasions of sin

These occasions of sin are those in which there is a slight danger of sinning. They can be overcome by an ordinary effort. In a sense everyone is in a remote occasion of sin throughout his life. The only way in which one can escape these occasions of sin is by death. In life as we know it today there is always a remote danger that one will be knocked down and killed or injured if one ventures out of the house in a busy street. The only way to escape such a danger is not to go out. Life would be intolerable if we had to keep avoid-ing remote occasions of sin.

Proximate occasions of sin

These are the main concern of the penitent and the confessor.

St Alphonsus and others take a proximate occasion of sin to mean one in which men for the most part sin, or one in which a man knows by experience that he has frequently fallen into sin. If he finds himself in such an occasion it is at least probable that he will sin. A greater effort is required to escape a proximate occasion than is required to escape a remote occasion of sin.

These occasions of sin can be absolute or relative. An occasion is said to be *absolute* when it constitutes a grave danger of sinning for people in general according to their standard of education, their sex, whether they are mature or immature, teenagers or adults, married or single, etc.[28]

An occasion is said to be *relative* when a particular individual knows by experience that if he finds himself in such an occasion he will very likely commit sin, e.g. drink to excess, lose his temper, etc.

Necessary occasions of sin

An occasion is said to be necessary when it is either physically or morally impossible to avoid it.

Physical impossibility arises when the occasion cannot be avoided in any way, e.g. being locked up in a prison cell with some-one who is an occasion of sin.

Moral impossibility arises when the occasion can be avoided but only with great difficulty, i.e. danger to one's life, health, repu-tation or some serious material loss. A husband and wife, for ex-ample, are obliged to live together for their own sakes and for the sake of their children, yet their being together may be the occasion of serious quarrelling or loss of temper at times. If they were to leave each other, they would be neglecting their duty and would also risk losing their good name. They are in a morally necessary occasion of sin.

Unnecessary occasions of sin

An occasion of sin can be unnecessary when there is no need to

H

go into it or to stay in it. It can easily be avoided with relatively little difficulty. These occasions are also called free occasions of sin.

If the penitent or confessor does not want to be left to the whim of the moment in forming a judgment about a particular situation, it is necessary to decide what sort of occasion of sin is involved.

A penitent who comes back to confession time and time again with the same sin because he is in a necessary occasion of sin will not be refused absolution provided he has a proportionate reason for remaining in the occasion of sin and that he is doing his best not to commit sin. It may take time before the desired effect or end is attained. One must try and examine every angle of the problem in an attempt to devise ways and means of overcoming it. It must be remembered that one is dealing with frail human nature and that this will sometimes call for great patience from all concerned.

A penitent who refuses to avoid a proximate unnecessary occasion of sin is not disposed to receive absolution and the confessor has no alternative but to refuse it. The intention to remain in an unnecessary occasion of grave sin is itself a grave sin. One has a grave obligation to keep away from such occasions. Emotional signs of sorrow in this case are not enough. We have already seen that genuine sorrow is at a deeper level than the emotional one. The confessor will accept a promise from the penitent that he will avoid such occasions a few times but if the penitent keeps coming back with the same sin and the confessor judges that he is really not trying he cannot give him absolution.

In dealing with particular cases prudence will suggest the best way to proceed. In some cases the only thing for the penitent to do will be to give up the occasion at once. In other cases it may be necessary for the confessor to make the penitent realise the gravity of the situation and get him to promise not to frequent the occasion of sin for a definite period of time, say, until his next confession. Psychologically this may have better results in the long run.[29]

Quite apart from occasions of sin a penitent may commit the same sin repeatedly because of his particular make-up, his tendency to sin and the fact that he has contracted a habit with regard to some particular sin. This is especially true of sins against the virtue of chastity. In this case he will be falling through human weakness. Such people fight against the temptation for a time and through weakness of will and the heat of passion they fall again. They usually detest the sin and are sorry immediately they have fallen. The tendency to sin is not a sin in itself and this can exist with good dispositions. Such people can be helped by being given fresh motivation. The confessor will congratulate them on the efforts they make to improve and it is hoped that through the grace of the sacrament they will eventually get the strength to overcome their weakness.

It is relevant here to quote from the Declaration of the Sacred Congregation for the Doctrine of the Faith 'On Certain Questions Concerning Sexual Ethics': "It is true that in sins of the sexual order, in view of their kind and their cause, it more easily happens that free consent is not fully given; this is a fact which calls for caution in all judgment as to the subject's responsibility. In this matter it is particularly opportune to recall the following words of Scripture: 'Man looks at appearances but God looks at the heart' (cf. 1 Sam 16:7). However, although prudence is recommended in judging the subjective seriousness of a particular sinful act, it in no way follows that one can hold the view that in the sexual field grave sins are not committed".

"Pastors of souls must therefore exercise patience and goodness; but they are not allowed to render God's commandments null, nor to reduce unreasonably people's responsibility. 'To diminish in no way the saving teaching of Christ constitutes an eminent form of charity for souls'. But this must ever be accompanied by patience and goodness, such as the Lord himself gave example of in dealing with people. Having come not to condemn but to save, he was indeed intransigent with evil, but merciful towards individuals".[30]

The real recidivist is the one who is still attached to his sin and because of this he falls frequently through his own fault. He gives the impression of making no effort to give up the sin(s). In practice it is sometimes difficult for the confessor to form a judgment about such people. Their dispositions are often doubtful, if not nonexistent. One must avoid being too lax or too strict in one's judgment. The guidelines we have already given about giving and refusing absolution will apply in cases of this kind.

The role of the confessor

The revised Rite of Penance speaks of the confessor's role in the following terms: "In order to fulfil his task properly, a confessor must learn to recognise the diseases of the soul and to be able to apply appropriate remedies. He must acquire the requisite knowledge and prudence to be able to act as a wise judge, by means of diligent study under the guidance of the Church's teaching authority, and especially through prayer. The discernment of spirits consists of a deep knowledge of the works of God in the human heart, and is a gift of the Holy Spirit and one of the fruits of charity" (n.10a).

"The priest is acting as a father when he welcomes a penitent sinner and leads him to the light of truth. He reveals the heart of God the Father to men and acts in the image and likeness of Christ the good shepherd" (n.10c). "He will give him (the penitent) any counsel that may be useful for beginning a new life, and if necessary, instruct him in the duties of the Christian life" (n.18).

The new Code of Canon Law is even more specific about the role of the confessor. It states that the priest should remember that in hearing confessions he plays the part of a judge and a physician and that he has been made by God a minister of divine justice and mercy at the same time so that he may have at heart the honour due to God and the salvation of souls (cf. c.978 n.1).

With these texts in view moralists discuss the confessor as a spiritual father, a physician of souls, a teacher and a judge.

A spiritual father

It is as a spiritual father especially that the confessor can show himself to be the minister of God's justice and mercy. This role calls for patience, understanding and approachability. Bearing in mind the love of Christ for sinners, the confessor should have a genuine and generous love for them. He should have the heart of a father who is forgetful of himself and is ready to spend himself for the good of sinners. Of him one should be able to say what was said of Christ: "This man receives sinners". The confessor will treat all with the utmost patience and bearing in mind that he is a minister of God's justice he will make no distinction between the various classes of penitent. Even if he has to deal with great sinners he will try to make confession as easy as possible for them. He should remember the words of St Philip Neri: "There go I but for the grace of God". He will put himself in the place of the penitent in so far as it will help him to show great kindness and understanding. He will respect the dignity of the penitent and will in no way be arrogant with him. He will have a great delicacy of approach. If the penitent is hesitant the confessor will be prepared to wait and if necessary he will put some helpful questions which will put the penitent at his ease. He will give the penitent time to explain the circumstances, if necessary. He won't hurry the penitent thus running the risk of making him forget his sins and depriving him of the devotion he should experience in the reception of the sacrament. Nor will he interrupt the penitent unless this becomes absolutely necessary, e.g. when he feels he will forget an important question he ought to put, if he waits until the penitent has finished. The penitent has a right to make a fruitful confession. Penitents must be treated with mercy. The sacrament of Penance was instituted for sinners who without sacramental absolution cannot obtain forgiveness of their sins. "I have come not to call the just but sinners" (cf. Mt 9:13). This is especially the sacrament of mercy.

Physician of souls

The work of the confessor as a physician of souls is to heal and not to kill! He must be prudent and skilled at his task. First of all he must know the spiritual state of the penitent so that he may be able to apply appropriate and effective remedies. The business of the confessor will be to suggest means which will help the penitent to avoid sin and practise virtue. This is why he has to study the causes of sin and the teaching on dangerous occasions of sin. This is necessary if he is to direct the penitent effectively. In theory the penitent may have a certain knowledge but he has to be shown to apply it in practice. The confessor will put strong natural and supernatural motives before his penitents to help them to practise virtue. It is good to recall such motives in time of temptation, e.g. God's love for us, his many blessings including that of health, the faith, good parents and friends, etc.

General remedies for avoiding sin are prayer and the sacraments, humility, the practice of the presence of God, trust in the mercy of God, avoidance of bad company and dangerous occasions of sin, reflection on the four last things — death, judgment, hell and heaven — regular examination of conscience, a solid devotion to our Lord in the Blessed Sacrament and to Our Lady, frequent renewal of one's purpose of amendment and the imposition of a voluntary penance on oneself if one happens to fall into sin.

In addition to these remedies the confessor will counsel each penitent according to his particular needs taking account of his special circumstances.

Teacher

In enlightening and guiding the penitent it is the duty of the confessor to instruct him about the things he ought to know for the Christian life. This calls for a certain competence on the part of the confessor. If he is lacking in this there is no question of the Church supplying it. As a preparation for his confessional work the confessor has been able to acquire sufficient knowledge of moral and pastoral theology to enable him to deal with the ordinary cases that are brought to him. He is not expected to carry around in his head all that is contained in the manuals of theology but he should know the general principles which he will have to apply to particular cases such as: the laws governing the responsibility for human acts; what sin is; the circumstances which can alter the gravity of sins; the teaching concerning occasions of sin; the principles concerning the duty of restitution; those governing scandal, etc. He is presumed to have a correct and up-to-date knowledge. Hazy notions would not be sufficient for a proper administration of the sacrament. He must be able to recognise a difficult case when he meets it and should have no hesitation in asking the penitent to come back after he has had time to study the matter. His task is not merely the negative one of showing people how to avoid sin and the occasions of sin. He has the positive role of helping his penitents to practise virtue and to grow in the Christian life by imitating and following Christ.

Judge

The confessor acts with a view to absolving the penitent who is properly disposed. As minister of the sacrament he must see that it is rightly administered. Sometimes the penitent does not give the confessor the information he requires to make a proper judgment. He must know the essential points of each case. If he prudently judges that something is lacking to make the confession an integral one, he has a duty to ask questions. On this point the new Code of Canon Law reminds the confessor that in putting questions he must proceed with prudence and discretion taking into consideration the condition and age of the penitent. He must not ask the name of an accomplice (cf. c.979).

His questions should be short, discreet and to the point. In the context of making restitution he may need to know the circumstances of the penitent — whether he is in a position to make restitution here and now. The penitent is bound to answer truthfully any questions put by the confessor which concern a circumstance which is necessary or useful for the confessor to know so that he may form a judgment correctly about the state of the penitent.

Such questions may also be necessary for the confessor to fulfil his role as physician of souls when it is question of applying appropriate remedies in a particular case. The confessor will accept what the penitent says in answer to the questions put to him. From his questioning the confessor may also conclude that the penitent needs instruction on matters about which he/she is ignorant and should be informed. A penitent may, for example, through a rigorous upbringing accuse herself of 'company keeping' so many times. This may refer to a perfectly innocent courtship. If so, the penitent has an erroneous conscience about the matter and needs instruction. In another case, of course, it could be used to cover a multitude of sins! The confessor can only find out by asking the necessary questions in accordance with what has been said above. On the other hand, the confessor is forbidden to instruct penitents about the facts of life in the confessional. He will refer penitents who need such instruction either to their parents or to some competent person who will be qualified to give the necessary instruction in a Christian setting.

The place of confession

The proper place for hearing confessions is a church or oratory.

It is for the Episcopal Conference to issue directives about the confessional itself. Provision must be made for the traditional confessionals with a grill between the priest and the penitent to be set up in an accessible place and the faithful should be free to use these if they so wish.

Confessions should not be heard outside the confessional except for a just cause (cf. c.964 nn. 1, 2 and 3).

On February 17, 1976, a directive was issued to the clergy of the Diocese of Westminster which reads: "Traditional confessional boxes should be available in all churches. Another room or chapel can be set aside where the penitent need not necessarily use the grill, which however should be available if required".

First confession

When we were dealing with first Holy Communion we saw that the new Code of Canon Law assumes that a child will make his/her confession before first Holy Communion (cf. c.914). If anything the law is more explicit than that of the 1917 Code.

In a letter to the clergy dated May 20, 1968, Cardinal Heenan said: "Nobody thinks that children of seven are capable of mortal sin but everyone knows that they know right from wrong. The chief advantage of early confession is to form good habits before a child is old enough to sin seriously. To invite boys and girls to confess only when grave sins trouble their conscience could prove embarrassing and be spiritually and psychologically dangerous".

Pope Paul VI in a message to the twenty-sixth Liturgical Week in Florence which opened on August 25, 1975, laid particular stress on the confession of children, and especially the first confession which must always precede first Communion, even if separated from it by a suitable interval. "It is from childhood", the message continues, "that this evangelization of penance must start: it will subsequently make more valid and conscious the support of a living faith in the celebration of the sacrament and, above all, in a reliable and consistent approach to the Christian life".[31]

Allowing for differences from diocese to diocese and from country to country, the following report on the procedure for introducing children to their first confession prepared at the request of the Bishops' Conference of England and Wales by a small commission of parents, priests and teachers provides useful guidelines on the subject of first confession.

"The supernatural life received at Baptism gives young children a fundamental openness of heart to God which is perceptible when they reach the stage of self-awareness. Intimate relationship with God can be appreciated quite startlingly by children of seven years of age. They can often grasp more readily than grown-ups the truth that we love God when we wish to please him more than we wish to please ourselves. They are capable of moral and religious discernment, of distinguishing what is good and what is evil though they lack an adult understanding of moral guilt. Their misdemeanours viewed objectively may be no more than imperfections, but to their unsophisticated minds these imperfections are sufficient matter for absolution. The sacrament of Penance is not for them a necessary means for salvation, but it does remit subjective guilt and enables them to experience the loving care and mercy of God in a unique way".

It is the current practice of the Church to allow young children to confess as soon as there is sufficient matter and true contrition, i.e. as soon as they have committed a subjective sin and are sorry. Children have a right to the sacrament which God has instituted as a sensible sign of reconciliation. At an early age they need guidance to help them to recognise their faults, and this can best be given by the priest who is father and counsellor in the confessional.

At the meeting of the Bishops' Conference of England and Wales in October 1968, it was agreed that the general policy should be for first confession to come before first Communion except in cases where parents think that their child is not ready to profit by the formal sign of forgiveness in the sacrament of Penance.

It was further agreed that:

1. *There should be a distinct lapse of time — at least two or three months — between first confession and first Communion.* Education for confession should precede and lead up to education for Communion. This would give children time to assimilate the characteristics of each sacrament and help them to comprehend two completely new experiences. The interval of time would be welcomed by priests, parents and teachers whose responsibility it is to prepare young people for these sacraments.

2. *The rite and procedure of confession should be simplified.* The first public act in life which is such an important step in the 'growing up' process should be made as informal as possible. Priests should hear first confessions in the sacristy or another room rather than in the confessional. They can do so much to set the child at ease, encourage him to signify his sorrow in a very simple way, and enable him more readily to discover God's mercy at work. Inevitably this will take more time. If confessors are to show interest and give encouragement to each child, they should not be expected to hear large numbers of children's confessions at one session. This informal approach to the sacrament of Penance will not only result in putting the emphasis where it should always lie, namely, on the openness to God, it will also avoid the danger of giving the child the impression that the formula and mechanics of the rite are the things that really matter.

3. *Education for confession should be a continuous process.* The aim of education for all the sacraments is that the child should be instructed according to his intelligence. Bearing this in mind, education for confession should not be a once for all affair. It should be a continuous process by both teacher and confessor to ensure that the child's understanding of the sacrament is deepening in a way consistent with his advancing intellectual powers. Happily it is much easier to give children instruction after they have made their first confession, and the best education for confession is given in confession itself, if possible by a regular confessor.

4. *Preparation for the sacraments should begin at home.* Parents undoubtedly are the persons who can best help in the long-

term preparation for confession. It is in the home that children form ideas of sin, sorrow and forgiveness. When they offend parents, brothers and sisters they are made aware that they have offended: when they make some gesture of regret, they are pardoned and restored to friendship. In each case they associate the offence, the sorrow and the pardon with someone they love, someone in whose good graces they are eager to stand. It is on this basis of personal relationship with God that they can be trained to understand sin, contrition and God's forgiveness of sin in confession.

If parents appreciate that on the natural plane sorrow and the wish to 'make up' are contingent upon the previous growth of the love-dependency relationship, they will come closer to the ideal for teaching for confession. Children must be helped to see their faults not so much as wrong-doing but as wrong-doing against God, a saying 'no' to God, a turning away from God. They must be taught that if they turn back to the Heavenly Father with confidence, sorrow and love, they are sure of being forgiven.

5. *Parent-teachers associations*. The majority of our teachers and an increasing number of parents are beginning to realise the importance of close co-operation between school, parish and home if religious education is to be effective. In the Decree on Christian Education, art. 6, the Vatican Council recommends team-work between home and school in the specific form of parent-teacher associations. The by-product of this co-operation is an understanding which greatly helps towards the formation of a balanced dynamic Christian.

When parents are instructed on the knowledge required, the preparation needed and the spirit of prayer which should animate the child before the reception of the sacraments, their own approach to the sacraments will be become more realistic.

The community aspect of penance

This aspect of penance and of the sacrament of Penance is referred to by Pope John Paul II in his Encyclical Letter 'Redemptor Hominis' and what he has to say will form a fitting conclusion to this chapter.

"In the last years much has been done to highlight in the Church's practice — in conformity with the most ancient tradition of the Church — the community aspect of penance and especially of the sacrament of Penance. We cannot however forget that conversion is a particularly profound inward act in which the individual cannot be replaced by others and cannot make the community be a substitute for him. Although the participation by the fraternal community of the faithful in the penitential celebration is a great help for the act of personal conversion, nevertheless, in the final analysis there should be a pronouncement by the individual himself with the whole depth of his conscience and with the whole of his sense of guilt and of trust in God, placing himself like the Psalmist before God to confess: 'Against thee, thee alone, have I sinned' (cf. Ps 50(51):4). As is evident, this is also a right on Christ's part with regard to every human being redeemed by him: his right to meet each one of us in that key moment in the soul's life constituted by the moment of conversion and forgiveness . . . The sacrament of Penance is the means to satisfy man with the righteousness that comes from the Redeemer himself".[32]

In another place Pope John Paul II says: "In this sacrament (Penance) each person can experience mercy in a unique way, that is the love that is more powerful than death".[33]

Penitential services

These emphasise the community aspect of penance and are a preparation for the celebration of the sacrament of Penance. Pope John Paul II mentions them as one of the means "which are pastorally effective for evoking in people's hearts sentiments of sorrow for faults committed".[34]

In addition they help to develop in the Christian community a deep spirit of repentance and a sense of responsibility for the sins committed by the members of the community. These penitential services can inspire the members of the Christian community to undertake some special social and charitable work which will counteract the social aspects of sin and will keep alive in the community the spirit of penance which should be part and parcel of the daily life of the Christian.

Personal conversion to God and the renewal of society

Finally Pope John Paul II shows how personal conversion has its repercussions in society itself, when he states that "at the root of the moral evils that divide and wound society is sin. Thus the whole human life is seen to be a struggle, often a dramatic one, between good and evil. Only if the roots of evil are taken away can true reconciliation be attained. And so personal conversion to God is at the same time the best path to a lasting renewal of society: for in every act of true reconciliation with God through repentance there is intrinsically present the social dimension side by side with the personal one".[35]

References

1. Pope John Paul II, Encyclical Letter 'Redemptor Hominis', 4.3.79, n.20, L'Osservatore Romano (English Edition), 19.3.79, pp.11–12.
2. Pope Paul VI, General Audience, 1.3.72, L'Osservatore Romano (English Edition), 9.3.72, p.1.
3. Pope John Paul II, Encyclical Letter 'Dives in Misericordia', 30.11.80, n.13, L'Osservatore Romano (English Edition), 9.12.80, p.16.
4. J. D. Chrichton, *The Ministry of Reconciliation* (Geoffrey Chapman, London, 1974), p.72.
5. Pope Paul VI, General Audience, 26.2.75, L'Osservatore Romano (English Edition), 6.3.75, p.1.
6. P. Galtier, *Sin and Penance* (Sands, London), p.175.
7. ibid., pp.172–3.
8. J. D. Crichton, op. cit., p.59.
9. Clergy Review, Vol. IV (1932), p.470.
10. J. D. Crichton, op. cit., p.60; Publisher's note: for a deeper study of 'Fundamental Option' see Bernard Häring, *Free and Faithful in Christ*, vol. I (St Paul Publications, Slough, 1978), pp.164–222.
11. Sacred Congregation for the Doctrine of the Faith, Declaration on Certain Questions Concerning Sexual Ethics (Vatican Press, 1975), n.10, pp. 13–15.
12. Pope Paul VI, General Audience, 8.3.72, L'Osservatore Romano (English Edition), 16.3.72, p.1.
13. Pope Paul VI, General Audience, 2.8.72, L'Osservatore Romano (English Edition), 10.8.72, p.8.
14. Pope Pius XII, Encyclical Letter 'Mystici Corporis Christi', C.T.S., n.18.
15. ibid., n.22.
16. Alfred Wilson, C.P., *Pardon and Peace* (Sheed and Ward, 1961), p.151.
17. H. A. Ayrinhac, *Legislation on the Sacraments* (Longmans, Green, London, 1928), p.263.
18. H. A. Ayrinhac, op. cit., p.267.
19. Instruction on the Worship of the Eucharistic Mystery, A. Flannery, op. cit., p.123.
20. Sacred Congregation for the Doctrine of the Faith, Pastoral Norms for the Administration of General Absolution, 16.6.1972, n.XII.
21. Pope John Paul II, Letter to the Bishops of the World on the occasion of the presentation of the working paper 'Instrumentum Laboris' in preparation for the 1983 Synod, 25.1.83, n.2, L'Osservatore Romano (English Edition), 21.2.83, p.5.
22. B. Häring, C.SS.R., *The Law of Christ*, Vol. I (The Mercier Press, Cork, 1965), pp.465–6; Publisher's note: cf. also B. Häring, *Free and Faithful in Christ*, vol. I (St Paul Publications, Slough, 1978), pp.426–460.
23. Instruction on the Worship of the Eucharist, A. Flannery, op. cit., p.123.
24. Pope Pius XII, Encyclical Letter 'Mystici Corporis Christi', C.T.S., n.87.
25. B. Häring, C.SS.R., *Shalom Peace* (Image Books, 1969), p.319.
26. B. Häring, C.SS.R., *Christian Renewal in a changing World* (Mercier Press, Cork), p.448; Publisher's note: cf. also B. Häring, *Free and Faith-*

ful in Christ, vol. I (St Paul Publications, Slough, 1978), pp.426–460.
27. Karl Rahner, *The Teaching of the Catholic Church* (Mercier Press, Cork), n.583, p.322.
28. John C. Ford, S. J., and Gerald Kelly, S.J., *Contemporary Moral Theology* (Mercier Press, Cork), vol. I, ch.9.
29. Gerald Kelly, S.J., *The Good Confessor* (Sentinel Press, New York), p.84.
30. Sacred Congregation for the Doctrine of the Faith, Declaration on Certain Questions Concerning Sexual Ethics (Vatican Press, 1975), n.10, p.15. Cf. also: Paul VII, Encyclical Letter 'Humanae Vitae', 29, *AAS* 660 (1968), p.501.
31. L'Osservatore Romano (English Edition), 18.9.75, p.10.
32. Pope John Paul II, Encyclical Letter 'Redemptor Hominis', 4.3.79, n.20, L'Osservatore Romano (English Edition), 19.3.79, p.12.
33. Pope John Paul II, Encyclical Letter 'Dives in Misericordia', 30.11.80, n.13, L'Osservatore Romano (English Edition), 9.12.80, p.15.
34. Pope John Paul II, Letter to the Bishops of the World on the occasion of the presentation of the working paper 'Instrumentum Laboris', in preparation for the 1983 Synod, 25.1.83, n.5, L'Osservatore Romano (English Edition), 21.2.83, p.5.
35. ibid., n.2.

6

THE ANOINTING OF THE SICK

The Anointing of the sick by which the Church commends the faithful who are dangerously ill to the suffering and glorified Lord, that he may bring them relief and save them, is conferred through the anointing with oil accompanied by the words prescribed in the liturgical books. Only a priest can validly administer this sacrament (cf. c.998 : 1003).

It will be noticed that the law of the Church speaks of those who are 'dangerously ill' and not those who are 'seriously ill'. For members of the medical profession there *is* a difference between the two. With serious illness no danger is thought to be present but with dangerous illness the patient is in some danger. The whole tenor of the recent documents of the Church has in mind a situation where there is some danger of death even though a certain latitude is allowed in the matter, as we shall see.

In the Apostolic Constitution accompanying the new Rite of Anointing dated November 30, 1972, Pope Paul VI states that "the Council of Trent declared its divine institution and explained what is taught in the Letter of James concerning the holy anointing, especially with regard to the reality and effects of the sacrament".[1]

The Council of Trent was first of all concerned to affirm the doctrine that the Anointing of the sick is a true sacrament in answer to those who denied this teaching. The Fathers of Trent also stated that the term 'elders of the Church', which is found in the Letter of James, chapter 5, verse 14, referred to consecrated ministers, so that no one who is not a priest could confer this sacrament.

Referring to the work of the Council of Trent at the Press Conference on the new Rite for the Anointing of the sick in Rome on January 18, 1973, Monsignor Aimé Georges Martimort had this to say: "The change of attitude (brought about by the new rite) is the continuation of the guidelines already traced out by the Council of Trent. It would in fact be seriously wrong to consider the Council of Trent as too remote in time or its decrees lapsed. Far from opposing Trent, the Second Vatican Council takes up that Council's work of reform and doctrinal deepening, in order to carry it further. That is why the Apostolic Constitution *Sacram Unctionem* bases itself, from its opening sentences, on the teaching of the sixteenth session of Trent, of which a part is reproduced. It is known from the history of the debate that this text indicated a desire on the part of the Fathers to move away from the view of mediaeval theology and a refusal to see in Extreme Unction the sacrament only for those who are dying. Profiting from the great light that patristic and liturgical studies had thrown upon the tradition of this sacrament, the Second Vatican Council was able to take a further step. Without disavowing the mediaeval term 'Extreme Unction', it indicated its preference for the term 'Anointing of the sick".[2]

The subject of the sacrament

The law of the Church states that the Anointing of the sick can be given to any member of the faithful who having attained the use of reason, begins to be in danger because of illness or old age (cf. c.1004 n.1).

It is to be noted that there is no mention here of a minimum age. The mere fact that a child has not yet reached the age of seven years is not proof that he does not enjoy the use of reason. In any case, it is not necessary for children to have attained the full use of reason.

Secondly, the sacrament can be repeated if the sick person recovers and becomes gravely ill again or if during the same illness the danger becomes more grave (cf. c.1004 n.2).

The sacrament may be administered if there is a doubt as to whether the sick person has attained the use of reason, is dangerously ill or is actually dead (cf. c.1005).

In accordance with the guidelines given in chapter I, the sacrament would be administered conditionally. At the same time, Directive n.15 in the introduction to the new Rite for the Anointing of the sick states that "when a priest has been called to a person who is already dead, he should pray for the dead person asking that God forgive his sins and graciously receive him into his kingdom. But the priest is not to administer the sacrament of Anointing".

Nor is the Anointing of the sick to be administered to those who obstinately persevere unrepentant in a clear state of grave sin (cf. c.1007).

This sacrament may be administered to those who are unconscious if they would have asked for it at least implicitly when they were in control of their faculties (cf. c.1006).

Danger of death

At the Press Conference already referred to, Monsignor Martimort commenting on the preference of the Second Vatican Council for the term 'Anointing of the sick' had this to say: "On two occasions, namely in the Constitution *Sacrosanctum Concilium* (the Constitution on the Sacred Liturgy), n.73, and in the Dogmatic Constitution *Lumen Gentium* (on the Church), n.1,1, it is suggested that this was more than just a question of words: 'As soon as any one of the faithful begins to be *in danger of death* from sickness or old age [italics mine], the appropriate time for him to receive this sacrament has certainly already arrived' ".[3]

Studying the text of the introduction to the new rite and the references contained in the footnotes it is hard to escape the conclusion that there must be some danger of death for the use of this sacrament. Admittedly the danger need not be imminent as is clear from the reference to the Constitution on the Sacred Liturgy. It is equally clear that it is sufficient to make a prudent and probable judgment that there is a danger. On this point the reader is referred to a letter dated February 2, 1923, authorised by Pope Pius XI and signed by Cardinal Gasparri, Secretary of State, where the judgment referred to is precisely about the danger of death (de periculo).[4] All the guidelines given on the subject imply that the sick person is in some danger. Referring to the communal celebration of the sacrament at his Press Conference, Monsignor Martimort speaks of people who are in *serious danger of death* [italics mine] through illness or old age. The view holding that no danger of death of any kind is required and that 'dangerous illness' is equated with 'serious illness' is not supported by the text. In fact the term 'serious illness' is not used.

The grace and effects of this sacrament

The introduction to the new rite tells us that "this sacrament provides the sick person with the grace of the Holy Spirit by which the whole man is brought to health, trust in God is encouraged, and strength is given to resist the temptations of the Evil One and anxiety about death".[5]

The words of the blessing of the oil of the sick indicate that the grace given is the work of the Holy Spirit and reflect the purpose and effect of the blessing. The bishop prays: "O God, Father of all consolation, who through your Son willed to heal the weakness of the sick, in your mercy hear our prayer of faith: Send, we beg you, your Holy Spirit the Paraclete from heaven into this rich substance of oil which you have deigned to produce from the green wood to restore the body, so that by your holy blessing all who are anointed with this oil may experience the benefit of it in body, mind and soul and be freed from all pain, infirmity and sickness".

At the Press Conference already referred to, Monsignor Martimort stated that "this sacrament is in effect meant to give to the sick person the graces proper to his condition — those which the Apostle James describes in the fifth chapter of his Epistle, quoted universally by the Magisterium and the liturgies: 'The prayer of faith will save the sick man and the Lord will raise him up again; and if he has committed any sins, he will be forgiven' ".

These effects are now given greater prominence by the significant change in the formula to be used when conferring the sacrament. The priest now says: "Through this holy anointing and his most loving mercy may the Lord assist you by the grace of the Holy Spirit, so that when you have been freed from your sins he may save you and in his goodness raise you up". The old formula which this new one replaces, emphasised rather the penitential effect of the sacrament. It does have a penitential effect even to the point of replacing the sacrament of Penance if it is impossible for the sick person to receive this sacrament. In this case it will even remit grave sins. But apart from this situation it is not meant to be a substitute for the sacrament of Penance. It is a sacrament of the living and the sick person should be in a state of grace before receiving it. The sacrament of Penance brings about a certain purification but the work of purification does not end with this sacrament. The anointing on the forehead and on the hands signifies the renewed purification and consecration of the thoughts and actions of the sick person and his openness to God.

The normal function of the Anointing is to remit venial sins and the remnants of sin, i.e. frailty and lack of vigour in pursuing the good; the inclination to evil; weakness of will and spiritual sloth as a result of past sins. Much depends on the life the sick person has led but a sinful life leaves its mark even after the sins have been forgiven.

The new rite reminds us that "the man who is dangerously ill needs the special help of God's grace in this time of anxiety, lest he be broken in spirit and subject to temptations and the weakening of faith. Christ, therefore, strengthens the faithful who are afflicted by illness with the sacrament of Anointing providing them with the strongest means of support".[6]

Combats spiritual inertia

For most people a dangerous illness is spiritually weakening. It does not help them to turn their minds to God and to spiritual things. The sickness causes them to be preoccupied with their own bodily distress. The sick person needs both patience and courage. His sickness can be exhausting to the point of making it more difficult for him to give a Christian witness in faith, hope and charity. This sacrament combats the spiritual inertia brought about by sickness. It brings with it the grace of salvation, comfort and consolation. It gives the spiritual strength and relief which are necessary if the sick person is to live a fully Christian life in the midst of his difficulties. It has a re-invigorating effect and effects a renewal of one's Christian vitality. Through it "the sick person is able not only to bear his suffering bravely, but also to fight against it".[7]

A sacrament of faith

"The anointing of the sick, which includes the prayer of faith (cf. Jas 5 : 15) is a sacrament of faith. This faith is important for the minister and particularly for the one who receives it. The sick man will be saved by his faith and the faith of the Church which looks back to the death and resurrection of Christ, the source of the sacrament's power (cf. Jas 5 : 15), and looks ahead to the future kingdom which is pledged in the sacraments".[8] The sacrament, then, should be received with the fullness of faith. This also enables the sick person to make an act of love of God by which he accepts his will with all its implications.

Raises morale

A Christian who has a proper appreciation of this sacrament will experience what theologians tell us when they say that the Anointing re-establishes order and tranquillity in the faculties and that by the removal of the remnants of sin the sick person also experiences a restoration of spiritual freedom. Furthermore, the Council of Trent states that the grace of this sacrament raises the morale of the sick person by arousing his confidence in the boundless mercy of God. All this establishes favourable conditions for a recovery to bodily health if this would be profitable to the sick person's salvation. If this happens, it would be a case of grace aiding nature. This is not surprising in view of the modern understanding of the psychosomatic nature of many diseases.

For the whole of one's illness

In view of all that has been said it is easy to see why the sacrament should be given at the beginning of a dangerous illness. The law of the Church urges pastors of souls and those who are close to the sick to see that the sick are given the support of this sacrament at the appropriate time (cf. c.1001). The sick person should be given the opportunity of the benefits of the sacrament throughout the whole of his illness. If it is left until the sick person is at the point of death, it is expecting too much perhaps for the sick person to be restored to bodily health, although God's goodness is operative right up till the end.

The sick person may be called upon to endure the illness and may not recover. The sacraments are primarily intended to help the Christian to live well but this does not mean that they are not intended to help the Christian to die well. We have already mentioned one effect of the sacrament which is to strengthen the sick person who is anxious about death.

The healing power of Christ at work

Clifford Howell says: "Sometimes a sick man's spiritual difficulties can be met without so much bodily alleviation as to lead to his recovery, and his sickness ends in death. But the sacrament will have enabled him to turn his mind to God, to renew his faith, hope and love, to be sorry for his sins without any despair, to be resigned to God's will and to accept death willingly as Christ did upon the cross. So in this case, as in others when recovery results, the healing power of Christ has been at work, leading him gently towards the full healing power which can only come at the resurrection".[9] In this context the Anointing can be also looked upon as a preparation for glory in so far as the sacrament has an eschatological significance — the hope and certitude that the entire person, body and soul, will share in the resurrection of Jesus Christ.

The specific sacrament for the dying is Viaticum but it can happen that the priest is called to someone who is unconscious and his ministrations will consist in a conditional absolution and the sacrament of the Anointing of the sick.

The need for instruction

All that we have seen so far bears out what Monsignor Martimort said on February 18, 1973, namely, that "the theological, spiritual and pastoral importance of the decisions taken deserves to be underlined, because they necessarily involve in many instances a change of attitude on the part of priests and laity and consequently an intense work of instruction".[10] At the same Conference it was also stated that "these various innovations demonstrate the necessity of urging priests to make a pastoral effort and the faithful to acquire a deeper spiritual awareness".

The introduction to the new rite touches this aspect when it states: "In public and private instruction the faithful should be taught to ask for the Anointing, and as soon as the opportune time for the Anointing comes, to receive it with complete faith and devotion, not to follow the bad custom of putting off receiving it. All who care for the sick should be taught the meaning and purpose of the Anointing".[11] In a later section of the rite the point is made that "the faithful should clearly understand the meaning of the Anointing of the sick and Viaticum so that these sacraments may nourish, strengthen, and express faith more fully. It is important for the faithful in general, and above all for the sick, to be prepared for the celebration of this sacrament and their actual part in it by suitable instructions which explain the rite, especially if it is to be carried out in a large gathering of the faithful. The prayer of faith which accompanies the celebration of the sacrament is supported by the profession of this faith".[12]

The communal celebration of this sacrament provides a suitable opportunity for instructing the faithful about the meaning and importance of the Anointing of the sick. There may also be other occasions when the liturgy lends itself to a discussion of this kind. It is important that this sacrament should be explained to the people when they are well. They will be more receptive to this when they are in good health than when they are ill. If the faithful are properly instructed they will see that the sacrament of the Anointing of the sick is administered to their sick relatives and friends as soon as they begin to be in any danger in accordance with the law of the Church which has already been quoted and with what is written in the introduction to the new rite: "If the sickness grows worse, the family and friends of the sick and those who take care of them have a duty to inform the parish priest and tactfully and prudently to dispose the sick person to receive the sacraments at the appropriate time".[13] The ideal, of course, will be for the sick themselves to ask for this sacrament as soon as they perceive or are informed that the appropriate time has come for them to receive it.

The Christian attitude towards sickness

Sickness and sin. Whilst sickness is closely connected with man's sinful condition, the new rite reminds us that it cannot be considered a punishment which has been inflicted on man for his personal sins. On seeing the man who was born blind, the disciples asked Christ: "Rabbi, who sinned, this man or his parents, that he was born blind". Jesus answered: "It was not this man that sinned, or his parents, but that the works of God might be made manifest in him" (cf. Jn 9:1–3). It is also stated that: "Christ himself who is without sin bore the sufferings of his passion and shared in all the sorrows of men (cf. Is 53:4–5); indeed in his members, who are made like to him, he is tormented and suffers still when we suffer hard things; 'For this slight momentary affliction is preparing us for an eternal weight of glory beyond all comparison' (cf. 2 Cor 4:17)".[14]

The meaning of human suffering in the mystery of salvation

"Sickness and pain have always been considered among the greatest problems which trouble the consciences of man. Although Christians feel and experience the same things as other men, they are helped by the light of faith, to understand more deeply the mystery of suffering and to bear their sufferings with greater courage. For not only do they know from the words of Christ what is the meaning of sickness and what value it has for their own salvation and that of the world but also they are not unaware of the fact that the sick are dear to the heart of Christ himself, who during his life on earth often visited the sick and healed them".[15]

The difference between the Christian and the non-believer in the face of sickness and suffering is that the former by believing in the message of salvation has hope and an assurance of eternal life and together with faith and hope he also has love.[16]

The teaching given above is drawn from that of the Second Vatican Council which when speaking of the Anointing of the sick tells us that "by the sacred Anointing of the sick and the prayer of the priests the whole Church commends those who are ill to the suffering and glorified Lord that he may raise them up and save them (cf. Jas 5 : 14–16). And indeed she exhorts them to contribute to the good of the people of God by freely uniting themselves to the passion and death of Christ. 'When we cry: Abba! Father! it is the Spirit himself bearing witness with our spirit that we are children of God, and if children then heirs, heirs of God and fellow heirs with Christ, provided we suffer with him, in order that we may also be glorified with him' (Rom 8 : 17). 'The saying is sure: If we have died with him (in baptism) we shall also live with him (in glory); if we endure (the difficulties and sufferings of life), we shall also reign with him' (2 Tim 2 : 11–12). 'But rejoice in so far as you share Christ's sufferings, that you may also rejoice and be glad when his glory is revealed' (1 Pet 4 : 13)".[17]

We are also told that "in a special way, those who are weighed down by poverty, infirmity, sickness and other hardships should realise that they are united to Christ, who suffers for the salvation of the world".[18]

The Council teaching shows us the contribution that Christians who are sick can make for the spiritual good of the People of God. Their contribution consists in offering to God their sufferings (and death) in union with the sacrifice of Christ. This implies the communication of spiritual benefits between the members of the Church in a very special way.

The Christian who has been vitally incorporated into the Mystical Body of Christ is given a special mission, the serious responsibility to conform himself, his interior life, his many external activities to the mysteries of Christ, his head. He is called in a special way to conform himself to the redemptive passion and death of Christ. This fundamental and inescapable duty has been strongly emphasised in the texts from St Paul and St Peter given above.

The sharing of the sorrowful mysteries of the head of the Mystical Body, not only assures him that he will attain eternal life but redounds to the spiritual advantage of the whole People of God. By joining his sufferings (and death) to the sufferings and death of Christ he makes of his state of sickness and eventually of his death a pleasing sacrifice to God for the benefit of the whole Church.

The death of a Christian in some way resembles the death of

Christ. Just as the Father did not remain indifferent to the death of his Son, so he cannot remain indifferent to the death of the Christian. When the Church uses the words of the Apocalypse: "Blessed are the dead who die in the Lord", she expresses a very deep reality.

Whilst saying all this the new rite also reminds us that "it is part of the plan of divine providence that man should struggle against sickness of any kind and diligently seek the blessing of health, so that he may be able to fulfil his role in human society and in the Church, provided that he is always ready to complete in his flesh what is lacking to Christ's afflictions (Col 1:14) waiting to enjoy freedom and glory as the children of God (Rom 8:19–21)".

"Moreover in the Church it is the duty of the sick by the witness they give to remind others not to lose sight of the essential and higher things and to show that the mortal life of man must be redeemed through the mystery of Christ's death and resurrection".[19]

Sickness the concern of the whole Christian community

"In the body of Christ, which is the Church, if one member suffers, all the members suffer with him (1 Cor 12:26). For this reason compassion towards the sick and works of charity and mutual help for the relief of every human need, should be held in special honour. Every effort of science to prolong life and every heartfelt attention given to the sick by any man can be considered as a preparation for the Gospel and in some way a sharing in the healing ministry of Christ".

"Thus it is especially fitting that all the baptised share in this ministry of mutual charity within the body of Christ both in the struggle against disease, by love shown towards the sick and in the celebration of the sacraments for the sick. Like the other sacraments, these have a community aspect which should be portrayed as much as possible when they are celebrated".[20]

"Not only the sick person should fight against sickness, but also doctors and all who are in any way associated with the sick should consider it their duty to do whatever they think will bring relief to the sick spiritually and physically. In doing this they fulfil the command of Christ to visit the sick, as if Christ were to say that the whole man had been committed to those visiting him so that they might bring him help for his body and refresh him with spiritual comfort".[21]

Visiting the sick

"The family and friends of the sick and those who for any reason take care of them have a special part to play in this ministry of comfort. In the first place it is their task to strengthen the sick with words of faith and by praying with them, to commend them to the suffering and glorified Lord, and especially to exhort them to associate themselves freely with the passion and death of Christ for the good of the People of God".[22]

"Priests, particularly parish priests and their assistants, priests who care for the sick or aged in hospitals, and superiors of clerical religious institutes, should remember that it is their duty to visit the sick regularly and to help them in a spirit of genuine charity. But especially in administering the sacraments should they stir up the hope of those present and foster their faith in Christ who suffered and was glorified, in such a way that by expressing the love of mother Church and the consolation of the faith, they comfort the believers and raise the minds of others to higher things".[23]

The new rite gives a selection of Scripture readings and prayers which can be said when visiting the sick. Lay people are encouraged to visit the sick. This is an expression of true Christian love and compassion. The length of the visits will depend very much on the condition of the sick person. It is often a misplaced compassion that causes people to stay too long, thus tiring the sick and defeating the very object of their visit. But visiting the sick in itself can make the sick person feel that someone cares and that they are a very real part of the Christian community. This apostolate should not be left to the older members of the community. Teenagers should be encouraged to take an interest in the sick especially those of their own age. Even when it is a question of those who have passed their teens and the elderly, a visit from a young person can do a great deal to raise the morale of the sick. Visiting the sick is one of the works of mercy by which we shall be judged at the end of our lives. "I was sick and you visited me" (Mt 25 : 36).

References

1. *Ordo Unctionis Infirmorum*, p.8.
2. L'Osservatore Romano (English Edition), 1.2.73, p.7.
3. ibid.
4. *Acta Apostolicae Sedis*, Vol. XV (1923), p.105.
5. *Ordo Unctionis Infirmorum*, n.6, p.14.
6. ibid., n.5, p.14.
7. ibid.

8. ibid., n.7, pp.14–15.
9. Clifford Howell, S.J., *The Work Of Our Redemption* (Geoffrey Chapman, London, 1969), p.87.
10. L'Osservatore Romano (English Edition), 1.2.73, p.7.
11. *Ordo Unctionis Infirmorum*, n.13, p.15.
12. ibid., n.36, p.20.
13. ibid., n.34, p.20.
14. ibid., n.2, p.13.
15. ibid., n.1, p.13.
16. Dogmatic Constitution on Divine Revelation, n.1, Walter M. Abbott, op. cit., p.111.
17. Dogmatic Constitution on the Church, n.11, Walter M. Abbott, op. cit., p.28.
18. ibid., p.70.
19. *Ordo Unctionis Infirmorum*, n.3, p.13.
20. ibid., nn.32 & 33, pp.19–20.
21. ibid., n.4, pp.13–14.
22. ibid., n.34, p.20.
23. ibid., n.35, p.20.

7

HOLY ORDERS

*The priesthood of the laity
and the ministerial priesthood*

The dignity and equality which all the faithful share by reason of their baptism (cf. c.208) does not entitle them to perform any task whatsoever in the Church.

Pope John Paul II points out that "although all the Christian faithful share in the kingly, prophetic and priestly function of the head, nevertheless the clergy and laity receive distinct functions according to their social activity, functions regulated and safeguarded by the will of Christ by 'sacred law' (ius sacrum), in such a way that the common good of the whole Church may be provided for".

"Not only is the People of God made up of different peoples but even in its inner structure it is composed of various ranks".

"This 'variety of members' is certainly of *divine law* and in effect the distinction which the Lord made between sacred ministers and the rest of the People of God implies a twofold and public way of living in the Church".

"From this also follows the other 'diversity': that of 'functions' or social functions, since the whole body, mutually supported and upheld by joints and sinews, achieves a growth from this source which comes from God' (Col 2:19): not all the members have the same function' (Rom 12:4)".[1]

"Though the common priesthood of the faithful and the ministerial or hierarchical priesthood differ 'essentially and not only in degree' they are ordered to one another, each in its own proper way shares in the one priesthood of Christ. The ministerial priest, by the sacred power he has, forms and rules the priestly people. In the person of Christ he effects the Eucharistic sacrifice and offers it to God in the name of all the people. The faithful indeed by virtue of their royal priesthood participate in the offering of the Eucharist. They exercise their priesthood too by the reception of the sacraments, prayer and thanksgiving, the witness of a holy life, abnegation and active charity".

"The fact that they differ not only in degree but in essence is a fruit of a particular aspect of the richness of the very priesthood of Christ which is the one centre and the one source both of that participation which belongs to all the baptised and of that other participation which is reached through a distinct sacrament. By virtue of its very nature and everything it produces in the life and activity of the priest this sacrament serves to make the faithful aware of their common priesthood and to activate it (Eph 4:11–12). The sacrament reminds them that they are the People of God and enables them to offer spiritual sacrifices through which Christ himself makes us an everlasting gift to the Father".[2]

The sacramental priesthood

The Code of Canon Law tells us that through the sacrament of Holy Orders, which is of divine institution, some of the faithful by the indelible character with which they are signed are constituted sacred ministers. They are consecrated and deputed, each according to his particular rank in the person of Christ the head, to nourish the people of God by fulfilling the duties of teaching, sanctifying and ruling them (cf. c.1008).

The three Orders involved are the episcopate, the priesthood and the diaconate (cf. c.1009 n.1).

Bishops enjoy the fullness of the sacrament of Holy Orders. Priests and deacons are dependent upon the bishops in the exercise of authority.[3]

The sacramental priesthood is called 'hierarchical' because it is connected with forming and governing the priestly people. It is also called 'ministerial' because it constitutes a special 'ministerium', that is, a service in relation to the community of believers. The priest is called to serve others. He carries out this office through which Christ himself unceasingly 'serves' the Father in the work of man's salvation.

A special grace and specific vocation

Pope John Paul II speaks of the sacrament of Holy Orders as "the fruit of the special grace of vocation and the basis of the priest's identity". Because the sacramental priesthood differs in essence and not only in degree "the words of the Author of the Letter to the Hebrews about the priest who has been 'chosen from among men . . . appointed to act on behalf of men' (Heb 5 : 1) take on their full meaning".

"Although the priesthood constitutes a special service to the community of believers, it does not take its origin from that community as though it were the community that 'called' or 'delegated'. The sacred priesthood is truly a gift for this community and comes from Christ himself from the fullness of his priesthood. This fullness finds its expression in the fact that Christ while making everyone capable of offering the spiritual sacrifice, calls some and enables them to be ministers of his own sacramental sacrifice — the Eucharist — in the offering of which all the faithful share, in which are taken up all the spiritual sacrifices of the People of God".[4]

The supreme exercise of the 'kingly priesthood'

In the Apostolic Letter on the Eucharist 'Dominicae Coenae' Pope John Paul II reminds us that "the priest fulfils his principal mission and is manifested in all his fullness when he celebrates the Eucharist. This is the supreme exercise of the 'kingly priesthood', the source and summit of all the Christian life".

"The priest offers the Holy Sacrifice in *persona Christi*: this means more than offering 'in the name of' or 'in the place of' Christ. *In persona* means in specific sacramental identification with 'the eternal, High Priest', who is the author and principal subject of this sacrifice of his, a sacrifice in which, in truth, nobody can take his place. Only he — only Christ — was able and is always able to be the true and effective 'expiation for our sins and . . . for the sins of the whole world'. Only his sacrifice — and no one else's — was able and is able to have a 'propitiatory power' before God, the Trinity and the transcendent holiness".

The priestly character

"Awareness of this reality", the Pope continues, "throws a certain light on the character and significance of the priest celebrant who, *by confecting the Holy Sacrifice and acting 'in persona Christi'*, is sacramentally (and ineffably) brought into that most profound *sacredness*, and made part of it, spiritually linking with it in turn all those participating in the Eucharistic assembly".

"Although all those who participate in the Eucharist do not confect the sacrifice as he does, they offer with him, by virtue of the common priesthood their own *spiritual sacrifices* represented by the bread and wine from the moment of their presentation at the altar. For this liturgical action . . . has a 'spiritual value and meaning'. The bread and wine become in a sense a symbol of all that the Eucharistic assembly brings, on its own part, as an offering to God and offers spiritually".[5]

In another place Pope John Paul II speaks of the priestly character as 'a special sign from God' "which gives the priest a share in the pastoral charism, which is a sign of a special relationship of likeness to Christ the Good Shepherd. Priests are expected to have a care and commitment for the salvation of others which are far greater than those of any lay person because his sharing in the priesthood of Christ differs from theirs essentially and not only in degree".

"The priesthood of Jesus Christ is the source and expression of an increasing and ever effective care for man's salvation which enables the priest to look to him precisely as the Good Shepherd".

The Good Shepherd is one who lays down his life for his sheep (cf. Jn 10: 11). These words refer to the Sacrifice of the Cross, the definitive act of Christ's priesthood. They tell the priest that his vocation is a singular solicitude for the salvation of his neighbour which is the special raison d'être of his priestly life, and gives it meaning. It is only through this solicitude that the priest can find the full significance of his own life, perfection and holiness.

Finally, Pope John Paul II tells us that the indelible character, the mark impressed in the depths of the being of the priest has its 'personalistic' dynamism. "The priestly personality must be for others", the Pope says, "a clear and plain sign and indication". This is the first condition for his pastoral service. The people from among whom he has been chosen and for whom he has been appointed, want above all to see in him such a sign and indication, and to this they have a right.[6]

Bishops

In the Code of Canon Law we read that bishops, who by divine institution are the successors of the apostles through the Holy Spirit which has been given them, are constituted pastors in the Church so that they may be teachers of doctrine, priests for divine worship and ministers for governing the Church.

In virtue of their episcopal consecration they also receive the mission to sanctify in addition to the duties mentioned above. But of their very nature they can only exercise these functions in hierarchical communion with the head and members of the College of Bishops (cf. c.375 nn. 1 and 2).

To be appointed a bishop, a priest must have been ordained at least five years and be 35 years old.

Pope John Paul II enlarges on what is stated in Canon Law when he says that:

1) the Holy Spirit has chosen and called bishops to preside over the Church with apostolic solicitude.

2) Bishops are called, after the apostles, to take upon themselves care for a) the Church; b) the flock; c) the vocation of the whole People of God; d) the proclamation of God's Word; e) the whole sacramental and moral order of Christian living; f) priestly and religious vocations; g) the functional spirit of the community.

He is also called to serve the cause of evangelization.[7]

Finally in his letter to the Bishops of Nicaragua, Pope John Paul II tells them that "the bishop is like Jesus Christ made present in the midst of his Church as the living and dynamic principle of unity. Without him this unity does not exist or is falsified and therefore is inconsistent and ephemeral".[8]

Priests

In addition to what has been said already it will be useful to list the following points made by Pope John Paul II when he speaks specifically about priests.

1) Priests have been consecrated by their ordination to represent Christ the Priest, for this reason their hands like their words and their will, have become the direct instruments of Christ.[9]

2) Priests have a specific vocation to give themselves to the service of the Church.

3) And in the Church to the service of man for the salvation of the most important problems and especially those regarding man's salvation.

4) They are the closest collaborators in the pastoral office of bishops.

5) The priest's vocation unites him to his bishop in a special communion of sacrament and ministry through which the Church, the Mystical Body of Christ, is built up.

6) He must be ready to humbly accept the gifts of the Holy Spirit.

7) He is to transmit to others the certainty of faith. From this derives a deep understanding of the meaning of human existence and the capacity to introduce the moral order into the life of individuals and of society.

8) He is to transmit to others the fruits of love and peace.

The priesthood is given so that the priest can serve others after the example of the Lord.

1) Celibacy is a "gift of the Holy Spirit".

2) Celibacy for the sake of the kingdom is an eschatological sign.

3) It also has a great social meaning in the present life, in the service of the People of God.

Through his celibacy, the priest becomes 'a man for others'.

By renouncing the fatherhood proper to married men, he seeks another fatherhood. The people entrusted to his solicitude by the Good Shepherd are the children of his spirit.

The pastoral vocation of priests is great, it is directed towards the whole Church, and therefore it is of a missionary character.

Normally it is linked to the service of a particular community of the People of God, in which each individual expects attention, care and love. In order that the heart of the priest may be available for this service, it must be free.

Celibacy is a sign of a freedom that exists for the sake of a service.[10]

According to the new Code of Canon Law, the age for ordination to the priesthood is 25 years. The candidate must be sufficiently mature (c.1031 n.1).

Deacons

1) The Second Vatican Council teaches that deacons "are ordained for service and minister to the People of God in communion with the bishop and his priests".[11]

2) For this service "they are strengthened by sacramental grace".

3) They are the servants of the mysteries of Christ and the Church.[12]

4) They serve the People of God in the ministry of the liturgy, of the Word and of charity.

It is the duty of the deacon to the extent that he has been authorised by competent authority to:

a) administer Baptism solemnly;

b) be custodian and dispenser of the Eucharist;

c) assist at and bless marriages in the name of the Church;
d) bring Viaticum to the dying;
e) read the Sacred Scripture to the faithful;
f) instruct and exhort the people;
g) preside at the worship and prayer of the faithful;
h) administer sacramentals;
i) officiate at funerals and burial services;[13]

j) the pastoral care of the family can be entrusted by the bishop to deacons as well as to priests.[14]

The permanent diaconate

Now that this has been restored in the Church, the new Code of Canon Law (cf. c.1031 n.2) gives the following guidelines:

a) The age for the ordination of a permanent deacon who is single is 25 years;
b) he binds himself by the obligation of celibacy;
c) the age for the ordination of a permanent deacon who is married is 35 years;
d) he must also obtain the consent of his wife.

References

1. Pope John Paul II, Address at the official presentation of the new Code of Canon Law, 3.2.83, L'Osservatore Romano (English Edition), 14.2.83, p. 6.
2. Pope John Paul II, Letter to all the priests on the occasion of Holy Thursday 1979, 8.4.79, L'Osservatore Romano (English Edition), 17.4.79, pp. 6–7.
3. Decree on the Bishops' Pastoral Office in the Church, n.15, Walter M. Abbott, op. cit., p.406.
4. Pope John Paul II, Letter to all the priests on the occasion of Holy Thursday 1979, 8.4.79, L'Osservatore Romano (English Edition), 17.4.79, p.7.
5. Pope John Paul II, Letter to all the Bishops of the Church on the Mystery and Worship of the Eucharist, 'Dominicae Coenae', 24.2.80, L'Osservatore Romano (English Edition), 24.3.80, pp.7–8.
6. Pope John Paul II, Letter to all the priests on the occasion of Holy Thursday 1979, 8.4.79, L'Osservatore Romano (English Edition), 17.4.79, p.7.
7. Pope John Paul II, Letter to all the Bishops of the Church on the occasion of Holy Thursday 1979, 8.4.79, L'Osservatore Romano (English Edition), 17.4.79, p.9.
8. Pope John Paul II, Letter to the Bishops of Nicaragua, 29.6.82, L'Osservatore Romano (English Edition), 6.9.82, p.6.
9. Pope John Paul II, Letter to all the Bishops of the Church on the Mystery and Worship of the Eucharist, 'Dominicae Coenae', 24.2.80, L'Osservatore Romano (English Edition), 24.3.80, p.9.

10. Pope John Paul II, Letter to all the priests on the occasion of Holy
    Thursday 1979, 8.4.79, L'Osservatore Romano (English Edition), 17.4.79,
    p.8.
11. Decree on the Bishops' Pastoral Office in the Church, n.15, Walter M.
    Abbott, op. cit., p.406.
12. Dogmatic Constitution on the Church, n.48, Walter M. Abbott, op. cit.,
    p.69.
13. ibid., n.29, p.55.
14. Pope John Paul II, Apostolic Exhortation 'Familiaris Consortio',
    22.11.81, L'Osservatore Romano (English Edition), 21-28.12.81, p.15.

8

MATRIMONY

Marriage — part of God's plan for man

Although marriage is looked upon today by many as a purely secular contract, which can be made and unmade by the State, it is in fact something sacred and religious because it has been instituted by God (cf. Genesis 2 : 22-24) and from the dawn of creation has been part of God's plan for man. On this point Cardinal Gasparri says that even the marriages of unbaptised people are sacred and religious because apart from their divine institution they reflect in some way the union of Christ with the Church of their very nature. For just as a man leaves his father and mother and cleaves to his wife and they become one flesh, so Christ came forth from the Father and came into the world (cf. Jn 16 : 28) on account of the Church. In this sense marriage is a sacrament in a wide sense, that is, it is a sign of a sacred thing. The Cardinal quotes Pope Leo XIII who stated that from the beginning marriage bore a certain resemblance to the Incarnation of the Word of God.[1]

Speaking of marriage, the Second Vatican Council tells us that "the intimate partnership of married life and love has been established by the Creator and qualified by his laws". "God himself is the author of marriage".[2] The new Code of Canon Law also states that the marriage of Catholics, even if only one of the parties is baptised, is governed not only by divine law, but also by Canon Law. The civil authority has competence over the purely civil effects of the same marriage (cf. c.1059).

Like all divine laws, the laws concerning marriage favour and promote the full development of the human person.

Marriage has been instituted by God first of all as a *natural* institution for the good of the spouses and the children. Pope John Paul II speaks of marriage as "the fruit and sign of a profoundly human need".[3] It is also a *social* institution for the good of society. The laws relating to marriage are aimed at protecting its existence and achieving the purposes for which it has been instituted.

The marriage consent

A marriage is brought into being through the irrevocable consent freely and lawfully given by two people who are considered in law capable of giving it (cf. c.1057 n.1).

Those who are about to marry should know and not exclude from their matrimonial consent the elements so essential to Christian marriage, that to exclude any of them would be to exclude marriage and so render their consent null. These elements are (1) the essence of the matrimonial consent itself, namely, the exchange of the right to sexual intercourse which is open to the generation of new life; (2) the unity of marriage, namely, that this right is to be exchanged with no other person while the marriage lasts; (3) the permanence of marriage, namely, that this right is intended to remain as long as both live (cf. c.1056, c.1057, c.1096).

The marriage consent is an act of the will, a decision made by the parties to commit themselves to one another by an irrevocable covenant for the purpose of setting up a marriage (cf. c.1057 n.2).

The following are considered in law to be incapable of giving a true marriage consent:

1) Those who have not a sufficient use of reason.

2) Those who are impeded by a serious lack of judgment about the essential rights and duties of marriage which parties exchange with each other.

3) Those who for reasons of a psychic nature are incapable of assuming the obligations of marriage (cf. c.1095).

A marriage exists from the moment the parties give a consent that is valid in Canon Law.

Addressing the members of the Tribunal of the Sacred Roman Rota, Pope Paul VI after quoting the teaching of the Second Vatican Council — which states that "by the human act whereby the spouses mutually bestow and accept each other, a relationship arises which by the divine will and in the eyes of society too is a lasting one. For the good of the spouses and their offspring as well as of society, the existence of this sacred bond no longer depends on human decisions" — went on to say: "It must be absolutely denied then that with the cessation of any subjective element, such as is especially conjugal love, the marriage no longer exists as a juridical reality, originating in a consent that is once and for all juridically effective. This reality, on the juridical level, continues to exist independently of love and endures even if the sentiments of love have completely disappeared. In fact, the spouses, by giving their free consent, have entered and are part of an objective order or 'institution' which transcendends and is independent of them, both by its nature and the laws proper to it". "From a spontaneous sentiment, love becomes a binding obligation (cf. Eph 5 : 25)".

"All this should not be understood as in any way diminishing the importance and dignity of married love, for the rich abundance of values inherent in the institution of marriage does not consist of its juridical element alone. Conjugal love, even if it has no place in the area of law, has nonetheless a sublime and indispensable role in marriage".[4]

A covenant

The Second Vatican Council chose the word 'covenant' in preference to others to describe marriage because it fits in more easily with the biblical associations connected with marriage.

Pope John Paul II reminds us that "the communion of love between God and his people, a fundamental part of Revelation and faith experience of Israel, finds a meaningful expression in the marriage consent which is established between a man and a woman. For this reason, the central word of Revelation 'God loves his people', is likewise proclaimed through the living and concrete word whereby a man and a woman express their conjugal love. Their bond of love becomes the image and the symbol of the covenant which unites God and his people".[5]

In making a covenant of love and fidelity with his people God chose to illustrate his love for them by taking as his model the love that exists between husband and wife. All through the Bible God speaks of his love for his people in terms of marriage. First of all God is looked upon as the husband and bridegroom of Israel (cf. Hosea ch.2; Ezekiel ch.16). The sins of infidelity of the chosen people are likened to adultery (cf. Jer 3 : 8). God loves his people as a husband loves his wife (cf. Jeremiah ch. 2). The chosen people have not always been faithful to their love but God's love for them is not lessened on that account. His dealings with them show him inflicting heavy punishments at one time and sending great blessings at another. The whole history of Israel is one of alternating joys and sorrows. Through these God binds himself more completely to his people.

The word covenant also better illustrates the relationship between Christ and the Church of which Christian marriage is a symbol. In Christ the place of love and marriage in God's plan becomes more sublime. In the New Testament the bridegroom is Christ, the Son of God. The bride is the Church, the new people of God (cf. Mt 9:15). In the Book of Revelation (19:17–8; 21:2,9), the Church is represented as the bride of the Lamb. St Paul (Eph 5:25–27) sees the Church as the bride whom Christ loved and for whom he sacrificed himself to purify her in his own blood and make her all resplendent without spot or stain.

This notion is enriched and developed in the Apostolic Exhortation 'Familiaris Consortio' of Pope John Paul II where we read that "the communion between God and his people finds its definitive fulfilment in Jesus Christ, the Bridegroom who loves and gives himself as the Saviour of our humanity uniting it to himself as his body".

"He reveals the original truth of marriage, the truth of the 'beginning'. . . This revelation reaches its definitive fullness in the gift of love which the Word of God makes to humanity in assuming a human nature and in the sacrifice which Jesus Christ makes of himself on the Cross for his bride, the Church. In this sacrifice there is entirely revealed that plan which God has imprinted on the humanity of man and woman since their creation: the marriage of baptised persons thus becomes a real symbol of that new and eternal covenant sanctioned in the blood of Christ".[6]

The new Code of Canon Law reflects the constant teaching of the Church when it states that the marriage covenant between the baptised has been raised to the dignity of a sacrament by Christ our Lord (cf. c.1055 n.1).

"The conjugal communion is the fruit and sign of a profoundly human need. But in the Lord Christ, God takes up this human need, confirms it, purifies it and elevates it, leading it to perfection through the sacrament of Matrimony".[7]

"The sacrament of Marriage gives the natural conjugal love a new significance which not only purifies and strengthens it, but elevates it to the point of making it the expression of specifically Christian values".[8]

The purposes of marriage

This is also referred to as the 'unitive' aspect of marriage. Through the institution of marriage at the human level, husband and wife are perfected as human beings.

From the human standpoint marriage is already a means through which husband and wife are perfected as human beings.

If they live their married lives as they should, they complement and complete each other. They act as a refining influence on each other and they mature together as human beings. Through the mutual self-giving and the intellectual endowments which each of the spouses brings to the marriage they enrich and complete each other physically and mentally. They develop a certain refinement and become more mature through the joys and difficulties of life, the responsibilities, preoccupations and even the sufferings which marriage involves.

Throughout the course of their married lives Christian couples help each other to grow and mature. In their Pastoral Letter for May 1975 (n.125) the Irish Bishops refer to this process when they say, "Many moral problems — whether it be in the area of justice, of charity, of business, of politics, of sex or whatever — can be perplexing and in human terms may offer no easy solution. One must remember that it is precisely in coping with problems and indeed in suffering through them that one develops as a person and as a Christian. It is in this way that in St Paul's words, 'We live by truth and in love' and 'grow in all ways into Christ' becoming 'fully mature with the fullness of Christ himself' (Eph 4 : 16,13). A moral problem should be seen not just as an obstacle to the moral life but as an opportunity for growth in that life. The life of the Church herself is one of ongoing and never ending renewal. The life of the individual Christian is one of ceaselessly renewed effort, of endless beginning again. Success for the Christian lies in refusing to give up the effort, refusing to admit defeat. It is victory through and beyond failure. In the struggle we are sustained by the all-powerful Spirit which raised Jesus from the dead. We are given the certitude of victory by 'Christ among us, our hope of glory' (Col 1 : 25)".

The married love of Christians

Love is at the root of every marriage but the love of Christian husbands and wives for each other has a special significance and has many qualities which we will now consider. It is :

1) *God-like.* This love is a sharing in the love of God. All human love is a sharing in the love of God but the love of husband and wife is seen to do this in a very special way. It is a love that unites two people in such a way that the one is completely for the other. It is a reflection, if even a faint one, of the life of the Blessed Trinity in so far as the love in the Trinity is a love which makes

Father, Son and Holy Spirit one so that they exist one for the other.

Pope John Paul II tells us that "the love of husband and wife is a unique participation in the mystery of life and of the love of God himself".[9]

2) *Christ-like and ecclesial.* It is an efficacious symbol of the love of Christ for the Church and of the love and fidelity of the Church for Christ. The relationship of Christ with the Church is not merely a symbolic relationship but a real one. By the will of Christ conjugal love between Christians is sacramental. It is a sign of grace which produces in those who receive the sacrament the effect it signifies. It produces a love that is in every sense Christian. In other words the sacrament of Marriage gives the husband the grace to love his wife with a love that is deep and generous, similar to the love with which Christ loved the Church. It is a love that is ready to sacrifice itself. It involves the utter giving of oneself and the rising above selfishness and a love that is purely erotic. Man tends to be selfish, hedonistic, to turn in upon himself, to become wrapped up in himself instead of opening himself to God and to others.

The sacrament gives the wife the grace to love her husband and to be faithful to him with a love and fidelity similar to the love which the Church has for Christ. Christ loved the Church to the point of giving his life for it. The Church has shown her love for and fidelity to Christ to the point of the martyrdom of some of her members. This is the model of love and fidelity for both husband and wife. Through the sacrament of Marriage the spouses are given a share in the love with which Christ and the Church love each other — a love that is real charity in the theological sense. This means that human love is taken up into the divine love and purified, strengthened and reinvigorated.

3) *Fully human.* It is a love that is eminently human. It is directed from one person to another through an affection of the will. Speaking of conjugal love, Pope Paul VI says that "It is a force of the psychological order, originally preordained by God to achieve the purposes of matrimony; and certainly where love is wanting the spouses lack the strong incentive for sincerely accomplishing all the duties and obligations of the marital community".[10]

In the Encyclical Letter 'Humanae Vitae' Pope Paul VI describes the human aspect of this love in the following words: "This love is a compound of sense and spirit. It is not, then, merely a question of natural instinct or emotional drive. It is also and above all, an act of free will, whose dynamism ensures that not only does it endure through the joys and sorrows of daily life, but also that it grows, so that husband and wife become in a way one heart and one soul, and together attain their human fulfilment".[11]

When viewed in this way conjugal love is seen to be something higher than the type of love which arises from instinct or passion. It is enriching and ennobling. It respects the personal values of the one being loved.

But like every other human reality married love has been affected by original sin which means that it can degenerate into lust. This happens when one of the spouses seeks his/her own selfish pleasure and satisfaction. He is really using the other to serve his own ends. This is why the Council tells us that Christ has healed and perfected this love. Through the grace of the sacrament this human love goes beyond human limits and enters into the divine sphere of charity.[12]

4) *Total, unique, exclusive.* The Second Vatican Council tells us that this love involves the good of the whole person. It is not just limited to physical attraction. Therefore, it can enrich the expressions of body and mind with a unique dignity, ennobling these expressions as special ingredients and signs of the friendship distinctive of marriage. Pope Paul VI speaks of it as "that very special form of personal friendship in which husband and wife generously share everything, allowing no unreasonable exceptions or thinking just of their own interests. Whoever really loves his partner loves not only for what he receives but loves that partner for her own sake, content to be able to enrich the other with the gift of himself".[13]

The total aspect of conjugal love also relates to one of the essential qualities of marriage, namely its unity.

Pope John Paul II spells out for us the significance of this totality of love when he says, "The Christian communion of two married persons represents the mystery of Christ's incarnation and the mystery of his covenant. Because husband and wife share in Christ's life, conjugal love involves a totality into which all the elements of the persons enter — appeal of the body and instinct, power of feeling and loving, aspirations of the mind and of will. It aims at a deeply personal unity that goes beyond union in one flesh and leads to forming one heart and soul".[14]

Pope John Paul II also points out that: "The gift of the Spirit is a commandment of life for Christian spouses and at the same time a stimulating impulse so that every day they may progress towards an ever richer union with each other on all levels — of the body, of the character, of the heart, of the intelligence and will, of the soul (47) — revealing in this way to the Church and to the world the new communion of love, given by the grace of Christ".

"Such a communion is radically contradicted by polygamy. This, in fact, directly negates the plan of God which was revealed from the beginning, because it is contrary to the equal personal dignity of men and women who, in matrimony, give themselves with a love that is total and therefore unique and exclusive. As the Second Vatican Council writes: 'Firmly established by the Lord, the unity of marriage will radiate from the equal personal dignity of husband and wife, a dignity acknowledged by mutual and total love (48)' ".[15]

5) *Faithful*. The fact that conjugal love is exclusive means that it involves mutual fidelity. When two people truly love each other they automatically desire and even demand that there shall be only one love in their lives. Their love requires that it be exclusive and this in turn calls for fidelity.

The mutual fidelity of the spouses is but the consequence of the gift each has made to the other of him/her self. It is also a sign of the respect and love they have for each other. Bernard Häring writes: "The love that binds husband and wife together is absolutely exclusive of any parallel relationship between either of them and another woman or man; such a relationship would at once falsify the love between them".[16]

Pope Paul VI states that "Married love is *faithful* and *exclusive* of all other, and this until death. This is how husband and wife understood it on the day on which, fully aware of what they were doing, they freely vowed themselves to one another in marriage. Though this fidelity of husband and wife sometimes presents difficulties, no one can assert that it is impossible, for it is always honourable and worthy of the highest esteem. The example of so many married persons down through the centuries, shows not only that fidelity is connatural to marriage but also that it is the source of profound and enduring happiness".[17]

It is not always easy to be faithful and as Pope John Paul II observes: "Fidelity at times becomes difficult for married people and requires sacrifice, mortification and self-denial".[18]

He also states that "a person's freedom, far from being restricted by this fidelity, is secured against every form of subjectivism or relativism and is made a sharer in creative wisdom".[19]

6) *Chaste love*. Chastity is a special moral virtue which governs

the sexual instinct in man so that it may serve and guide him without harming him and also that it may achieve the purposes intended by the Creator. The sex instinct and the desires that go with it are very strong. They can easily be abused. They need to be controlled. It is the function of chastity to control the use of sex.

The Council states that: "The actions within marriage by which the couple are united intimately and chastely are noble and worthy ones. Expressed in a manner which is truly human, these actions signify and promote that mutual self-giving by which spouses enrich each other with a joyful and thankful will".[20]

Chastity causes husband and wife to limit the use of sex to what is lawful in marriage and to refrain from what is contrary to the order established by God, e.g. adultery, masturbation, unnatural vice.

The marital act is a human act inspired by love and accompanied by expressions of tenderness and loving solicitude. The union on the physical level strengthens and deepens the union at the emotional and spiritual level.

The Vatican Council refers to the sacrifices that must be made by married couples if they are to practise conjugal chastity and reminds them that this will only be possible if they have learnt to exercise self-control over themselves in all that concerns their sex life, moderating their sex drives out of respect for the other partner.

7) *Fruitful and creative.* First of all when married love is fruitful it reflects the very life of the Church. The Church forms generations of men for Christ. She introduces them to the life of grace by means of Baptism and the other sacraments. She is able to do this through the sacrament of Marriage. The Dogmatic Constitution on the Church reminds us that "Christian spouses, in virtue of the sacrament of Matrimony, signify and partake of the mystery of that unity and fruitful love which exist between Christ and his Church (cf. Eph 5 : 32)".[21]

Moreover, "the gift of the Spirit, accepted and responded to by husband and wife, helps them to live their human sexuality in accordance with God's plan and as a sign of the unitive and fruitful love of Christ for his Church".[22]

Married love is creative because it is a special sharing in the love of God which is at the source of its creative work. As procreative it reflects the creative activity of God in the Godhead itself. The love of God is essentially fruitful in the Godhead since the Son is generated from the love of the Father, and the Holy

Spirit proceeds from the mutual love of the Father and the Son. All paternity (which includes motherhood) has its origin in God himself, St Paul tells the Ephesians: "This, then, is what I pray, kneeling before the Father, from whom every family, whether spiritual or natural, takes its name" (Eph 3 : 14–15). Outside the Godhead the love of God is also fruitful in that from it the whole of creation springs. In becoming fathers and mothers the spouses are living and free instruments of the love of God, who through them increases the number of children. This is a great and noble vocation.

Fruitfulness or creativity are built into the very structure of married love and the community of life which arises from it. Husband and wife are truly and fully 'one' when they become 'three'. True love naturally causes husband and wife to want children.

In their Pastoral Letter for May 1975 the Irish Bishops point out that: "Love in marriage ordinarily finds its highest fulfilment in bringing new life into the world. When God blesses marriage with children, these should be and grow up knowing themselves to be the living expression of the love of husband and wife for one another. The child usually bears traces of the physical appearance and the character traits of both the husband and the wife, blended together in a new human face and personality. The child is thus a new bond of love between the partners. The love of husband and wife lives on in a third mutually loved and shared little one. In the child and around the child, husband and wife become in a way one".

Bernard Häring sees this procreative openness to children, this assent to childbirth as constituting "the specific and differentiating characteristic of married love, the characteristic that sets it apart from every other form of love between human persons; and it is precisely this procreative openness that safeguards married love from becoming an 'egoism between two' ".[23] For the same writer human sexuality has a sacredness because through it "man is privileged to enjoy a creative partnership with Almighty God".[24]

With reference to the fruitful aspect of conjugal love, Pope John Paul II tells us that "With the creation of man and woman in his own image and likeness, God crowns and brings to perfection the work of his hands: he calls them to a special sharing in his love and in his power as Creator and Father, through their free and responsible co-operation in transmitting the gift of human life, 'God blessed them, and God said to them, Be fruitful and multiply, fill the earth and subdue it' (Gen 1 : 28)".

"Conjugal love, while leading the spouses to reciprocal 'know-ledge' which makes them 'one flesh', does not end with the couple, because it makes them capable of the greatest possible gift, the gift by which they become co-operators with God for giving life to a new human person. Thus, the couple, while giving themselves to one another, give not just themselves but also the reality of children, who are a living reflection of their love, a permanent sign of con-jugal unity and a living and inseparable synthesis of their being a father and a mother".

"Fecundity is the fruit and the sign of conjugal love, the living testimony of the full reciprocal self-giving of the spouses: 'While not making the other purposes of matrimony of less account, the true practice of conjugal love, and the whole meaning of the family life which results from it, have this aim: that the couple be ready with stout hearts to cooperate with the love of the Creator and the Saviour, who through them will enlarge and enrich his own family day by day' (82)".

Responsible parenthood

The Second Vatican Council and subsequent documents speak of the spouses acquitting themselves of the duty to procreate with a generous and human Christian sense of responsibility.

The Church does not require married couples to have as many children as they can physically manage. John Marshall points out that "to produce a child for which the parents cannot provide is to fulfil only a part of this purpose of marriage. They procreate but they do not educate. Parents must consider their obligation to educate as well as to procreate. Feckless or irresponsible parent-hood is not part of the Catholic concept of marriage.[26] This is perfectly in accord with the teaching of the Second Vatican Council that 'Parents should regard as their proper mission the task of transmitting human life and educating those to whom it has been transmitted' ".[27]

The Council does not define the responsibility of the parents in terms of the number of children they should have. It says they must approach the matter with "docile reverence towards God". This means that they must pray for light to see what is the will of God and for the strength to carry it out, so that the decision about the number of children they should have, which must be theirs, will not be a selfish one. When left to himself man can be both blind and weak.

With regard to the number of children they should have "the parents should themselves ultimately make this judgment in the sight of God. But in their manner of acting spouses should be aware that they cannot proceed arbitrarily. They must always be governed according to a conscience dutifully conformed to the divine law itself and should be submissive towards the Church's teaching office, which authentically interprets that law in the light of the Gospel. That divine law reveals and protects the integral meaning of conjugal love, and impels it towards a truly human fulfilment".[28]

In coming to a decision they will take into consideration reasons of a medical nature (danger to the mother of another pergnancy; illness of the father or mother, or of a child already born, that would make it exceptionally difficult to care for another child); eugenic nature (probability that future children would be mentally defective or have some serious hereditary defect); an economic nature (parents may be financially unable to provide for more children according to the standards of decent living outlined by the Church and the ability to save reasonably for the future); a social nature (proper housing facilities, decent living conditions, the possibility of properly educating the children). Some of these reasons could be permanent, others might be temporary.

In addition to what has already been said, the Council says that parents should consult the interests of the temporal society and of the Church herself. The former could refer to the population problem. But it must be remembered that a problem can be caused not only by irresponsible parenthood but also by an appreciable fall in the birth-rate. The strict limiting of one's family to one or two children and adherence to a rigid policy of birth-control will result in a preponderance of old people in due course. Some countries are already worried about this problem.

Commenting on this aspect of the Council teaching, Bernard Häring says: "Responsible parenthood has nothing in common with arrogant planning or birth-control inspired by unwillingness to have children. The Christian attitude is one of 'docile reverence', and basic to it are the respect for the gifts and possibilities bestowed by God and the mutual regard of the married couple for one another".[29]

The mention of the interests of the Church is taken to refer to the need for vocations to the priesthood and the religious life. Parents should not rule out the possibility that one or more of their children may be given such a vocation. Again this is a matter about which they should pray and if any of their children is given a vocation, they should not stand in the way but encourage them and leave them perfectly free to follow such a calling, once it is clear that the call is a genuine one and not just a passing fancy.

Parents, then, should take this decision in common agreement and with generosity. They may take advice about the matter but the final decision rests with them. It is their duty and their right which others must respect.

In this matter they cannot act arbitrarily. They must form their conscience by taking into account both the law of God and the official teaching of the Church.

Sex in marriage

By speaking of marital acts as noble and worthy ones the Council wants to dispel any suspicion about the moral goodness of the sex act in marriage. It also wants to correct current views about sex. There are those who distrust sex and limit the function of sex to the procreation of children instead of seeing it also as an expression of love between husband and wife.

A false spirituality

In this context Bernard Häring points out that the totality of married love can be shattered through a false spirituality. "False spirituality regards with suspicion the joy of body and soul which the Creator has bestowed on a man as a natural consequence of married love. The pleasure of the senses is suspect because it is not seen as forming a totality with the self-giving that bears it along, and because there is no appreciation of the fact that this pleasure is all the purer and gladder the less selfishly it is sought for its own sake by husband and wife. In pastoral work we sometimes encounter a falsely spiritual form of selfishness in this sphere. . . In marriage intercourse the satisfaction of the senses belongs to the full expression of each partner's self-giving and to the grateful acceptance by each one of the self-giving of the other. The decisive factor is, of course, that this pleasure is not sought for its own sake but as the consequence of true love. Love, being good, is and should be a bringer of joy from its very nature. Consequently, the joy of body and soul that marriage brings is itself lovable as an essential result of married love in its totality".[30]

At the other end of the scale there are those who extol sex

above everything else. The Council teaches that it must be controlled and put at the service of charity. This is why the Council
stresses the 'spirituality' of married love. It assigns the right place
to sex and reminds married couples of the responsibility they have
to value their married love rightly.

In its 'Statement Concerning Moral Questions', the Bishops'
Conference of England and Wales answers the oblique objection
that the Church is obsessed with sex when it says: "An obsession
with sex is more characteristic of society at large today than of the
Church. Bookstalls, theatre and cinema, even advertisements for
cars and other unlikely merchandise, are full of sex. It is not the
Church but the mass media which in Christian marriage see only
the question of the 'pill'; in the priesthood only the question of
celibacy".

"For a morality of sex the Christian looks to Christ. He said:
'He who made them from the beginning made them male and
female, and said, For this reason a man shall leave his father and
mother and be joined to his wife, and the two shall become one,
so they are no longer two but one. What therefore God has joined
together, let no man put asunder' (Mt 19: 4–6; Mk 10: 6–9)
[R.S.V.]."

"He gives us here two fundamental principles: first, that sex
is part of God's design for living and is therefore good; secondly,
that the context for the sexual union of man and woman is
marriage".[31]

St Paul sees the use of sex in marriage as something that is
perfectly good and he refers to the marital act as a debt, that is,
something that is due, something to which the spouses have a right
(cf. 1 Cor 7: 1–7). The state of marriage gives the spouses the
right to *natural* sexual intercourse. This is something that is due
in justice from one partner to the other. But in all that concerns
this right the spouses should show consideration for one another,
should study how to please one another and do everything in a
spirit of charity. Charity is violated if either of the partners is
unreasonable in his/her demands.

In this matter the spouses have equal rights and as often as
etiher of them *reasonably* and seriously requests the exercise of
his/her marital rights the other partner is bound in justice to
acquiesce.

One does not wish to give the impression that the sexual aspect
is the only one to be considered in marriage but, in the words of
Bernard Häring, "As an expression of love the sexual relations of

husband and wife have a quite fundamental importance. Continual effort is required on their part in order to integrate sexual relations ever more fully into love, so that they may grow in love alike through their self-giving and through the renunciations which may be required of them".[32] If this is not understood, "the over-demanding husband may increase his wife's resistance and ultimately limit his own satisfaction. The over-resisting wife frustrates the free expression of her husband's love and may create a problem area".[33] The faithful sometimes need instruction on these points. Serious harm can result from an unreasonable refusal on the part of either partner, such as the danger of infidelity, solitary sin, the lessening of the love that should exist between the spouses and in some cases the breaking-up of the marriage. Women are said to be more given to this defect because they do not want the inconvenience of pregnancy; they fear the pains of childbirth; they are apprehensive of the difficulties of rearing children and in some cases they are afraid of a miscarriage. People with a history of miscarriages should consult the Catholic Marriage Advisory Council with a view to getting advice and pre-natal care from the first moment of pregnancy.

The deliberate refusal to have sexual relations when they are reasonably requested is a violation of the virtues of justice and charity.

Requests are said to be unreasonable when the person making them has not shown due consideration for his partner. It would be unreasonable, for example, for a husband who comes home in the early hours of the morning from night work when his wife is asleep, to expect her to make love to him at that juncture.

Other instances of unreasonable requests would be: 1) when they would be dangerous for the mother or the fetus; 2) when the husband irresponsibly leaves the care of the whole family to the wife. In this case he is simply using his wife for his own selfish ends; 3) when sexual intercourse is sought too frequently. One cannot lay down a hard and fast rule. For some once a week would be frequent enough, for others once a night would be the norm. Sexual intercourse is said to be too frequent when it would be harmful to the spiritual or physical well-being of either spouse; 4) when the other partner is suffering from serious psychic depression or from some illness which makes sexual intercourse difficult, e.g. disease of the genital organs; 5) when there is a danger of catching some disease, e.g. venereal disease; 6) when the other partner wants to perform the sexual act indecently; e.g. in an unnatural way. The rights enjoyed by the spouses extend only to sexual activity in keeping with the requirements of the virtue of chastity; 6) when sexual activity will be attended by cruelty or lack of control. This could happen when one of the parties is drunk. The love, in this case, cannot be said to be expressed in a manner which is truly human.

Harmonizing conjugal love with the responsible transmission of life

One of the pressing problems today arises from the need for married couples to express their love for one another in an intimate way while at the same time having to limit the size of their families. This causes a conflict in the lives of many spouses. The Council alludes to this problem and recognises as no other such document has done the dangers that are present if married life does not have at its disposal the means of communication proper to it. "As a result", the Council declares, "the faithful exercise of love and the full intimacy of their lives are hard to maintain. But where the intimacy of married life is broken off, it is not rare for its faithfulness to be imperilled and its quality of fruitfulness ruined. For then the upbringing of the children and the courage to accept new ones are both endangered".[34] Dissensions can arise between the spouses. They can grow cold towards each other. This can make it more easy for them to yield to temptations to be unfaithful. A climate can be created which is ill-suited for the bringing up and education of children.

The Council first states a fact and then refers to the solutions proposed for this situation. It speaks of 'dishonourable solutions' only to reject them. It states that a true contradiction cannot exist between the divine laws pertaining to the transmission of life and those pertaining to the fostering of genuine conjugal love. Because of an imperfect interpretation of the two divine laws by those involved in an emotive situation there may well be an apparent contradiction in people's minds. The reaction to 'Humanae Vitae' would seem to indicate that many people fail to see that there cannot be a real contradiction between the two divine laws in question.

Having laid down the general principle that the two divine laws cannot contradict each other, the Council goes on to say that "God, the Lord of life, has conferred on men the surpassing ministry of safeguarding life — a ministry which must be fulfilled in a manner which is worthy of man. Therefore, from the moment of its concep-

K

tion life must be guarded with the greatest care, while abortion and infanticide are unspeakable crimes".[35] From this it is deduced that man is not the master concerning anything to do with human life. He cannot dispose of it at will. His high mission is to safeguard it, not to use it simply for his own pleasure or self-interest, still less to destroy it even to benefit other people. We are reminded of what Pope Pius XII said to the Family Associations in 1951, namely, that "Marriage appears as an institution at the service of life. In close connection with this principle, we have illustrated, following the constant teaching of the Church, a thesis which is one of the essential foundations not only of conjugal morality, but of social morality in general: namely, that any direct attempt on an innocent human life as a means to an end — in this case to the end of saving another life — is unlawful".

"Innocent human life, in whatsoever condition it is found, is withdrawn from the very first moment of its existence from any direct deliberate attack. This is a fundamental right of the human person, which is of universal value in the Christian concept of life".[36]

The Council speaks of the mission to safeguard life being fulfilled in a manner worthy of man. This means taking account of his nature and his sexuality, which is an integral part of his human nature. Human sexuality cannot be put on the same plane as the sexuality of animals. In animals the function of sexuality is reproduction. It is totally at the service of the species. Sex in man, judging from the structure of its biological mechanisms, has also the function of reproduction but this is not its exclusive function. Besides being for the good of the species it is also for the good of the person. It serves to perfect and enrich the person. Above all, it serves as an expression of love touching the highest value in human beings. Looked upon in this way, human sexuality differs from sex in animals. Acts of sexual intercourse between married people have a special dignity and are worthy of particular respect. From this we get the norm governing sex, namely, that sexual activity between married couples cannot be performed if they cannot be the expression of married love or if they do not respect the value of the person.

"Therefore when there is question of harmonizing conjugal love with the responsible transmission of life", the Council tells us, "the moral aspect of any procedure does not depend solely on sincere intentions or on an evaluation of motives. It must be determined by objective standards. These, based on the nature of the human person and his acts, preserve the full sense of mutual self-giving and human procreation in the context of true love. Such a goal cannot be achieved unless the virtue of conjugal chastity is sincerely practised. Relying on these principles, sons of the Church may not undertake methods of regulating procreation which are found blameworthy by the teaching authority of the Church in its unfolding of the divine law".

"Everyone should be persuaded that human life and the task of transmitting it are not realities bound up with this world alone. Hence they cannot be measured or perceived only in terms of it, but always have a bearing on the eternal destiny of men".[37]

The Council restricts itself to general principles and goes on to explain the norms for resolving the problem of harmonizing married love with respect for the transmission of human life. A human action is moral if it is in conformity with human nature. Nature must be considered in all its aspects, in all its relations. In man nature is ultimately bound up with the person. In practice this means that married people who love one another and wish to show this love by sexual intercourse, but for good reasons cannot have more children, at least for the time being, cannot appeal only to their sincerity and to the good reasons they have for acting. They must take into account the *objective* norms which govern conjugal relations. These norms are taken from human nature and are for the good of the individual. They protect and respect the full meaning of marriage as a mutual self-giving and as a means of a truly human procreation. Such objective norms, the Council says, in effect condemn the use of practices aimed at preventing generation. Where Catholics are concerned the moral norms for the use of marriage are indicated authoritatively by the teaching authority (Magisterium) of the Church. By the will of Christ, the Church is authorised to interpret the moral law, the law of God.

The question of intention

With regard to the question of the intention of the spouses mentioned by the Council, Pope Paul VI asks the question: "Could it not be accepted that the intention to have a less prolific but more rationally planned family might not transform an action which renders natural processes infertile into a licit and provident control of birth? Could it not be admitted, in other words, that procreative finality applies to the totality of married life rather than to each single act? It is being asked whether, because people are more conscious today of their responsibilities, the time has not come when the transmission of life should be regulated by their intelligence and will rather than through the specific rhythms of their own bodies".[38]

Before the Encyclical 'Humanae Vitae' some theologians tried to solve the problem by suggesting that openness to life applied to sex in marriage as a whole and not the individual acts of sexual intercourse. Others taught that *ideally* Christian couples should leave the act open to life but that if they found themselves in a difficult situation they would be entitled to make use of contraception. This approach to the problem has been ruled out by the teaching of the Second Vatican Council, the Encyclical 'Humanae Vitae', the Sixth Synod of Bishops held in Rome in September 1980 and by Pope John Paul II, as the following quotation testifies: "The Synod Fathers made the following declaration at their last assembly: 'This Sacred Synod, gathered together with the Successor of Peter in the unity of faith, firmly holds what has been set forth in the Second Vatican Council (cf. Gaudium et Spes, 50) and afterwards in the Encyclical 'Humanae Vitae', particularly that love between husband and wife must be fully human, exclusive and open to new life ('Humanae Vitae', 11; cf. also 9,12)' (83)".

"Moreover, Paul VI affirmed that the teaching of the Church 'is founded upon the inseparable connection, willed by God and unable to be broken by man on his own initiative, between the two meanings of the conjugal act: the unitive meaning and the procreative meaning (88).' And he concluded by re-emphasizing that there must be excluded as intrinsically immoral 'every action which, either in anticipation of the conjugal act, or in its accomplishment, or in the development of its natural consequences, proposes, whether as an end or as a means, to render procreation impossible (89)' ".[39]

Furthermore, Pope John Paul II refers to this approach when he discusses the moral progress of married people in the following terms: "It is always very important to have a right notion of the moral order, its values and its norms; and the importance is all the greater when the difficulties in the way of respecting them become more numerous and serious".

"Since the moral order reveals and sets forth the plan of God the Creator, for this very reason it cannot be something that harms man, something impersonal. On the contrary, by responding to the deepest demands of the human being created by God, it places itself at the service of that person's full humanity with the delicate and binding love whereby God himself inspires, sustains and guides every creature towards its happiness".

"But man, who has been called to live God's wise and loving design in a responsible manner, is an historical being who day by day builds himself up through his many free decisions; and so he knows, loves and accomplishes moral good by stages of growth".

"Married people too are called upon to progress unceasingly in their moral life, with the support of a sincere and active desire to gain ever better knowledge of the values enshrined in and fostered by the law of God. They must also be supported by an upright and generous willingness to embody these values in their concrete decisions. They cannot however look on the law as merely an ideal to be achieved in the future: they must consider it as a command of Christ the Lord to overcome difficulties with constancy". "And so what is known as 'the law of gradualness' or step-by-step advance cannot be identified with 'gradualness of the law', as if there were different degrees or forms of precept in God's law for different individuals and situations. In God's plan, all husbands and wives are called in marriage to holiness, and this lofty vocation is fulfilled to the extent that the human person is able to respond to God's command with serene confidence in God's grace and in his or her own will" (95). On the same lines, it is part of the Church's pedagogy that husbands and wives should first of all recognize clearly the teaching of 'Humanae Vitae' as indicating the norm for the exercise of their sexuality, and that they should endeavour to establish the conditions necessary for observing that norm".

"As the Synod noted, this pedagogy embraces the whole of married life. Accordingly, the function of transmitting life must be integrated into the overall mission of Christian life as a whole, which without the Cross cannot reach the Resurrection. In such a context it is understandable that sacrifice cannot be removed from family life, but must in fact be wholeheartedly accepted if the love between husband and wife is to be deepened and become a source of intimate joy".[40]

In their Pastoral Letter for Lent 1969 the Irish Bishops point out that: "Modern theories of sexual freedom all take as their starting point the fact that contraceptives separate the personal relationship or unitive aspect of sex from its procreative aspect. To admit this separation is in fact to be inescapably committed to the very principle which lies at the root of contemporary sexual permissiveness. Pope Paul VI affirms that the only alternative to this neopagan view of sex is the teaching 'often expounded by the Magisterium of the Church, based on the inescapable connection, established by God, which man on his own initiative may not break, between the unitive and procreative significance which are both inherent to the marriage act' ".[41]

Pope John Paul II speaks of today's culture as one "which seriously distorts or entirely misinterprets, the true meaning of human sexuality, because it separates it from its essential reference to the person". He also refers to "the appearance of a truly contraceptive mentality" and the prevalence of "an anti-life mentality".[42]

"If we can regard a contraceptive act of sexual relations as a legitimate expression of the meaning and values of sex, it becomes difficult to see why sex must require marriage at all for its lawful exercise. For it is only by viewing sex in its natural integrity, that we come to see marriage as the only adequate expression of sexual love. Respecting the integrity of sex does not mean merely concern for biological or physiological integrity. It means respect for the human wholeness of sex. Love in its sexual expression is a longing for unreserved self-giving by two people who desire to belong to each other completely in life-long love and sharing of life, and who desire to love together into life children who will be the living image of their two-in-oneness. This is why it is only in marriage that sex finds its true personalist meaning and value and its human wholeness. Every form of sexual immorality can be defined by its deliberate exclusion of one or other aspect of this human wholeness of sexual love".

"Contraception alters the very meaning of sexuality, on which the meaning and value of marriage are based. If we can separate sexual activity from its procreative meaning there is no reason why we could not separate it also from its full unitive meaning. In other words, it would become impossible to find a decisive reason for condemning the use of sex outside of marriage. If the meanings and values of sex can be artificially divided by contraception within marriage, there seems no reason why they cannot be divided from marriage altogether".[43]

Pope John Paul II alludes to this very point when he says: "When couples, by means of recourse to contraception, separate these two meanings that God the Creator has inscribed in the being of man and woman and in the dynamism of their sexual communion, they act as 'arbiters' of the divine plan and they 'manipulate' and degrade human sexuality — and with it themselves and their married partner — by altering its value of 'total' self-giving. Thus the innate language that expresses the total reciprocal self-giving of husband and wife is overlaid, through contraception, by an objectively contradictory language, namely, that of not giving oneself totally to the other. This leads not only to a positive refusal to be open to life but also to a falsification of the inner truth of conjugal love, which is called upon to give itself in personal totality".[44]

Difficulties to be met with

Speaking of the specific social and cultural situations within which marriage and the family are lived today, Pope John Paul II states that "not infrequently ideas and solutions which are very appealing but which obscure in varying degrees the truth and the dignity of the human perron, are offered to the men and women of today in their sincere and deep search for a response to the important daily problems that affect their married and family life. These views are often supported by the powerful and persuasive organization of the means of social communication, *which subtly endangers freedom and the capacity for an objective judgment*"[45] (Italics mine).

The Pope also recognizes that "the teaching of the Church in our day is placed in a social and cultural context which renders it more difficult to understand and yet more urgent and irreplaceable for promoting the true good of men and women".[46]

Again we read that "living in such a world, under the pressures coming above all from the mass media, the faithful do not always remain immune from the obscuring of certain fundamental values, nor set themselves up as the critical conscience of family culture and as active agents in the building of an authentic family humanism".

"Among the more troubling signs of this phenomenon, the Synod Fathers stressed the following, in particular: the spread of divorce and of recourse to a new union, even on the part of the faithful; the acceptance of purely civil marriage in contradiction to the vocation of the baptised to 'be married in the Lord'; the celebration of the marriage sacrament without living faith, but for other motives; the rejection of the moral norms that guide and promote the human and Christian exercise of sexuality in marriage".[47]

Finally, Pope John Paul II refers to the role of the Church as Teacher and Mother when he says, "In the field of conjugal morality the Church is Teacher and Mother and acts as such".

"As Teacher, she never tires of proclaiming the moral norm that must guide the responsible transmission of life. The Church is in no way the author or the arbiter of this norm. In obedience to the truth which is Christ, whose image is reflected in the nature and dignity of the human person, the Church interprets the moral norm and proposes it to all people of good will, without concealing its demands of radicalness and perfection".

"As Mother, the Church is close to the many married couples who find themselves in difficulty over this important point of the moral life: she knows well their situation, which is often very arduous and at times truly tormented by difficulties of every kind, not only individual difficulties but social ones as well; she knows that many couples encounter difficulties not only in the concrete fulfilment of the moral norm but even in understanding its inherent values".

"But it is one and the same Church that is both Teacher and Mother. And so the Church never ceases to exhort and encourage all to resolve whatever conjugal difficulties may arise without ever falsifying or compromising the truth: she is convinced that there can be no true contradiction between the divine law on transmitting life and that on fostering authetic married love (91). Accordingly, the concrete pedagogy of the Church must always remain linked with her doctrine and never be separated from it. With the same conviction as my predecessor, I therefore repeat: To diminish in no way the teaching of Christ constitutes an eminent form of charity for souls" (92).[48]

Subjective guilt

All this has a bearing on the subjective guilt of those who practice contraception.

In their Pastoral Letter for May 1975 the Irish Bishops raise the question of the objective wrongness of contraception and the subjective guilt. They state in n 124: "When the confessor or pastor is asked, 'Is contraception wrong?', he must state clearly, 'It is wrong'. In assessing the degree of moral failure in a particular case, of course, one must not exclude from this area (the area of contraception) the traditional moral principles which recognise that circumstances may sometimes diminish or even exclude subjective guilt (or culpability). It is a grave responsibility of conscience on the penitent and on the confessor to decide whether, or to what

extent, culpability has been diminished in a particular case. In all
circumstances the faithful should continue to have recourse to
God's mercy and to his strengthening grace in the sacrament of
Penance".

Francis Frost touches on some of the factors the Irish Bishops
have in mind when he states that "It must be remembered, however, that the individual is conditioned in varying degrees, not only
by his own psychosomatic make-up and that of his partner in marriage, but also by society, which may bring to bear on both partners
a host of subtle pressures only half-understood by them and
beyond their control. Since they make their decision to use contraception in this context, however deliberate it may seem to them
from the standpoint of their subjective awareness of their thought
processes, feelings and psychic drives, from the moral point of view
their responsibility may be relatively slight. The statement of the
objective moral norm is a statement about responsibility shared by
the whole environment and not incurred by the individual in isola-
tion. Therefore the individual who practises contraception may not
necessarily be held guilty of grave sin".[49]

Bernard Häring describes the effect of the environment on the
individual conscience when he says: "The great temptation today
is to yield blindly and instinctively to the pattern of one's environment, or to the life style advocated on movie and television screens.
Today, motion pictures and television have an uncanny influence
over many of our young people. They are continually confronted
by a celluloid world setting prime value on the beauty and pleasures
of the body. Worse still, many of these celluloid heroes portrayed
by the actors are either violent individuals or simply free-lance
lovers, and the cameras manage to catch only the comic effects
of their escapades".

"There is, then, an urgent need to help people form a mature
conscience. The man who has a properly formed Christian conscience experiences the freedom of the children of God. This
experience fortifies him against mediocrity and self-centredness,
and makes him less likely to fall a prey to the unenlightened pat-
terns of his environment. He recognises that his contribution to
his environment will serve the common good only so long as he
preserves his own personality and lives according to his own conscience as a Christian".[50]

The principles for assessing subjective guilt or the lack of it
with regard to immoral actions must be applied in the same way
to all sins and not more strictly to the sin of contraception. In this

connection it is also well to remember what was said about the dispositions of the penitent when we discussed the sacrament of Penance.

Natural family planning

Pope John Paul II points out that "the responsible regulation of fertility in accordance with natural methods is in conformity with human dignity and the teaching of the Church".[51]

Pope Paul VI teaches that "If there are reasonable grounds for spacing births, arising from the physical or psychological condition of husband or wife, or from external circumstances, the Church teaches that then married people may take advantage of the natural cycles immanent in the reproductive system and use their marriage at precisely those times that are infertile, and in this way control birth, a way which does not in the least offend moral principles".[52]

Pope Pius XII told the Midwives: "It is your office, and not that of the priest, to instruct married people by private consultation or through serious publications, on the medical and biological aspects of the theory".[53] What the Pope said earlier to his audience applies to Catholic members of the medical profession in general, namely, that "You are rightly expected to be well informed, from the medical point of view, of this well-known theory and of the progress which can still be foreseen in this matter; and moreover, your advice and help are expected to be based, not on simple, popular publications, but on scientific facts and the authoritative judgment of conscientious specialists in medicine and biology".[54]

In a later address Pope Pius XII referred to the use of the infertile period and said: "One may even hope (yet in this matter the Church naturally leaves the judgment to medical science) that science will succeed in providing this lawful method with a sufficiently secure basis. The most recent information seems to confirm such a hope".[55]

A further reference to natural family planning is made by the Council when it expresses the hopes held by Pope Pius XII and encourages further research into the matter. "Those, too, who are skilled in other sciences, notably the medical, biological, social, and psychological, can considerably advance the welfare of marriage and the family, along with peace of conscience, if by pooling their efforts they labour to explain more thoroughly the various conditions favouring a proper regulation of births".[56]

Pope Paul VI in 'Humanae Vitae' makes a similar appeal to

men of science on the lines already indicated.[57]

When speaking about the necessity of imparting knowledge of the body's rhythms of fertility, Pope John Paul II had this to say: "Accordingly, every effort must be made to render such knowledge accessible to all married people and also to young adults before marriage, through clear, timely and serious instruction and education given by married couples, doctors and experts. Knowledge must then lead to education in self-control: hence the absolute necessity for the virtue of chastity and for permanent education in it. In the Christian view, chastity by no means signifies rejection of human sexuality or lack of esteem for it: rather it signifies spiritual energy capable of defending love from the perils of selfishness and aggressiveness, and able to advance it towards its full realization".[58]

The difference between artificial contraceptive methods and the use of natural rhythms

Pope John Paul II speaks of this as follows: "When, instead, by means of recourse to periods of infertility, the couple respect the inseparable connection between the unitive and procreative meanings of human sexuality, they are acting as 'ministers' of God's plan and they 'benefit from' their sexuality according to the original dynamism of 'total' self-giving, without manipulation or alteration (90)".

"In the light of the experience of many couples and of the data provided by the diffrent human sciences, theological reflection is able to perceive and is called to study further the difference, both anthropological and moral, between contraception and recourse to the rhythm of the cycle: it is a difference which is much wider and deeper that is usually thought, one which involves in the final analysis two irreconcilable concepts of the human person and of human sexuality. The choice of the natural rhythms involves accepting the cycle of the person, that is the woman, and thereby accepting dialogue, reciprocal respect, shared responsibility and self-control. To accept the cycle and to enter into dialogue means to recognise both the spiritual and corporal character of conjugal communion, and to live personal love with its requirement of fidelity. In this context the couple comes to experience how conjugal communion is enriched with those values of tenderness and affection which constitute the inner soul of human sexuality, in its physical dimension also. In this way sexuality is respected and promoted in its truly and fully human dimension, and is never 'used' as an 'object' that, by breaking the personal unity of soul and body, strikes at God's creation itself at the level of the deepest interaction of nature and person".[59]

Not an easy matter

Christian married couples must not be led into thinking that adhering faithfully to the teaching of the Church does not call for any adjustments to be made especially when they have recourse to the natural methods of regulating birth.

Speaking in general terms, Pope John Paul II had this to say: "Conjugal intimacy involves the wills of two persons, who are however called to harmonize their mentality and behaviour. This requires much patience, understanding and time. Uniquely important in this field is unity of moral and pastoral judgment by priests, a unity that much be carefully sought and ensured, in order that the faithful may not have to suffer anxiety of conscience".[60]

Adherence to the teaching of the Church will require honesty, persistence, patience, humility, self-control, strength of mind, filial trust in God and in his grace, frequent recourse to prayer, and to the sacraments of the Eucharist and Renconciliation.[61]

It must also be remembered that people are ready to sacrifice pleasure in many other spheres. Parents have to make sacrifices for their children; doctors and other professional people are called upon to make sacrifices in the exercise of their duty. An anonymous author, writing in a C.T.S. pamphlet, reminds us that: "Life isn't meant to be hard, it *is* hard. God is the answer, not the problem".[62] Christians cannot escape the cross in any walk of life. Not being able to have sexual intercourse when they like may be a cross married couples are called upon to bear, if not permanently, at least for a time. "If any man would come after me, let him deny himself, take up his cross and follow me" (Mt 16:24).

The Catholic Marriage Advisory Council has done a great deal of research into the natural methods of family planning and it is continuing to study the problem. There are a number of Centres in the British Isles where Catholics can go and get expert advice which is in accordance with the teaching of the Church. Similar organisations exist in other countries where Catholics can go with their problems.

Other expressions of love

Sexual intercourse is not the only expression of love open to married people. Bernard Häring writes: "Since marriage is a total communion of life, married love has far more forms of expression than that of sexual intercourse. A very important factor in married life is the sharing of meals, which is a symbol of the eucharistic communion of love enjoyed by the family of God in Jesus Christ. Since marriage as a sacrament points to the eucharistic celebration of the alliance of love, it should be clear how necessary it is that family meals should form a genuine expression of love in the home. Other forms of expression of married love are to be found in the educative and formative function of marriage, in its protective function, in the mutual economic help that goes with it, in community of material goods, in a wise provision for old age, in the domesticity (devotion to home and family life) of the wife through which love becomes the very atmosphere of the home. The variety and richness of family functions are of great importance for married love".[63]

A love that sanctifies

Following on what has been said above about love being faithful and creative, it is relevant to quote Pope John Paul II on other aspects of the faithfulness of conjugal love: "However, the fruitfulness of conjugal love is not restricted solely to the procreation of children, even understood in its specifically human dimension: it is enlarged and enriched by all those fruits of moral, spiritual and supernatural life which the father and mother are called to hand on to their children, and through the children to the Church and to the world".

Pope John Paul II also reminds us that marriage is a sacrament of mutual sanctification: "The sacrament of Marriage is the specific source and original means of sanctification for Christian married couples and families. It takes up again and makes specific the sanctifying grace of Baptism. By virtue of the mystery of the death and resurrection of Christ, of which the spouses are made part in a new way by marriage, conjugal love is purified and made holy: This love the Lord has judged worthy of special gifts, healing, perfecting and exalting gifts of grace and of charity" (138).

"The gift of Jesus Christ is not exhausted in the actual celebration of the sacrament of Marriage, but rather accompanies the married couple throughout their lives. This fact is explicitly recalled by the Second Vatican Council when it says that Jesus Christ 'abides with them so that, just as he loved the Church and handed himself over on her behalf, the spouses may love each other with perpetual fidelity through mutual self-bestowal. . . For this reason, Christian spouses have a special sacrament by which they are fortified and receive a kind of consecration in the duties and dignity of their state. By virtue of this sacrament, as spouses fulfil their conjugal and family obligations, they are penetrated with the Spirit of Christ, who fills their whole lives with faith, hope and charity. Thus they increasingly advance towards their own perfection, as well as towards their mutual sanctification, and hence contribute jointly to the glory of God' " (139).

"Christian spouses and parents are included in the universal call to sanctity. For them this call is specified by the sacrament they have celebrated and is carried out concretely in the realities proper to their conjugal and family life (140). This gives rise to the grace and requirement of an authentic and profound conjugal and family spirituality that draws its inspiration from the themes of creation, covenant, cross, resurrection, and sign, which were stressed more than once by the Synod".

"Christian marriage, like the other sacraments, 'whose purpose is to sanctify people, to build up the body of Christ, and finally, to give worship to God' (141), is in itself a liturgical action glorifying God in Jesus Christ and in the Church. By celebrating it, Christian spouses profess their gratitude to God for the sublime gift bestowed on them of being able to live in their married and family lives the very love of God for people and that of the Lord Jesus for the Church, his bride".

"Just as husbands and wives receive from the sacrament the gift and responsibility of translating into daily living the sanctification bestowed on them, so the same sacrament confers on them the grace and moral obligation of transforming their whole lives into a 'spiritual sacrifice' " (142).[65]

By the sacrament of Marriage human values are all taken up, purified and elevated. Through it they are made to serve not only the perfecting of the spouse at the human level but also their Christian sanctification — the perfecting of the spouses as Christians.

A kind of consecration

The Council reminds us that through the sacrament of Matrimony "the spouses are fortified and receive a kind of consecration in the duties and dignity of their state. By virtue of this sacrament, as spouses fulfill their conjugal and family obligations, they are penetrated with the spirit of Christ. This spirit suffuses their whole lives with faith, hope and charity. Thus they increasingly advance their own perfection, as well as their mutual sanctification, and hence contribute jointly to the glory of God".[66] Pope John Paul II speaks of the sacrament of Marriage consecrating parents for the strictly Christian education of their children.

A journeying together towards God — a journey of faith

The spouses sanctify each other together, Christian marriage is a journeying together towards God. Each of the spouses has his/her part to play in the sanctification of the other and they have the duty of helping each other to reach God by word and encouragement, example and sacrifice. They contribute jointly to the glory of God which is the end for which they were created. Their marriage will have attained its purpose fully only when in the joy of God the two spouses become companions for all eternity.

A life of virtue

Christian spouses have no need to go outside their own state in order to achieve holiness. But for this to be a reality in their lives they must in the words of the Council see that their lives are penetrated with the spirit of Christ. In other words they must co-operate with the grace of the sacrament. This means that they must strive to live their married and family life in the spirit of the Gospel, which is the spirit of Christ. This is a spirit of faith, hope and charity, the practice of the moral virtues, especially humility, the avoidance of worldliness and detachment from riches, even if they have them.

They exercise faith when as father and mother they see themselves as collaborators with the creativity of God. This saves them from the temptation of thinking that everything depends on them. Strong faith is also necessary when they are educating their children in the love of God and their neighbour.

The virtue of hope is brought into play when the parents are preparing their children, who are a projection of themselves, for the future. It is a future which is bound up with the hope expressed in the liturgy when after saying the 'Our Father' with the celebrant of the Mass we hear him pray on our behalf "as we wait in joyful hope for the coming of our Saviour Jesus Christ".

It is also the function of the grace of the sacrament to enable Christian couples to rise from the human plane of married love to the divine plane of true supernatural charity. It helps them to strive every day to aim at transforming their love for one another more and more into this higher form of married love. Grace does not destroy nature but elevates it. It brings it to completion and gives it a supernatural character. The same thing can happen in any human friendship but in the case of married love, this is supernaturalised by a special sacrament. It must also be remembered that the love which brought a husband and wife together can also diminish, as we have seen. If love were based on natural attraction alone, not necessarily an attraction which is limited to the senses, such a love would be unthinkable for the whole of one's life unless it were aided by the grace of the sacrament.

The deeper knowledge which married people come to have of each other as the years go by may reveal defects which were not evident at the outset of married life. Differences may appear because of different temperament, background, education, psychological make-up and standards. With advancing years the spouses will almost certainly lose some of the physical attraction that initially brought them together. The harmony of the home may be threatened by sickness and failure. There are also the disappointments which are incidental to every marriage and the weariness that most married people experience from time to time in their married life. In all these eventualities charity makes it easier as well as possible for love to continue and develop between the spouses. It tends to overlook inevitable defects and to concentrate on the good points and virtues of the other. True charity springs from the sense of dedication or surrender shared by the spouses. It will be intensified to the extent that it is disinterested in so far as oneself is concerned. Without charity the sacrifices demanded of both parties in the situations we have described would be impossible. Charity gives married love a stability it would not otherwise have.

There is also great scope in married life for the practice of the moral virtues especially the cardinal virtues of prudence, justice, fortitude and temperance.

Prudence is shown in the decisions which the partners have to make. St Thomas Aquinas says that if an act is not prudent it is not virtuous. The parties are bound in justice to be faithful to one another and to their respective duties. They will also need courage or fortitude to support them in the trials which are inescapable in all walks of life. There is also a wide field for the practice of the virtue of temperance, which means that the spouses will be called upon to show moderation in various ways.

It is not surprising, then, that in the same context the Council stresses the need for example on the part of the parents and the importance of family prayer as means for helping the whole family to reach maturity, salvation and holiness.[67]

Speaking of family prayer, Pope John Paul II tells us that "Family prayer has its own characteristic qualities. It is prayer offered in common, husband and wife together, parents and children together. Communion in prayer is both a consequence of and a requirement for the communion bestowed by the sacraments of Baptism and Matrimony. The words with which the Lord Jesus promises his presence can be applied to the members of the Christian family in a special way: 'Again I say to you, if two of you agree on earth about anything they ask it will be done for them by my Father in heaven. For where two or three are gathered in my name, there am I in the midst of them' (150)".[68]

"Far from being a form of escapism from everyday commitments, prayer constitutes the strongest incentive for the Christian family to assume and comply fully with all its responsibilities as the primary and fundamental cell of human society. Thus the Christian family's actual participation in the Church's life and mission is in direct proportion to the fidelity and intensity of the prayer with which it is united with the fruitful vine that is Christ the Lord (157)".

"The fruitfulness of the Christian family in its specific service to human advancement, which of itself cannot but lead to the transformation of the world, derives from its living union with Christ, nourished by the Liturgy, by self-oblation and by prayer (158)".[69]

Authority and love

In discussing this aspect of married love Bernard Häring writes: "Christ has redeemed marriage and woman from this distortion of authority (the husband lording it over the wife) through his authority of love over the Church displayed in his self-giving and in his obedience. In the Epistle to the Ephesians St Paul strongly emphasizes the fact that the husband's authority must be an expression of love, a love ready for service and self-giving. Corresponding to this is the loving obedience of the wife, after the manner of Christ and the Church (cf. Eph 5 : 21ff)".

"In the sacrament of Marriage husband and wife are reciprocally authors (auctores) of the alliance of love that unites them and so living instruments of that sacramental grace which gives them a special share in the New and Eternal Alliance. Through this fact the authenticity of love that belongs to marriage and the mutual process of self-adaptation that goes on in it are placed on the highest level".[70]

Authority and the family

Pope John Paul II speaks of the serious misconceptions in the world today regarding the relationship of authority between parents and children. He points out that parents will help their children to show love, respect and obedience if they exercise "their un-renounceable authority as a true and proper 'ministry', that is, as a service to the human and Christian well-being of their children, and in particular as a service aimed at helping them acquire a truly responsible freedom and if parents maintain a living awareness of the 'gift' they continually receive from their children".[71]

Marriage and the family as such

It would be impossible to treat of this question adequately in a book of this kind. The family is the subject-matter of the Apostolic Exhortation 'Familiaris Consortio' issued by Pope John Paul II on November 22, 1981. Many relevant passages have been quoted in these pages.

When speaking to the Clergy of Rome on February 17, 1983, Pope John Paul II described this document as the 'abc' of the family apostolate. He urged his hearers to read it and study it assiduously. The Pope added: "We must look to and follow the teaching of 'Familiaris Consortio' in its integrity: all the problems, all the moral principles which are found there, all the dogmatic and ethical doctrine which is expressed in this document".[72] Our readers are exhorted to follow this advice.

Apart from what has already been said, we give just one signi-ficant quotation from this important document: "According to the plan of God, marriage is the foundation of the wider community of the family, since the very institution of marriage and conjugal love are ordained to the procreation and education of children, in whom they find their crowning (34)".

"In its most profound reality, love is essentially a gift; and conjugal love, while leading the spouses to the reciprocal 'know-ledge' which makes them 'one flesh' (35), does not end with the couple, because it makes them capable of the greatest possible gift, the gift by which they become co-operators with God for giving life to a new human person. Thus the couple, while giving themselves to one another, give not just themselves but also the reality of children, who are a living reflection of their love, a permanent sign of conjugal unity and a living and inseparable synthesis of their being a father and a mother".[73]

Childless couples

They merit a word of encouragement, and on this point Pope John Paul II says: "It must not be forgotten however that, even when procreation is not possible, conjugal life does not for this reason lose its value. Physical sterility in fact can be for spouses the occasion for other important services to the life of the human person, for example, adoption, various forms of educational work, and assistance to other families, and to poor or handicapped children".[74]

The Second Vatican Council also stated that marriage does not lose its value if procreation, extremely important as it is, cannot be achieved. Obviously married couples will feel the lack of children very much. They feel that because they cannot have children the marriage is not a success. In so far as marriage is a community of love and destiny between husband and wife, if their lives are filled with love, they enrich each other, complete and perfect each other. They will achieve such perfection through the development and maturity of their love in all its manifestations. In this sense a marriage can be said to be successful as a personal relationship if the spouses are growing to maturity and perfecting each other.[75]

The ministers of the sacrament

It must not be forgotten that the bride and bridegroom are themselves the ministers of the sacrament even though for the marriage to be valid in the eyes of the Church it must take place before the bishop, parish priest or another priest or deacon, duly delegated by either of the first two, together with two witnesses.

The bishop, priest or deacon are said to assist at the marriage in the sense that they are there to ask and receive the consent of the parties in the name of the Church (cf. c.1108).

What has been said in Chapter 1 about the minister of the

sacraments applies to the bride and bridegroom with regard to the sacrament of Marriage.

When speaking of the celebrations of the marriage, Pope John Paul II refers to the moral and spiritual dispositions of those being married in the following terms: "Precisely because in the celebration of the sacrament very special attention must be devoted to the moral and spiritual dispositions of those being married, in particular to their faith, we must here deal with a not infrequent difficulty in which the pastors of the Church can find themselves in the context of our secularized society".

The faith of those seeking to be married

"In fact, the faith of the person asking the Church for marriage can exist in different degrees, and it is the primary duty of pastors to bring about a rediscovery of this faith and to nourish it and bring it to maturity. But pastors must also understand the reasons that lead the Church also to admit to the celebration of marriage those who are imperfectly disposed".

"The sacrament of Matrimony has this specific element that distinguishes it from all the other sacraments: it is the sacrament of something that was part of the very economy of creation; it is the very conjugal covenant instituted by the Creator 'in the beginning'. Therefore the decision of a man and a woman to marry in accordance with this divine plan, that is to say, the decision to commit by their irrevocable conjugal consent their whole lives in indissoluble love and unconditional fidelity, really involves, even if not in a fully conscious way, an attitude of profound obedience to the will of God, an attitude which cannot exist without God's grace. They have thus already begun what is in a true and proper sense a journey which the celebration of the sacrament and the immediate preparation for it can complement and bring to completion, given the uprightness of their intention".

"On the other hand it is true that in some places engaged couples ask to be married in church for motives which are social rather than genuinely religious. This is not surprising. Marriage, in fact, is not an event that concerns only the persons actually getting married. By its very nature it is also a social matter, committing the couple being married in the eyes of society. And its celebration has always been an occasion of rejoicing that brings together families and friends. It therefore goes without saying that social as well as personal motives enter into the request to be married in church".

"Nevertheless, it must not be forgotten that these engaged couples, by virtue of their Baptism, are already really sharers in Christ's marriage covenant with the Church, and that, by their right intention, they have accepted God's plan regarding marriage and therefore at least implicitly consent to what the Church intends to do when she celebrates marriage. Thus, the fact that motives of a social nature also enter into the request is not enough to justify refusal on the part of pastors. Moreover, as the Second Vatican Council teaches, the sacraments by words and ritual elements nourish and strengthen faith (168): that faith towards which the married couple are already journeying by reason of the uprightness of their intention, which Christ's grace certainly does not fail to favour and support".

"As for wishing to lay down further criteria for admission to the ecclesial celebration of marriage, criteria that would concern the level of faith of those to be married, this would above all involve grave risks. In the first place, the risk of making unfounded and discriminatory judgments; secondly, the risk of causing doubts about the validity of marriages already celebrated, with grave harm to Christian communities, and new and unjustified anxieties to the consciences of married couples; one would also fall into the danger of calling into question the sacramental nature of many marriages of brethren separated from full communion with the Catholic Church, thus contradicting ecclesial tradition".

"However, when in spite of all efforts engaged couples show that they reject explicitly and formally what the Church intends to do when the marriage of baptized persons is celebrated, the pastor of souls cannot admit them to the celebration of marriage. In spite of his reluctance to do so, he has the duty to take note of the situation and to make it clear to those concerned that, in these circumstances, it is not the Church that is placing an obstacle in the way of the celebration that they are asking for, but themselves".

"Once more there appears in all its urgency the need for evangelization and catechesis before and after marriage, effected by the whole Christian community, so that every man and woman that gets married celebrates the sacrament of Matrimony not only validly but also fruitfully".[76]

An indissoluble communion

We have left this aspect of marriage until now because it forms a fitting introduction to the question of divorce, the growing number of which Pope John Paul II lists among the signs of a disturbing degradation of some fundamental values.[77]

The teaching of the Church on the indissolubility of marriage has been summed up by Pope John Paul II as follows: "Conjugal communion is characterized not only by its unity but also by its indissolubility: as a mutual gift of two persons, this intimate union, as well as the good of children, imposes total fidelity on the spouses and argues for an unbreakable oneness between them (49)".

"It is a fundamental duty of the Church to reaffirm strongly, as the Synod Fathers did, the doctrine of the indissolubility of marriage. To all those who, in our times, consider it too difficult, or indeed impossible, to be bound to one person for the whole of life, and to those caught up in a culture that rejects the indissolubility of marriage and openly mocks the commitment of spouses to fidelity, it is necessary to reconfirm the good news of the definitive nature of that conjugal love that has in Christ its foundation and strength (50)".

"Being rooted in the personal and total self-giving of the couple, and being required by the good of the children, the indissolubility of marriage finds its ultimate truth in the plan that God has manifested in his revelation: he wills and he communicates the indissolubility of marriage as a fruit, a sign and a requirement of the absolutely faithful love that God has for man and that the Lord Jesus has for the Church".

"Christ renews the first plan that the Creator inscribed in the hearts of man and woman, and in the celebration of the sacrament of Matrimony offers 'a new heart'. Thus the couples are not only able to overcome 'hardness of heart" (51), but also and above all they are able to share the full and definitive love of Christ, the new and eternal Covenant made flesh. Just as the Lord Jesus is the 'faithful witness' (52), the 'yes' of the promises of God (53) and thus the supreme realization of the unconditional faithfulness with which God loves his people, so Christian couples are called to participate truly in the irrevocable indissolubility that binds Christ to the Church his bride, loved by him to the end (54)".

"The gift of the sacrament is at the same time a vocation and commandment for Christian spouses, that they may remain faithful to each other forever, beyond every trial and difficulty, in generous obedience to the holy will of the Lord: 'What therefore God has joined together, let not man put asunder' (55)".

"To bear witness to the inestimable value of the indissolubility and fidelity of marriage is one of the most precious and most urgent tasks of Christian couples in our time. So, with all my brothers who participated in the Synod of Bishops, I praise and encourage those numerous couples who, though encountering no small difficulty, preserve and develop the value of indissolubility; thus, in a humble and courageous manner, they perform the role committed to them of being in the world a 'sign' — a small and precious sign, sometimes also subjected to temptation, but always renewed — of the unfailing fidelity with which God and Jesus Christ love each and every human being. But it is also proper to recognize the value of the witness of those spouses who, even when abandoned by their partner, with the strength of faith and of Christian hope have not entered a new union. These spouses too give an authentic witness to fidelity, of which the world today has a great need. For this reason they must be encouraged and helped by the pastors and the faithful of the Church".[78]

The benefits of indissolubility

It will not be out of place to refer here to what Pope Pius XI had to say about this in his Encyclical Letter 'Casti Connubii' (n.36) on this subject: "The many precious benefits which flow from the indissolubility of marriage will be understood if we consider, even superficially, the welfare of husband and wife, of their children, and of society as a whole. In the first place husband and wife find in it a guarantee of that enduring stability which the reciprocal and generous surrender of their persons and of the deepest love of their hearts naturally requires; for true charity 'never falls away' (1 Cor 13:8). To chastity it affords a bulwark against temptations to infidelity, whether from within or from without. It banishes the fear of being deserted in adversity or old age, and establishes instead a quiet feeling of security. It provides an effective safeguard to the dignity of each party and ensures that they will always be at hand to help each other, the indissoluble bond which unites them serving as a constant reminder that it is not for the sake of transitory goods nor for mere satisfaction of desire, but in order to obtain for each other higher and everlasting goods, that they have contracted this matrimonial union which can be dissolved only by death. Excellent provision is also made for the instruction and education of the offspring, which has to be prolonged over many years a task involving weighty and enduring responsibilities which the united efforts of both parents will make easier to bear. Equal advantages are afforded to the whole of society. For experience shows that the inviolable indissolubility of marriage is a most fruitful source of upright living and of moral integrity. If this is observed the happiness and prosperity of the State are secured: for the State is what it is made to be by the individuals and families which compose it, as a body is composed of its members. Consequently those who strenuously defend the permanent stability of marriage render a great service to the individual welfare of married persons and their children, and to the public welfare of society".

Divorce — the teaching of 'Casti Connubii'

The Church's teaching on divorce is based on the divine law establishing the marriage covenant as an indissoluble bond between the two parties. This teaching is clearly set out by Pope Pius XI in his Encyclical Letter 'Casti Connubii' (nn.33–36). This important teaching is also reflected in the documents of the Second Vatican Council. "But this inviolable stability, though not always in equal measure nor always with the same degree of perfection, is the attribute of every true matrimonial bond; for the words of the Lord, 'What God has joined together let no man put asunder', were spoken concerning the nuptual union of our first parents, the prototype of all future marriages, and are consequently applicable to every true marriage. It is true that before the coming of Christ the perfection and strictness of the original law were modified to the extent that Moses, because of the hardness of their hearts, allowed even the members of God's people to give a bill of divorce for certain reasons. But Christ, in virtue of his power as supreme Lawgiver, revoked this concession and restored the law to its original perfection by those words which must never be forgotten: 'What God has joined together let no man put asunder'. 'Wherefore it is evident', wrote Pius VI, Our predecesor of happy memory, to the Bishop of Agria, 'that even in the state of nature, and at all events long before it was raised to the dignity of a sacrament properly so called, marriage was divinely consituted in such a way as to involve a perpetual and indissoluble bond, which consequently cannot be dissolved by any civil law. Therefore, although a marriage may exist without the sacrament, as in the case of marriage between infidels, even so, being a true marriage it must and does retain the character of a perpetual bond, which from the very beginning has been by divine law inseparable from marriage and over which no civil power has any authority. Therefore if a marriage is said to be contracted, either it is so contracted as to be a true marriage, in which case it carries with it that perpetual bond which by divine law is inherent in every true marriage; or else it is deemed to be contracted without this perpetual bond, in which case it is not a true marriage at all, but an illicit union objectively contrary to the divine law, which consequently may not be entered into or maintained' ".

"If the stability of marriage appears in some rare cases to be subject to exception — as in certain natural marriages contracted between infidels, or between Christians, in the category of marriages ratified but not consummated — such exception does not depend upon the will of man or of any merely human power, but upon the divine law, of which the Church of Christ is the sole guardian and interpreter. But no such dissolving power can ever, or for any cause, be exercised upon a Christian marriage ratified and consummated. In such a marriage the matrimonial contract has attained its final perfection, and therefore by God's will exhibits the highest degree of stability and indissolubility which no human authority can put asunder".

"If we seek with reverence to discover the intrinsic reason of this divine ordinance, Venerable Brethren, we shall easily find it in the mystical signification of Christian wedlock, seen in its full perfection in consummated marriage between Christians. The Apostle, in the epistle to the Ephesians which we quoted at the beginning of this Encyclical (Eph 5 : 32), tells us that Christian wedlock signifies that most perfect union which subsists between Christ and the Church: 'This is a great sacrament; but I speak in Christ and the Church'; and this is a union which certainly, as long as Christ lives and the Church lives by him can never cease or be dissolved. The same teaching is thus set forth by St Augustine: 'This is what is observed in Christ and in the Church: married persons must never break their married life by any divorce. This sacrament is esteemed so highly in the City of our God, that is in the Church, that when women marry or are married for the purpose of procreating offspring it is not lawful to leave a wife, even though she be sterile, to marry another who may bear children. If anyone were to act in this way he would not be condemned by the law of this world, which by divorce permits him to contract another marriage. Indeed our Lord tells us that the holy Lawgiver Moses made the same concession to the Israelites by reason of the hardness of

their hearts. But according to the law of the Gospel such a man is
guilty of adultery; and so too is his wife if she marry another man".

*From the Joint Pastoral Letter of the Hierarchy of England
and Wales (1952)*

It will be relevant to quote the following passages from the
Joint Pastoral Letter of the Hierarchy of England and Wales on
Marriage and Divorce. The teaching it contains is as valid today
as when it was first given.

"The main teaching of the Church on marriage is contained in
a single sentence: 'What, therefore, God has joined together, let no
man put asunder' (Mark 10:9). If this is thought to be either
strict or strange, the blame cannot be put upon the Church of
God. But it is blasphemy so to regard this law. For these are the
words of Christ. It is idle to pretend that he did not foresee modern
conditions. He is the Son of God. No social conditions, modern or
ancient, here or elsewhere, can alter the fundamental truth that
upon stable family life the strength of a nation is built".

"It is not the Church which has changed in regarding the
family as sacred and indivisible. What is new is the modern view
of marriage as a temporary union. The present divorce rate in this
country means a broken home for thousands of men, women and
children every year. It is even proposed and supported by otherwise responsible bodies that the reward of adultery should be the
right to divorce an innocent wife or husband. It is all too easy to
forget that those who seek fresh unions after civil divorce are
living in adultery. For no civil law can alter the law of God".

"The growth of crime, among the young, is in no small measure
due to the removal of parental control and the disregard of the
obligations of marriage. Current literature and films tend to give
a false picture of love. Catholics are taught to regard sex as sacred
because this faculty is given, in trust, for the good of the whole
human race. Being sacred, its use is enshrined in a holy sacrament.
In simple terms the issue is between consecrated love and free love.
Easier divorce inevitably extends and legalises lust".

Remedies in Canon Law

"When married men and women are unable to live at peace, the
Church has authority to offer them only the remedy of legal
separation. We are told that separation is cruel — especially when

there is only one guilty party. The innocent partners are deserving of all compassion. But it is a false compassion which seeks to give them relief by destroying the whole institution of Christian marriage. The husband or wife who is betrayed will receive the grace to live a chaste life by earnestly seeking it from God. That is the Christian solution. That is the law of Christ. It is said that this is a hard doctrine. Even the first disciples complained that it was too hard. 'If the case of a man with his wife be so', they said, 'it is not expedient to marry' (Mt 19:10). But our Lord did not relax his law. Neither may those who speak in his name. To do otherwise would be to open the floodgates to passion and sweep away the very foundation of family life".

"No one who has studied the evidence can maintain that increased facility for divorce in English-speaking countries has produced happier or healthier family relations. On the contrary, where divorce has been made easy, marriage as an institution has been brought into contempt. . . If divorce is made more easy, couples will become even more ready to rush thoughtlessly into marriage. Every divorce inflicts a fresh wound on the whole of society".

Whilst safeguarding the teaching of Sacred Scripture and applying the principles of sound theology and jurisprudence the Church goes as far as she can in granting relief in difficult cases by allowing converts from paganism to avail of the Pauline privilege, if the necessary conditions for doing so can be fulfilled, by dissolving the natural bond of marriage in favour of the faith, and by granting dispensations with regard to the valid but non-consummated marriages of two Christians when the conditions for doing so can be met. But as has already been stated by Pope Pius XI the Church has no power to dissolve a valid marriage between two Christians that has been consummated (cf. the new Code of Canon Law, ch. IX art. 1 and 2).

Invalidly married Catholics and admission to the sacraments

A marriage can be invalid for a variety of reasons. Firstly, it may be invalid because one of the parties has given a consent that is defective but which is known only to him and cannot be proved publicly. Such a marriage is presumed to be a valid one in the eyes of the Church and the partner who has given the defective consent has a duty to remove the invalidity by renewing his consent and thus causing a valid marriage to come into being. He owes this to the other partner who was unaware of the situation at the time of the marriage. Once a marriage has been entered into it is for the Church to decide the question of invalidity, if it is alleged that the marriage is invalid. Today the Church makes use of the findings of the biological, medical, psychiatric, psychological and social sciences in dealing with cases of alleged invalidity of marriage. If the alleged invalidity cannot be satisfactorily proved the parties are not free to separate and re-marry. Such a procedure would only provide a pretext for the unscrupulous to abandon a valid marriage and to contract a subsequent invalid one. This would be tantamount to allowing the parties to a valid marriage to divorce each other at will. It has always been the teaching of the Church that the parties may not of their own free will set aside a valid marriage. This was tried in Russia some years ago but it has been discontinued. Although human consent makes the marriage, it may not break the marriage once it has been made. The good of the spouses, of the children and of society requires that no marriage should be capable of dissolution at the will or caprice of the parties themselves.

Secondly, a marriage may be invalid because of the existence of some impediment which may or may not be able to be dispensed by the Church. We have in mind impediments which can be proved publicly to exist. The invalidity in these cases can be removed by dispensing these impediments which the Church has the power to dispense. If it is a question of an impediment which the Church has no power to dispense, nothing can be done to make the invalid marriage a valid one. Such is the impediment of a previous marriage bond. This impediment exists during the lifetime of the other partner to the previous marriage. It follows from this that if two validly married Catholics (or a Catholic who has validly married a non-Catholic in the Church) obtain a civil divorce and either or both of them subsequently contract(s) a civil union, by the law of God they are not entitled to live as man and wife. Should they presume to exercise the rights proper to married people, they would be committing adultery, and, adultery is one of the immutable prohibitions laid down by God to which there is no exception.

All that has been said so far is relevant to the question now being discussed whether Catholics who have contracted a valid marriage and after obtaining a civil divorce have contracted a civil contracted a civil union should be admitted to the sacraments.

This question reminds us of the interventions by Cardinal Hume and Archbishop Derek Worlock at the 1980 Synod of

Bishops which was held in Rome to discuss matters relating to the
family.

Cardinal Hume spoke of the vision he had of the Church as a
pilgrim and he reflected that "the pilgrim is always in search, and
that can be painful. The leaders, too, of the pilgrimage are often
themselves not clear. They must sometimes co-agonize with the
other pilgrims. Co-responsibility will always involve co-agonizing".

The following quotation from the intervention made by Archbishop Worlock gives the section that is relevant to our purpose:
"Many pastors nowadays are faced with Catholics whose first marriages have perished and who have now a second and more stable
(if legally only civil) union in which they seek to bring up a new
family. Often such persons, especially in their desire to help their
children, long for the restoration of full Eucharistic communion
with the Church and its Lord. Is this spirit of repentance and
desire for sacramental strength to be for ever frustrated? Can they
be told only that they must reject their new responsibilities as a
necessary condition of forgiveness and restoration to sacramental
life?"

"Some pastors argue that the Church's teaching on marital
fidelity and contractual indissolubility are here at risk. They fear
lest other Catholics would be scandalised and the bond of marriage
weakened. Our pre-synodal consultation would question this asser-
tion. Those who vigorously uphold the Church's teaching on
indissolubility, also ask for mercy and compassion for the repentant who have suffered irrevocable marital breakdown. There is no
easy answer. But our Synod must listen seriously to this voice of
experienced priests and laity pleading for consideration of this problem of their less happy brethren. They ask that the Church should
provide for the spiritually destitute to the same degree as it strives
today to meet the material needs of those physically starving".

Before the 1980 Synod and the publication of the Apostolic
Exhortation 'Familiaris Consortio' by Pope John Paul II, the
Bishops of England and Wales expressed their solidarity with the
sentiments of the delegates to the National Pastoral Congress held
in Liverpool in 1980. In their message known as 'The Easter
People' the Bishops stated that: "There are, however, other situations in which there may be moral certainty that the previous marriage was not valid even although this cannot be adequately established in the matrimonial courts, or in which a first valid marriage
has broken down irretrievably but a second union is stable. The
question of the reception of the sacraments in such cases is one

which the Bishops' Conference has been considering for some time. We have a most serious responsibility to witness to the life-long and exclusive commitment of a Christian marriage. Yet as pastors and loving servants of our brothers and sisters in the local churches of England and Wales, we take to heart the sympathy and the compassion expressed by the Congress delegates as we continue our deliberations on this very sensitive doctrinal and pastoral issue" (no.111).[78*] The author has been assured that as yet no further statement has been issued by the Bishops.

Pastoral care: considerations to be borne in mind

The following suggestions have been made by Walter Kasper in his book *Theology of Christian Marriage:*

"Many Christian theologians and pastors . . . believe that the facilities for pastoral help are insufficient in the present situation and that not enough provision is made for them in canon law as it now stands. Generally speaking, they do not advocate, of course, that a second marriage should receive a liturgical blessing or be solemnized sacramentally, thus putting it on the same level as the first marriage. Such an action should not be reconciled with the whole tradition of the Church. The more moderate authors who have written about this question therefore believe in a policy similar to the practice of 'tolerance' and 'leniency' that emerges from many documents of the early Church and similar to (though not identical with) the practice of the Eastern Church, which was not formally excluded by the Council of Trent and which amounts to an order of penance. The God proclaimed by Jesus Christ reveals to all men, including sinners, when they turn back to him, a possibility of salvation".

"The Church should act in accordance with God's way of acting and for this reason, it should be possible to admit divorced people who have remarried to the sacraments on three conditions: 1) when they are sorry for their guilt and have made amends for it as well as they can; 2) when everything humanly possible has been done to achieve reconciliation with the first partner; and 3) when the second marriage has become a morally binding union that cannot be dissolved without causing fresh injustice".

"A solution of this kind would seem at least to do justice to the teaching of Jesus, the complexity and difficulty of the situation in which such people often find themselves today and the human and Christian values that may well be present in a civilly contracted second marriage. It ought to be possible to avoid both giving scandal to others and causing indifference in those concerned by following a sensible and responsible pastoral policy which makes it clear that all men are in need of conversion and reconciliation and that no one has reason to point critically at others. Such a programme ought also to lead to a deepening of the spiritual life of the community as a whole, especially with regard to the need for conversion and reconciliation".

"These theological considerations cannot, of course, establish norms for pastoral activity. They are, however, necessary in view of the complex pastoral situation today, in which theological understanding is of great importance. This is, after all, from the point of view of theology at least a question that is not simply already resolved. It is rather subject to the ultimate decision of the Church's pastoral office. The final decision can only be made in accordance with the whole Church. In this decision making, two points of view must have the highest priority: a renewal and a deepening of our understanding of the human and Christian value of faithfulness in marriage and a renewal and deepening of our need for penance. Both of these viewpoints are concerned ultimately with God's faithfulness, by which human faithfulness is sustained and made holy and which also remains faithful to people when they become unfaithful and, by means of conversion offers them a possibility of salvation. Avoiding rigidity on the one hand and laxity on the other, the Church has the task of bearing witness to this divine faithfulness as God's way of saving all people. It is only in this way that it can act in accordance with Jesus' words and practice".[79]

In general the following points should not be forgotten:

It is claimed that such people have a right to the sacraments. They certainly have a right to the sacraments if they are properly disposed to receive them. But those who are not ready to do what the Church requires cannot be said to be properly disposed and therefore it cannot be claimed on their behalf that they have a right to receive the sacraments in question.

Another argument put forward is that if such people are sorry for what they have done they should be given the sacraments. Sorrow for sin in the sacrament of Penance involves a firm purpose of amendment. This means the serious intention to do one's best in the future to avoid sin and the occasions of sin. But people who are not validly married in the eyes of the Church and who continue to live as if they were and have no intention of doing otherwise cannot be said to have the sorrow that is required for the valid reception of the sacrament of Penance.

It is also alleged that these people more than others have need of the sacraments. This is true. But if they are not properly disposed to receive them, the very sacraments they seek can have no effect in their lives because of the obstacle there is to the grace of the sacraments helping them personally. The principle involved in these cases is the principle governing the use of sex. According to the order established by God the sex faculty can lawfully be used only in a marriage that is a true or valid marriage and in an act of intercourse which is said to be 'natural'. A person who is not willing to cease having sexual intercourse with a partner to whom he/she is invalidly married is not properly disposed to receive the sacraments.

It is further pointed out that it is the Christian thing to forgive and that the Church should forgive these people and let them start afresh. It is certainly Christian to forgive and one hopes that this is the attitude of every Christian with regard to such situations. But to allow such people to act towards each other as those who are validly married would not just be forgiveness, it would be to condone an irregular situation, the sign of such condonation being their admission to the sacraments when they are not properly disposed to receive them.

It is said that we all make mistakes in life. These people have made a mistake. They acknowledge this and should be allowed to learn from their last experience and start all over again. This is certainly possible when it is a question of human affairs depending on human laws. But even where human laws are involved some mistakes cannot be rectified and it is also said that two wrongs cannot make a right. But here one is dealing with the laws of God which man has no power to tamper with even to help his unfortunate situation.

Finally, it is argued that the conditions imposed by the Church before such people can be admitted to the sacraments are impossible to fulfil. They would certainly be impossible to fulfil if man were to trust in his own unaided efforts. On this point Pius XII once stated that complete abstinence *is* possible with the grace of God. Admittedly this requires a high degree of spirituality.

Commenting on this situation the late Cardinal Heenan instructed his priests to "treat persons in these circumstances with very great sympathy and understanding. For many of them it is morally impossible to separate. It is not for us to apportion blame in individual cases. . . The teaching of the Church makes it clear that no justification for admitting such to confession and Holy Communion is to be found by questioning the doctrine of indissoluble marriage".

We show our compassion in these cases first of all by putting these people in touch with those in the Church whose business it is to discover if any genuine grounds exist for declaring the first marriage null and void so that the second union may be regularized by the Church. In practice this means referring them to the Diocesan Marriage Court.

A deeper understanding of marriage and research into the breakdown of many marriages has resulted in a development in recent years of genuine grounds for nullity.

W. P. Denning writes: "Lack of due discretion is a new ground for nullity, introduced largely as a consequence of the teaching of Vatican II that marriage is a 'community of love'. It is therefore important to understand exactly what the phrase means as interpreted in the Courts of the Catholic Church. It means the inability of one party (or both parties) to establish and sustain a normal marital relationship, or in other words, inability to undertake and carry out the obligations and responsibilities of marriage".

"Like impotence — a far narrower concept — it may be absolute or relative: absolute if the inability precludes a relationship with any partner, relative if it precludes a relationship with a particular person".

"It also resembles impotence in that if it is to cause nullity it must be antecedent to the marriage. It is not enough to prove that a couple did not get on well together. It has to be proved that from the very beginning there was something in one party that would make it impossible for them to get on together. In many cases, however, this inability may not have been apparent at the time of the marriage and subsequent conduct may be one of the strongest proofs of its existence".

"Examples of cases that have succeeded in the courts are homosexuality, serious immaturity, severe psychopathy, inadequate personality, obsessional-compulsive illness, depressive illness with obsessions, as well as the case of a compulsive liar".[80]

Pope John Paul II discusses the various situations that can arise in the life of people who are bound by a valid marriage bond, and so we have on this matter the clear statement from the supreme authority in the Church. Two situations are envisaged:

M

a) *Separated or divorced persons who have not remarried*:

"Various reasons can unfortunately lead to the often irreparable breakdown of valid marriages. These include mutual lack of understanding and the inability to enter into interpersonal relationships. Obviously, separation must be considered as a last resort, after all other reasonable attempts at reconciliation have proved vain".

"Loneliness and other difficulties are often the lot of separated spouses, especially when they are the innocent parties. The ecclesial community must support such people more than ever. It must give them much respect, solidarity, understanding and practical help, so that they can preserve their fidelity even in their difficult situation; and it must help them to cultivate the need to forgive which is inherent in Christian love, and to be ready perhaps to return to their former married life".

"The situation is similar for people who have undergone divorce, but, being well aware that the valid marriage bond is indissoluble, refrain from becoming involved in a new union and devote themselves solely to carrying out their family duties and the responsibilities of Christian life. In such cases their example of fidelity and Christian consistency takes on particular value as a witness before the world and the Church. Here it is even more necessary for the Church to offer continual love and assistance, without there being any obstacle to admission to the sacraments".

b) *Divorced persons who have remarried*:

"Daily experience unfortunately shows that people who have obtained a divorce usually intend to enter into a new union, obviously not with a Catholic religious ceremony. Since this is an evil that, like the others, is affecting more and more Catholics as well, the problem must be faced with resolution and without delay. The Synod Fathers studied it expressly. The Church, which was set up to lead to salvation all people and especially the baptised, cannot abandon to their own devices those who have been previously bound by sacramental marriage and who have attempted a second marriage. The Church will therefore make untiring efforts to put at their disposal her means of salvation".

"Pastors must know that, for the sake of truth, they are obliged to exercise careful discernment of situations. There is, in fact, a difference between those who have sincerely tried to save their first marriage and have been unjustly abandoned, and those who through their own grave fault have destroyed a canonically valid marriage. Finally, there are those who have entered into a second union for the sake of the children's upbringing, and who are sometimes subjectively certain in conscience that their previous and irreparably destroyed marriage had never been valid".

"Together with the Synod, I earnestly call upon pastors and the whole community of the faithful to help the divorced, and with solicitous care to make sure that they do not consider themselves as separated from the Church, for as baptised persons they can, and indeed must, share in her life. They should be encouraged to listen to the word of God, to attend the Sacrifice of the Mass, to persevere in prayer, to contribute to works of charity and to community efforts in favour of justice, to bring up their children in the Christian faith, to cultivate the spirit and practice of penance and thus implore, day by day, God's grace. Let the Church pray for them, encourage them and show herself a merciful mother, and thus sustain them in faith and hope".

"However, the Church reaffirms her practice, which is based upon Sacred Scripture, of not admitting to Eucharistic Communion divorced persons who have remarried. They are unable to be admitted thereto from the fact that their state and condition of life objectively contradict that union of love between Christ and the Church which is signified and effected by the Eucharist. Besides this, there is another special pastoral reason: if these people were admitted to the Eucharist, the faithful would be led into error and confusion regarding the Church's teaching about the indissolubility of marriage".

"Reconciliation in the sacrament of Penance, which would open the way to the Eucharist, can only be granted to those who, repenting of having broken the sign of the covenant and of fidelity to Christ, are sincerely ready to undertake a way of life that is no longer in contradiction to the indissolubility of marriage. This means, in practice, that when, for serious reasons such as for example the children's upbringing, a man and a woman cannot satisfy the obligation to separate, they 'take on themselves the duty to live in complete continence, that is, by abstinence from the acts proper to married couples' ".

Religious ceremony forbidden

"Similarly, the respect due to the sacrament of Matrimony, to the couples themselves and their families, and also to the community of the faithful, forbids any pastor, for whatever reason or pretext even of a pastoral nature, to perform ceremonies of any kind for divorced people who remarry. Such ceremonies would give the impression of the celebration of a new sacramentally valid marriage, and would thus lead people into error concerning the indissolubility of a validly contracted marriage".

"By acting in this way, the Church professes her own fidelity to Christ and to his truth. At the same time she shows motherly concern for these children of hers, especially those who, through no fault of their own, have been abandoned by their legitimate partner".

"With firm confidence she believes that those who have rejected the Lord's command and are still living in this state will be able to obtain from God the grace of salvation, provided that they have persevered in prayer, penance and charity".[81]

A. Regan, CSSR, points out that "In a situation such as the one visualized — impossibility of physical separation on the one hand and the persistence of a previous bond on the other — the brother and sister relationship is a clear imperative of the divine law. Therefore, its observance must, with the aid of prayer, be possible. Frequent lapses are possible and likely, and in that indeed is an imperfect response. Still there must be the resolution, broken maybe many times, but then constantly renewed in a struggle that if persevered in will meet with eventual success. In the meantime, wise old casuists whose 'legalism' has sometimes a habit of reflecting the charity of the Gospel have left golden counsel for the confessor who has to deal with material *recidivi* in a necessary occasion of sin (see, for example, St Alphonsus, *Praxis Confessarii*, n.67–9, where one will find prudent advice flexible enough to be adapted to the conditions and mentality of today). Among other things he should advise and exhort them to pray, not to know the will of God, which is already clear, but to do it".

"It was not the casuists or Canon Law that introduced the dilemma: either they must live as brother and sister or be guilty of adultery. St Paul saw the quasi-marital cohabitation of a woman with any other than her lawful husband precisely as adultery. 'She will be called an adulteress if she lives with another while her husband is alive' (Rom 7:3). And he was promulgating the law of

Christ (cf. 1 Cor 7 : 10–11, 39; Mk 10 : 11–12)".

"Can there be a basis for thinking that in a situation so difficult, where physical separation is impossible, where the good of a family requires that their parents live with them under the same roof, God has really relaxed a law proclaimed by his Son as the only one in harmony with the divine institution of marriage? One wonders if we are really being told that such is the case, or that evidence that it is can be found in the subjective conviction of the couple concerned, which sounds very like the theology of the 'funny internal feeling'. Such a dispensation on the part of God would be in its own genus a miracle more astounding than the superseding of the laws of nature. Would the miracle in question be a dissolution of the previous bond, a permission to live in concubinage, or finally permission for polygamy or polyandry, as the case may be? Each supposition would have its special difficulties (cf. St Thomas, 3rd Part, Supplement, q. 85–7) and in any case miracles are not wrought for the private convenience of individuals. Finally what is the point or function of the Church's Magisterium, if there can be as many magisteria as individuals?"[82]

In recommending the 'brother and sister' solution one is not shutting one's eyes to the fact that it may not be easy and may be more difficult in some cases than in others, but it is possible with the grace of God and has been tried with success by those who are genuinely anxious to do God's will and not their own. It does, of course, call for a deep spirit of faith and love of God, which may in a particular case be lacking in an age when it is fashionable to question everything, even the most necessary and God-given teachings of the Church for the salvation of man. Those who are disposed to do what this teaching requires will be given spiritual peace and comfort which will help them to keep in contact with God by prayer, by participating in the sacred liturgy and by doing their best to bring up their children in the knowledge and practice of the faith in their difficult situation.

The true pastor will also try to help such people in every possible way. He will visit them and encourage them in their striving to live the Christian life and he will avoid the excessive emotional approach to such problems which has occasioned much of the muddled thinking in this matter and has been responsible for proposing some solutions which cannot be of any real help to the parties concerned because they are clearly contrary to what God requires in the whole context of Christian marriage.

Christian burial

An Instruction dated May 28, 1973, issued by the Sacred Congregation for the Doctrine of the Faith states that Catholics who have contracted irregular marriages are not to be forbidden ecclesiastical burial (this means the funeral Mass and all that follows) provided they remained members of the Church and before their death gave some sign of repentance and provided that no public scandal will be given to the faithful by their being allowed to have Christian burial. This is perfectly in accord with the terms of canon 1184 of the new Code of Canon Law. In doubt, the matter should be referred to the bishop, whose decision is final (c.1184 n.2).

For completeness it will be useful to quote the Pope on the question of trial marriages and on Catholics in civil civic marriages.

Trial marriages

"A first example of an irregular situation is provided by what are called 'trial marriages', which many people today would like to justify by attributing a certain value to them. But human reason leads one to see that they are unacceptable, by showing the unconvincing nature of carrying out an 'experiment' with human beings, whose dignity demands that they should be always and solely the term of a self-giving love without limitations of time or of any other circumstance".

"The Church, for her part, cannot admit such a kind of union, for further and original reasons which derive from faith. For, in the first place, the gift of the body in the sexual relationship is a real symbol of the giving of the whole person: such a giving, moreover, in the present state of things cannot take place with full truth without the concourse of the love of charity given by Christ. In the second place, marriage between two baptised persons is a real symbol of the union of Christ and the Church, which is not a temporary or 'trial' union but one which is eternally faithful. Therefore between two baptised persons there can exist only an indissoluble marriage".

"Such a situation cannot usually be overcome unless the human person, from childhood, with the help of Christ's grace and without fear, has been trained to dominate concupiscence from the beginning and to establish relationships of genuine love with other people. This cannot be secured without a true education in genuine love and in the right use of sexuality, such as to introduce the human person in every aspect, and therefore the bodily aspect too, into the fullness of the mystery of Christ".

"It will be very useful to investigate the causes of this phenomenon, including its psychological and sociological aspect, in order to find the proper remedy".[83]

This situation is often associated with pre-marital sexual intercourse. On this point Bernard Häring says, "If young people today can realise that the marriage act essentially expresses irrevocable mutual self-giving and unity, they will also understand that pre-marital sexual intercourse is contradictory and profoundly false and inauthentic because it expresses complete unity 'being one body', when such a unity of persons does not exist".[84] The same must be said about the so-called trial marriages. They are a contradiction in terms because marriage by its very definition signifies a permanent relationship.

c) *Catholics in civil marriages:*

"There are increasing cases of Catholics who, for ideological or practical reasons, prefer to contract a merely civil marriage, and who reject or at least defer religious marriage. Their situation cannot of course be likened to that of people simply living together without any bond at all, because in the present case there is at least a certain commitment to a properly-defined and probably stable state of life, even though the possibility of a future divorce is often present in the minds of those entering a civil marriage. By seeking public recognition of their bond on the part of the State, such couples show that they are ready to accept not only its advantages but also its obligations. Nevertheless, not even this situation is acceptable to the Church".

"The aims of pastoral action will be to make these people understand the need for consistency between their choice of life and the faith that they profess, and to try to do everything possible to induce them to regularize their situation in the light of Christian principles. While treating them with great charity and bringing them into the life of the respective communities, the pastors of the Church will regrettably not be able to admit them to the sacraments".[85]

Preparation for marriage

Pope John Paul II points out that "More than ever necessary in our time is preparation of young people for marriage and family life. . .". "The changes that have taken place within almost all modern societies demand that not only the family but also society and the Church should be involved in the effort of properly preparing young people for their future responsibilities".

"Many negative phenomena which are today noted with regret in family life derive from the fact that, in the new situations, young people not only lose sight of the correct hierarchy of values but, since they no longer have certain criteria of behaviour, they do not know how to face and deal with the new difficulties. But experience teaches that young people who have been well prepared for family life generally succeed better than others".

"This is even more applicable to Christian marriage, which influences the holiness of large numbers of men and women. The Church must therefore promote better and more intensive programmes of marriage preparation, in order to eliminate as far as possible the difficulties that many married couples find themselves in, and even more in order to favour positively the establishing and maturing of successful marriages".

1) *For the marriage of Catholics*

"Marriage preparation has to be seen and put into practice as a gradual and continuous process. It includes three main stages: remote, proximate and immediate preparation".

a) *Remote preparation* begins in early childhood, in that wise family training which leads children to discover themselves as beings endowed with a rich and complex psychology and with a particular personality with its own strengths and weaknesses. It is the period when esteem for all authentic human values is instilled, both in interpersonal and in social relationships, with all that this signifies for the formation of character, for the control and right use of one's inclinations, for the manner of regarding and meeting people of the opposite sex, and so on. Also necessary, especially for Christians, is solid spiritual and catechetical formation that will show that marriage is a true vocation and mission, without excluding the possibility of the total gift of self to God in the vocation to the priestly or religious life".

b) "Upon this basis there will subsequently and gradually be

built up the *proximate preparation*, which — from the suitable age
and with adequate catechesis, as in a catechumenal process —
involves a more specific preparation for the sacraments, as if were
a rediscovery of them. This renewed catechesis of young people
and others preparing for Christian marriage is absolutely necessary
in order that the sacrament may be celebrated and lived with the
right moral and spiritual dispositions. The religious formation of
young people should be integrated, at the right moment and in
accordance with the various concrete requirements, with a preparation for life as a couple. This preparation will present marriage
as an interpersonal relationship of a man and woman that has to
be continually developed, and it will encourage those concerned
to study the nature of conjugal sexuality and responsible parent-
hood, with the essential medical and biological knowledge connected with it. It will also acquaint those concerned with correct
methods for the education of children, and will assist them in
gaining the basic requisites for well-ordered family life, such as
stable work, sufficient financial resources, sensible administration,
notions of house-keeping".

"Finally, one must not overlook preparation for the family
apostolate, for fraternal solidarity and collaboration with other
families, for active membership in groups, associations, movements
and undertakings set up for the human and Christian benefit of the
family".

c) "The *immediate preparation* for the celebration of the
sacrament of Matrimony should take place in the months and weeks
immediately preceding the wedding, so as to give a new meaning,
content and form to the so-called premarital enquiry required by
Canon Law. This preparation is not only necessary in every case,
but is also more urgently needed for engaged couples that still
manifest shortcomings or difficulties in Christian doctrine and
practice".

"Among the elements to be instilled in this journey of faith,
which is similar to the catechumenate, there must also be a deeper
knowledge of the mystery of Christ and the Church, of the meaning of grace and of the responsibility of Christian marriage, as well
as preparation for taking an active and conscious part in the rites of
the marriage liturgy".

"The Christian family and the whole of the ecclesial community should feel involved in the different phases of the preparation for marriage, which have been described only in their broad
outlines. It is to be hoped that the Episcopal Conferences, just as

they are concerned with appropriate initiatives to help engaged couples to be more aware of the seriousness of their choice and also to help pastors of souls to make sure of the couple's proper dispositions, so they will also take steps to see that there is issued a Directory for the pastoral care of the family. In this they should lay down in the first place the minimum content, duration and method of the 'preparation courses', balancing the different aspects — doctrinal, pedagogical, legal and medical — concerning marriage and structuring them in such a way that those preparing for marriage will not only receive an intellectual training, but will also feel a desire to enter actively into the ecclesial community".[86] [Publisher's note: cf. the very useful book *Love is your calling*: A book on marriage for the faithful/A manual of faith for lovers (St Paul Publications).]

2) *For those entering into a 'mixed marriage'*

In England and Wales 'mixed marriages' are regulated by the Revised Directory (1977) by the Bishops' Conference based upon the Apostolic Letter 'Matrimonia Mixta' of Pope Paul VI, Determining Forms for Mixed Marriages, the provisions of which have been incorporated into the new Code of Canon Law.

Pope John Paul II speaks of the appropriate preparation to be given for this type of marriage. To conclude it will be useful to quote the relevant passages from the papal document on the subject.

"Couples living in a mixed marriage have special needs, which can be put under three main headings".

"In the first place, attention must be paid to the obligations that faith imposes on the Catholic party with regard to the free exercise of the faith and the consequent obligation to ensure, as far as is possible, the Baptism and upbringing of the children in the Catholic faith".

"There must be borne in mind the particular difficulties inherent in the relationships between husband and wife with regard to respect for religious freedom: this freedom could be violated either by undue pressure to make the partner change his or her beliefs, for by placing obstacles in the way of the free manifestation of these beliefs by religious practice".

"With regard to the liturgical and canonical form of marriage, Ordinaries can make wide use of their faculties to meet various necessities".

'In dealing with these special needs, the following points should be kept in mind:

— "In the appropriate preparation for this type of marriage, every reasonable effort must be made to ensure a proper understanding of Catholic teaching on the qualities and obligations of marriage, and also to ensure that the pressures and obstacles mentioned above will not occur".

— "It is of the greatest importance that, through the support of the community, the Catholic party should be strengthened in faith and positively helped to mature in understanding and practising that faith, so as to become a credible witness within the family through his or her own life and through the quality of love shown to the other spouse and the children".

"Marriages between Catolics and other baptised persons have their own particular nature, but they contain numerous elements that could well be made good use of and developed, both for their intrinsic value and for the contribution that they can make to the ecumenical movement. This is particularly true when both parties are faithful to their religious duties. Their common Baptism and the dynamism of grace provide the spouses in these marriages with the basis and motivation for expressing their unity in the sphere of moral and spiritual values".

"For this purpose, and also in order to highlight the ecumenical importance of mixed marriages which are fully lived in the faith of the two Christian spouses, an effort should be made to establish cordial co-operation between the Catholic and the non-Catholic ministers from the time that preparations begin for the marriage and the wedding ceremony, even though this does not always prove easy".

"With regard to the sharing of the non-Catholic party in Eucharistic Communion, the norms issued by the Secretariat for Promoting Christian Unity should be followed".

The place of the marriage

Only those marriages of Catholics are valid which are contracted before the bishop of the place, the parish priest or a priest or deacon delegated by either of these to assist at the marriage together with two witnesses (cf. c.1108). This is known in canonical language as the form of marriage.

At the same time when it is a question of mixed marriages the law of the Church recognises that there may be serious difficulties which prevent the Catholic from complying with the ruling given above (cf. c.1127, n.2).

In this case the bishop of the Catholic party can lawfully dispense from the form of marriage.

Guidelines relating to marriages in non-Catholic Churches

In accordance with what has been said above the following guide-lines have been issued for the Diocese of Westminster:

A. It is forbidden by Church law to have two religious marriage services or to have a single service in which both the Catholic marriage rite and a non-Catholic marriage rite are celebrated jointly or successively, for the purpose of giving or renewing matrimonal consent (cf. c.1127, n.3).

B. When, with a dispensation from the canonical form, the wedding takes place in a non-Catholic church or chapel, the rite of the wedding will presumably be that of the church or chapel in which it is being celebrated. Although in no way legally necessary, it could be appropriate in these circumstances that the Catholic priest or deacon who has been preparing the couple for marriage, should, where possible, be present at the wedding. If invited to do so by the couple, with the consent of the minister in charge of the church, a Catholic priest or deacon may attend in the sanctuary, in 'choir dress', and, if further invited, take part in the rite, provided it is not part of the Eucharistic Rite, just as a non-Catholic minister may be invited to take part in a Catholic rite. When taking part in a non-Catholic rite, a Catholic priest or deacon should be in choir dress.

C. As already stated, it is forbidden to have the simultaneous performance of different rites, or the addition of any second rite which includes the giving or renewal of matrimonial consent. This is a measure of simple prudence, to ensure that consent is expressed only once, and so possible doubts about validity are excluded. A second service of blessing and thanksgiving in the church of the other party, provided it does not include the giving or renewing of matrimonial consent, is positively recommended. It provides this other party with the opportunity to give witness to his new responsibilities before the Christian community to which he belongs.

Marriages between Catholics and non-baptised persons

"Today in many parts of the world marriages between Catholics and non-baptised persons are growing in numbers. In many such marriages the non-baptised partner professes another religion, and his beliefs are to be treated with respect, in accordance with the principles set out in the Second Vatican Council's Declaration 'Nostra Aetate' on relations with non-Christian religions. But in many other such marriages, particularly in secularized societies, the non-baptised person professes no religion at all. In these marriages there is a need for Episcopal Conferences and for individual bishops to ensure that there are proper pastoral safeguards for the faith of the Catholic partner and for the free exercise of his faith, above all in regard to his duty to do all in his power to ensure the Catholic baptism and education of the children of the marriage. Likewise the Catholic must be assisted in every possible way to offer within his family a genuine witness to the Catholic faith and to Catholic life".[87]

The need to assist the faithful

Finally, the new Code of Canon Law, addressing itself to pastors of souls, tells them that they are bound to see that their particular ecclesial community comes to the assistance of the faithful, so that the married state may be maintained in a Christian spirit and that it may advance in perfection.

This assistance is given especially in the following ways:

1) by preaching, by catechesis suited to the needs of minors, young people and adults, by making use also of the mass media, so that the faithful may be informed about the meaning of Christian marriage and the mission of the spouses and of parents;

2) by personal preparation for marriage, so that the spouses may be prepared for the holiness and the duties of their new state;

3) by a fruitful liturgical celebration of marriage, which will enable the spouses to appreciate the fact that they signify and share in the mystery of the unity and the fruitful love between Christ and the Church;

4) by the help offered to those who are married, so that through faithfully keeping and safeguarding the marriage covenant, they may every day be enabled to live a holier and fuller life in the family circle (cf. c.1063).

References

1. Cardinal P. Gasparri, *De Matrimonio* (Vatican Press, 1932), Vol. I, ch. I, p.19.
2. Pastoral Constitution on the Church in the Modern World, n.48, Walter M. Abbott, op. cit., p.250.
3. Pope John Paul II, Apostolic Exhortation 'Familiaris Consortio', 22.11.81, n.19, L'Osservatore Romano (English Edition), 21-28.12.1981, p.4.
4. Pope Paul VI, Address to the Members of the Tribunal of the Sacred Roman Rota, 9.2.76, L'Osservatore Romano (English Edition), 26.2.76, p.4.
5. Pope John Paul II, Apostolic Exhortation 'Familiaris Consortio', n.12, loc. cit., p.3.
6. ibid., n.13, p.3.
7. ibid., n.19, p.4.
8. ibid., n.13, p.3.
9. ibid., n.29, p.6.
10. Pope Paul VI, Address to the Members of the Sacred Roman Rota, 9.2.76, loc. cit., p.4.
11. Pope Paul VI, Encyclical Letter on the Regulation of Birth, 25.7.68, n.9, (English trans. — S. Burns & Sons, p.8).
12. Pastoral Constitution on the Church in the Modern World, n.49, Walter M. Abbott, op. cit., p.252.
13. Pope Paul VI, Encyclical Letter on the Regulation of Birth, loc. cit., n.9, p.8.
14. Pope John Paul II, Apostolic Exhortation 'Familiaris Consortio', n.13, loc. cit., p.3.
15. ibid., n.19, p.4.
16. *The Meaning of Christian Marriage*, edited by Enda McDonagh (Gill, Dublin, 1963), p.64.
17. Pope Paul VI, Encyclical Letter on the Regulation of Birth, n.9, loc. cit., p.8.
18. Pope John Paul II, Apostolic Exhortation 'Familiaris Consortio', n.16, loc. cit., p.4.
19. ibid., n.8, p.2.
20. Pastoral Constitution on the Church in the Modern World, n.49, Walter M. Abbott, op. cit., p. 253.
21. Dogmatic Constitution on the Church, n.11, Walter M. Abbott, op. cit., pp.28–29.
22. Pope John Paul II, Apostolic Exhortation 'Familiaris Consortio', n.33, loc. cit., p.7.
23. *The Meaning of Christian Marriage*, p.64.
24. B. Häring, C.SS.R., *Shalom-Peace* (Image Books, 1969), p.212. See also: B. Häring, *Free and Faithful in Christ*, 3 vols. (St Paul Publications, Slough 1978/1981).
25. Pope John Paul II, Apostolic Exhortation 'Familiaris Consortio', nn.28 and 14, loc. cit., pp. 6 and 3.
26. John Marshall, *The Infertile Period* (Darton, Longman & Todd, 1963), p.96.
27. Pastoral Constitution on the Church in the Modern World, n.50, Walter M. Abbott, op. cit., p.254.
28. ibid.
29. Commentary on the Documents of Vatican II (Burns & Oates/Herder, 1969), Vol. V, p.241.

30. *The Meaning of Christian Marriage*, pp.71–72.

31. Catholic Truth Society pamphlet, Do. 432, pp.18–19.

32. *The Meaning of Christian Marriage*, p.73.

33. *Beginning Your Marriage* (Catholic Marriage Advisory Council, London, 1963), pp.91–92.

34. Pastoral Constitution on the Church in the Modern World, n.51, Walter M. Abbott, op. cit., p.255.

35. ibid., p.256.

36. *Marriage and the Moral Law* (C.T.S., S231), nn.6–7, pp.31–32.

37. Pastoral Constitution on the Church in the Modern World, n.51, Walter M. Abbott, op. cit., p.256.

38. Pope Paul VI, Encyclical Letter on the Regulation of Birth, n.3, loc. cit., p.4.

39. Pope John Paul II, Apostolic Exhortation 'Familiaris Consortio', n.29, loc. cit., p.6.

40. ibid., n.34, p.7.

41. Pope Paul VI, Encyclical Letter on the Regulation of Birth, n.12, loc. cit., p.10.

42. Pope John Paul II, Apostolic Exhortation 'Familiaris Consortio', nn.32, 6 and 30, loc. cit., pp.7, 3 and 6.

43. *Christian Marriage*, Lent 1969 (C.T.S. Dublin, EN48 3218), pp.22–23.

44. Pope John Paul II, Apostolic Exhortation 'Familiaris Consortio', n.32, loc. cit., p.7.

45. ibid., n.4, p.1.

46. ibid., n.30, p.6.

47. ibid., n.7, p.2.

48. ibid., n.33, p.7.

49. Francis Frost, D.D., L-es-L, *Contraception and Unholiness* (Samuel Walker, Hinckley), pp.5–6.

50. B. Häring, C.SS.R., *Shalom-Peace* (Image Books, D264), p.140, see also: B. Häring, *Free and Faithful in Christ*, 3 vols. (St Paul Publications, Slough 1978/1981).

51. Pope John Paul II, Apostolic Exhortation 'Familiaris Consortio', n.72, loc. cit., p.15.

52. Pope Paul VI, Encyclical Letter on the Regulation of Birth, n.16, loc. cit., p.13.

53. *Marriage and the Moral Law* (C.T.S. S231), n.30, p.17.

54. ibid.

55. ibid., n.15, p.35.

56. Pastoral Constitution on the Church in the Modern World, n.52, Walter M. Abbott, op. cit., p.258.

57. Pope Paul VI, Encyclical Letter on the Regulation of Birth, n.24, loc. cit., pp.19–20.

58. Pope John Paul II, Apostolic Exhortation 'Familiaris Consortio' n.33, loc. cit., p.7.

59. ibid.

60. ibid.

61. ibid.

62. *Facing Up To 'Humanae Vitae'* (C.T.S. S282), p.7.

63. *The Meaning of Christian Marriage*, p.72.

64. Pope John Paul II, Apostolic Exhortation 'Familiaris Consortio', n.28, loc. cit., p.6.

65. ibid., n.56, p.11.

66. Pastoral Constitution on the Church in the Modern World, n.48, Walter M. Abbott, op. cit., p.251.

67. ibid.
68. Pope John Paul II, Apostolic Exhortation 'Familiaris Consortio', n.59, loc. cit., p.12.
69. ibid., n.62, p.12.
70. *The Meaning of Christian Marriage*, p.73.
71. Pope John Paul II, Address to the Parish Priests and Clergy of Rome, 17.2.83, L'Osservatore Romano (English edition), 14.3.83, p.9.
73. Pope John Paul II, Apostolic Exhortation 'Familiaris Consortio', n.14, loc. cit., p.3.
74. ibid.
75. Pastoral Constitution on the Church in the Modern World, n.50, Walter M. Abbott, op. cit., p.255.
76. Pope John Paul II, Apostolic Exhortation 'Familiaris Consortio', n.68, loc. cit., p.13.
77. ibid., n.6, pp.2–3.
78. ibid., n.20, pp.4–5.
78*. Bishops' Conference of England and Wales, *The Easter People* (St Paul Publications, 1980), p.39.
79. Walter Kasper, *Theology of Christian Marriage* (Burns & Oates, 1980), pp.69–71.
80. Southwark Diocesan Bulletin, January 1973.
81. Pope John Paul II, Apostolic Exhortation 'Familiaris Consortio', nn.83 and 84, loc. cit., p.17.
82. Clergy Review, June 1970, pp.482–4.
83. Pope John Paul II, Apostolic Exhortation 'Familiaris Consortio', n.81, loc. cit., p. 17.
84. Commentary on the Documents of Vatican II (Burns & Oates/Herder), Vol. V, p.238.
85. Pope John Paul II, Apostolic Exhortation 'Familiaris Consortio', n.82, loc. cit., p.17.
86. ibid., n.66, p.13.
87. ibid., n.78, p.16.

INDEX